Making
Man's
Environment

Urban Issues

Leonard O. Gertler

VNR Van Nostrand Reinhold Ltd.
Toronto
New York, Cincinnati, London, Melbourne

For my sons, Denis, Meric, Kim and Neil—dreamers and searchers.

ISBN cloth 0 442 29920 6
     paper 0 442 29921 4
Library of Congress Catalogue number 75-5273
Design by Brant Cowie/Artplus
Printed and bound in Canada by The Bryant Press Limited
Cover and jacket photograph by permission of GAF Corporation Limited

76 77 78 79 80 81 82 8 7 6 5 4 3 2 1

Foreword

In the field of urban studies and community planning, Canada appears to be entering a period of prolific self-examination. After a long silence, we have in the early seventies been the beneficiaries of a stream of books, dealing with various aspects of the Canadian urban experience: some have been concerned with dissecting the structure of cities, some with the impact of urbanization on land and the biosphere, others with sounding alarms about a multitude of current problems, a few with the politics of governing, and fewer still with the examination of policies: what are we doing about our towns and cities?

While these works have generally shared a concern for "the crisis of urbanization", they have been very different in approach, style and reachable audience. Some bear, without apology, the scars of the seminar room and the Ph.D. thesis. Many are anthologies, either in the form of hasty contrivances—"scrambled eggs" or carefully selected works making a strong unified impact. Others are efforts, newly initiated, built around a problem (for example, pollution or housing) or a discipline theme (for example, geographical or social aspects), and are addressed to either a specialized or broad audience. Altogether this body of work is beginning to assume an impressive scope and to attain, at times, a level of excellence which is second to none, but not surprisingly gaps remain. And it is to some of these that the VNR Urban Planning series addresses itself.

This new series has several aims: (i) to relate urban environmental concerns and planning to the general forces, historical and contemporary, that shape Canadian society, (ii) to treat the major elements of human settlement, for example, the environments of work, shelter, leisure, etcetera from a base of human understanding and human need, that is, from the inside out—first man and woman and family, and then house and neighborhood and city implied by their expressed desires, behaviour patterns and struggles for something better, (iii) to bring these major elements together in a critical exploration of alternative forms of settlement, keeping an eye to the future, and (iv) through all of this taking part in the broader search for philosophical sanity—the relating of humane ends to effective means, on which environmental well-being ultimately depends.

To say that the reach of such an ambition runs the continual risk of exceeding its grasp, would be an understatement. The editor and the authors associated with him have no illusions concerning the difficulty of what they are undertaking. If, however, our collective effort serves only as a base, a footing however precarious, from which others will strike higher and see clearer, the exertion will have been entirely worthwhile.

This first book in the series takes as its mandate an introduction to aspects of all four of the series' stated aims, in a manner explained in the pages that immediately follow.

In writing a book of this nature, which is broad and exploratory, one is indebted to many people whose ideas and stimulation have become internalized and anonymous. This includes participants in the bull sessions of academia as well as the policy conferences of government. But the help of certain people is gratefully remembered: Jim MacNeill, Secretary of the Ministry of State for Urban Affairs, who read the entire original manuscript and offered, as is his custom, very good advice; Professor Peter Homenuck of the Urban Studies Programme, York University, whose critical comments were extremely helpful, and appreciated; Professor G.G. Mulamootil, School of Urban and Regional Planning, University of Waterloo, who offered valued criticism of ecological themes in the manuscript; Ian Bender, senior planner, Calgary Regional Planning Commission as a Master's graduate from the Waterloo Planning Program whose creative response to the dilemmas of urban land development, which I presented, made for a memorable association; Colin Fowlie, Man-Environment student, University of Waterloo, whose sharp unorthodox observations on the philosophy of education, Chapter 6, moved and will continue to move me off certain familiar turf; to the notorious "class of '72" whose stubborn nihilism drove me to those assertions in the first place; to Garry Lovatt, Executive Editor at Van Nostrand Reinhold and Diane Mew, editorial consultant, whose entreaties — general and specific, and most graciously administered — saved me from untold folly; and to my wife, Anita — alias Monkey and Charlie — whose constant encouragement meant so much to me.

Appreciation goes as well to the Central Mortgage and Housing Corporation which provided the original grant funds for the author's investigations of the process of new city planning and building, and which has given consent to the use of some material from the research report; and to the Publications Service Government of Ontario for agreeing to the adaption for this book, Chapter Four, of certain parts of a paper published in their *Micros and Macros of Our Urban Crisis,* 1971.

As is the custom in these matters, none of the above persons and agencies can be considered accomplices to the crime.

Len Gertler

Contents

Introduction

This book is presented at a time of increasing awareness of urban issues in Canada. The symptoms are all about us; at all levels of government urban problems are at the top of policy agenda. We are deep in the age of tri-level consultation. While this urban consciousness appears to have emerged suddenly, it is in fact the product of a long fermentation.

About the time that Prime Minister Laurier was claiming the twentieth century for Canada, an obscure Methodist minister, who was later to lead a national party, wrote a book about urban Canada: *My Neighbor, A Study of City Conditions*. In his book J. S. Woodsworth noted the drift of population to the cities: Winnipeg in 1901 already had one-quarter of the population of Manitoba; the population of Ontario had doubled between 1851 and 1901, while that of Toronto in the same period increased six times, and so on. And Woodsworth, not unsuitably for a man of prophetic tendencies, anticipated the coming dominance of the city: "Though Canada is so young a country it is being carried into the main current of modern social development. . . . Man has entered on an urban age. He has become a communal being. The increasing pressure of population is fast filling up the waste places of the globe. This, of itself, forecasts the life of the future. And in consequence, the city will no longer be an incidental problem. It has already become the problem of society and the measure of our civilization."

It is this kind of prescience which suggests the value of viewing the problems of our cities and towns within the broad flow of history. And this is the first thing that this book sets out to do, at least insofar as it is possible in an introductory overview. In this overview, we must distinguish between those conditions that are associated with urbanization anywhere in the industrial world, and those which are rooted in the Canadian environment. Amongst the first must be counted the surge of British overseas investment and the impact of the railway, which facilitated the concentration of production and people; the spatial segregation of functions and, to a degree, social classes in the industrial city; and the biases of the real estate market.

Amongst the more endemic influences should be noted the source of the centre-periphery syndrome: the dominance of a few big places, regional disparities, etcetera, in a colonial past which spawned one or two entrepôt cities, middlemen in the exchange of manufactured goods from the imperial centre for the staples of a sub-continent. Observe the beginnings of urban distress in the waves of immigrants who came to farm, to mine, to cut timber and build railways, and who ended up in the city, struggling but not always making it towards their middle-class nirvana.

The hand of the past lies particularly heavy on transportation in our cities. The normal operation of the real estate market, heated up by the speculative fever of a country on the pioneer fringe, produced the characteristic central city pyramid of land values. Much of what we have done in urban transportation has been connected with overcoming the development consequences of that, namely congestion in the centre and the push towards lower land prices on the fringe. In economic terms we have been trying to do the impossible: build a centripetal public system dependent on the concentration of passengers not too far from the main lines, while facilitating through a centrifugally-biased road system, the maximum of auto-mobility and dispersion of residential areas. Something's got to give. The Science Council sounds the knell — declining quality and rising costs of public transit, automobile and truck traffic congestion during travel peaks, noise, air pollution, neighbourhood blight, and so on.

While not offering any definitive solutions, this book does urge a certain approach to urban problems. For example, the transportation dilemma appears as a dead-end unless it is understood as a symptom of a deeper disorder: of an economic calculus which does not count indirect social costs, such as the additional cost in productive land and services of excessively low density development; of an energy-production cycle, which does not provide for the efficient re-use of its waste products; and of an urban structure which reflects a galloping change towards a new settlement form characterized by the expansion of volatile urban life spaces.

Attention is given to one form of urban reconstruction — new communities integrated within a regional system — as a demonstration of the potentials of positive planning. The concept is a species of regional city in which external costs, economic and ecological, are minimized by making a high-speed, non-polluting, environmentally buffered facility the backbone of the system. Transportation is "manipulated" to accommodate transcending environmental goals: development in the form of communities, wide choice in living areas, and access to a diverse array of work, leisure and business opportunities. The Toronto-Centred Plan has these potentials.

There are risks in this kind of intervention, but these can be minimized by taking care to evaluate our own experience as we go, and by being open to relevant outside experience. Noted are Stockholm's skill in managing the urban environment, and the techniques used to develop new towns in the Helsinki region — towns which are not havens for the comfortable middle-class but which represent the economic and social profile, blue collar and white collar, of their region.

3

The argument advanced by this book points to several other conditions essential to coping effectively with urban development. One is to recognize the saliency of land costs and to do something about it. Planning, as an instrument for enhancing our environment, leads to forward-looking concepts requiring the control of land for the public benefit, such as new communities forming a regional city, and the identification and protection of recreational corridors. To undertake these kinds of programs without prohibitive cost will require land policies specifically designed to deal with the problem of escalating land prices.

Another essential condition for an effective response to the urban challenge is that plans for the places in which we live, our blueprints for the good life, be developed in relation to regional potentials. The richness and diversity of the urban mosaic depends on giving full play to the history and geography of the different regional settings of this country. Where this dimension has been acknowledged in the institutions of a province, as in Alberta which has a comprehensive system of planning regions, then such regions should be plugged into the process of three-level consultation on national urban policy.

The final chapter of this book is based on the notion that we will not get very far with our shelf of remedies, performing like the apothecary with a sure-fire potion for gout that unfortunately shocks the heart, unless we develop an integrated view of what we are treating and how we will approach our task. We need a philosophy of planning. Some of the materials out of which this may be built are assembled. There is a concept of environmental planning that understands the creation of human community in ecosystem terms: a struggle towards an optimum mix and balance of people, resources and technology and of tradition and social change. There is the dual Canadian heritage of individualism and cooperation. There is the pinpointing of the interacting stresses — economic, resource and urban—which demand a societal response. And above all, there is a heritage of humanist thought which deserves our ardent attention.

Painful as the struggle towards philosophical poise may be, our success in meeting the challenges of urban development depends on just such an integrated view informing our policies and permeating our academic halls. It is argued that an approach to educating planners which places emphasis on understanding the social development of Canada, and of the choices we have to make in the continuum from individual fulfilment to collective action—such an approach is likely to be one which leads to cities in which our gadgetry, no matter how alluring, will take second place to human need. We will have our priorities straight.

4

1 Overview of the Canadian City

From Colonial/Merchant Towns to Industrial Cities

Many forces, reaching back to the beginning of this country, have shaped the character and form of Canadian cities. If our concern with the urban environment of our day starts with a retrospective view, it is to better understand the conditions which we now celebrate or deplore. For the influences of the past on the areas in which we live are pervasive, albeit not always obvious. The very layout of our urban places betrays the nature of the two original systems of rural land enclosure. There was the French type of Quebec, consisting of long narrow lots stretching back from frontage roads; and the English type, either in the form of broad oblong enclosures in Ontario and the Maritimes or of square sections in Western Canada. Since Canadian towns typically developed by gradual penetration into farm land, their internal patterns — the shapes and sizes of lots and blocks, the location of roads and of woodlots that could become open space amenities — were shaped by the original forms of colonial land survey.[1]

Not all of the influences, however, are of a direct physical nature. Some are general historic forces like industrialization; some are specific responses to the Canadian environment like massive immigration and settlement; others are institutional like the private ownership of property; and still others are systems of values, like competition or cooperation. Together these represent a complex evolution, not yet adequately documented, which deserves full treatment. Although this overview will be more provocative than inclusive, it should at the very least incite the enquiring reader to the rewards of personal discovery.

Urban development in Canada originated as a by-product of the Western European nation state, and of the Catholic Restoration. Both forces were mixed in the establishment of Quebec City in 1608 and Montreal in 1642, with the secular impulse strongest in the first and the sacred in the second. Ironically these roles were later reversed. The Hôtel Dieu hospital in Quebec City, founded in 1639 by the Duchess of Aiguillon, niece of the Cardinal de Richelieu, chief minister of Louis XIII, remains a tangible reminder of this dual heritage.[2]

The City of Quebec, from the Top of Prescott Gate, 1860

Quebec City, cradle of Canadian urbanism, demonstrates more clearly than any other Canadian city the way in which a city can express the continuity of human experience. This drawing, which appeared in Harper's Weekly *in August 1860, spans three centuries: the lower town, built in the seventeenth and eighteenth centuries during the French regime, and the walls and citadel, crowning Cape Diamond, built by the British in 1823-32.*

The European origins of the city, specifically the transplanting of the forms and pretensions of two imperial centres, are still expressed in the contemporary city's penchant for order and monumentalism. Many buildings were constructed in the French Renaissance style well into the last century and a few, such as the Château Frontenac, are contemporary.

Quebec City is still, in a physical sense, a link with the grandeur of the baroque city, the city of royal formality and order. Its walls; the citadel that crowns Cape Diamond over three hundred feet above the St. Lawrence; Château Frontenac, brilliant public relations coup of the CPR; and Dufferin Terrace, which provides a commanding view of the harbour and the spires and small formal squares of Lower Town — with their elaborate architecture, all contrive to preserve the illusion of the city's historic past.[3] We still experience something of Thoreau's culture shock when in 1850 he passed by the guardhouse and sentinal of Prescott Gate into Upper Town, and exclaimed, "I rubbed my eyes to be sure that I was in the nineteenth century. . . . "

Quebec's founder, the "royal geographer" Samuel de Champlain, exercised through an intermediary a patent to explore and develop trade in North America from Henri IV, whose regime participated in what one author has called "the frenetic adventuring of renaissance Europe." And later, when he was appointed commandant of New France in 1612, and in 1628 the representative in the new world of the Company of New France, he became the conscientious agent of Richelieu's mission to "make the king (Louis XIII) the most powerful monarch in the world." The foundation was laid for Quebec City's role as the centre of French interest in North America for more than a century—interests that revolved around the trinity of church, king and the fur trade.[4]

Although New France was declared a royal province in 1661 and enjoyed the benefits of some sophisticated institutions and social life, as well as "a sensitive scale in civic design," Quebec City was described after its capture by the British in 1763 as being like "a third or fourth rate country town in England; much hospitality, little society, cards, scandal, dancing and good cheer. . . . "[5] Nevertheless, the original influences survived even that extravagant derision—the old baroque magic lives on in the city's Grande Allée.

The fullest expression in contemporary Canada of this pre-industrial urban tradition is the city of Ottawa. The Gothic Parliament buildings, the avenues, great square and monumentalism of its centre and its parkways are a legacy of Victorian eclecticism, reasserted in our time by the Greber Plan, which curiously links Ottawa to the Paris of Haussman. Wedded to a city which in other respects enjoys comfortable civil service standards, the effect, in our prosaic age, is not without its appeal. But as an urban tradition, the baroque stands for the glory of absolute power, for the glory of the state and its need for military drill and display. It represented a scale of values that gave low priority to more basic human needs. Ottawa's present development on its earlier framework is well worth a close look. It demonstrates vividly how more populist influences can transform the use and meaning of an inheritied physical structure; a military canal becomes a channel for pleasure-boating and ice-skating, and on Parliament Hill, the pomp and circumstances of the changing of the guard becomes, in the setting of the city's centre, part of a "street carnival" that includes vendors of pottery and prints, flower girls, hari krishnas and many forms of vagabonding youth.

Industrialism in Canada originated in Montreal in the early nineteenth century. There, paradoxically, the conditions for manufacturing were created during a period of mercantilist restriction of local industry. The wealth accumulated in the staple trades — first furs, and then timber, ships, wheat and flour—provided the basis for two essential props of modern industrialism: a bank (The Bank of Montreal, founded in 1817) and an institution of higher learning (McGill University, established in 1829). In that period, the Montreal mercantile elite, spurred by competition from New York, which was linked up with the settlement and trade of the Great Lakes region by the Erie Canal, became the driving force behind the enlargement of the domestic market and the construction of an efficient canal system for the St. Lawrence—Great Lakes route (and later the transcontinental railway).

In the period preceding the first major thrust of industrialization, the Montreal mercantile interests shifted their attention from the far western hinterland of the fur trade, to the nearer hinterland of Upper Canada, and deliberately consolidated the city's entrepôt and trading function.[6]

This was the period, beginning in the twenties and thirties, when the economics of transatlantic transportation favoured immigration to Canada from Great Britain. The economic historian, Harold Innis, has explained one of the important consequences of the shift of Montreal trade to bulky commodities, particularly white pine timber: "With a heavy return cargo and empty space on the outbound voyage, its effects were the reverse of the fur trade, and large numbers of settlers were brought out in preference to ballast." This economic pull coincided with certain push factors in the British Isles: post-Napoleonic unrest, the new Poor Law (1834) that drastically reduced relief expenditures, the Irish potato famine in the forties, and the rising price of corn.[7]

Some of the consequences for urban Canada of that immigration have been immortalized in Lord Durham's report: "Many of these poor people have little or no agricultural knowledge, and they are all ignorant of the husbandry practised in the country. The consequence is that, after getting into the 'bush', as it is called, they find themselves

The Port of Montreal, late Nineteenth Century
By the sixth decade of the last century Montreal had emerged as the predominant industrial city of the country, from its harbour reaching the markets of the entire St. Lawrence–Great Lakes system. Trade and industry stamped its mark on the structure of the city. Symbolically, the warehouse and other props of the entrepôt function became more conspicuous than the church, as in later years the car was to become ubiquitous, taking over without ceremony such places as the Champs de Mars, a French regime military parade ground, as a parking lot.

McGill College Avenue, after 1850
Behind the hustle and sweat of nineteenth-century Montreal, there was a frieze of elegance and good living, which had its pre-industrial roots in the days of trader-philanthopist James McGill, after whom this avenue was named. These are typical of the town houses occupied by the commercial elite. Here, close to the salubrious environment of Mount Royal, was an almost perfect legacy of eighteenth-century baroque order: groups of houses built of common building materials, with a common roof-line punctuated by a point of accent in the form of a pediment in the middle of the block.

9

beset by privations and difficulties which they are not able to contend with, and, giving way under pressure, they abandon their little improvements, to seek a livelihood elsewhere. Many resort to the large towns in the Provinces, with their starving families, to eke out by day-labour and begging together a wretched existence."[8]

This early nineteenth-century migration was the first of several waves of large-scale immigration which were to exert a major influence on Canadian patterns of settlement and on the character of Canadian cities. Between 1815 and 1850, some 800,000 British immigrants arrived. Those that settled in Montreal and other towns became, as Durham has suggested, part of an emerging urban working class. And the others, more numerous, by clearing and occupying virtually all of the arable land of Upper Canada and the Eastern Townships had, willy-nilly, prepared the way for massive urbanization in the post-Confederation period.[9]

As far as Montreal's growth is concerned, the period of the take-off began after the trauma of the mid-century British shift to free trade, when the Canadian market became accessible to domestic manufactures. The city's population, rapidly augmented by the flow of habitants from the countryside, increased at the phenomenal rate of about 12 per cent a year between 1851 and 1861, to a total of 130,000. Industrial capital investment increased thirteen-fold in the next decade. With the rise of its first big city (Toronto at the time had less than half the above population), the country was well on its way to the over-centralized pattern of urbanization that is still the bane of policy-makers.[10]

There was a parallel pattern of early settlement in the Maritimes, beginning in 1605 with the first colonial settlement, a French trading post on the western shore of Annapolis Bay, and culminating in the Victorian period when Halifax achieved a prominence associated with "the golden years of the sailing ship." That heyday, between 1840 and 1879, left a legacy of nautical industries, from sailmaking to insurance. But as events conspired, that era of staple trade did not result in major industrial growth, as it had in Montreal.

The history of urban settlement in the Maritimes is nevertheless of interest because it demonstrates the complexity of the forces that originally shaped urban Canada, the very early tradition of "new town" building in Canada, and the predominance of certain American influences through New England and Loyalist immigrations. The main streams of settlement were Acadian, British, Hanoverian, New England, Loyalist and Scot. In each of these there is some feature that is of continuing interest.[11]

As a by-product of its military struggles with England early in the

Halifax from Dartmouth Cove, 1832
This is Halifax harbour on the eve of its ascendance as the site of a major shipbuilding industry, undermining "the entire eastern American shipbuilding shed." In this pre-Victorian period, Halifax as a military and naval base was reputed to have the strongest defences outside of Europe. Among the more prominent buildings making up its skyline was Dalhousie University, established in 1818. Citadel Hill dominates the scene. Notwithstanding its rocky rugged terrain a gridiron plan laid out in 1749 has established the pattern for central Halifax.

seventeenth century, France established a number of colonies in what is now called Nova Scotia. These colonists, known as Acadians (a derivation of Arcadian, referring to scenic beauty), initiated in the Annapolis Valley a pattern of orchard and mixed farming and prosperous market centres which has been perpetuated to this day by their New England successors, and by the descendants of the original settlers who returned after the expulsion by the British in 1755. The Acadians brought with them from the western coast of France a technique of land management—the diking and cultivation of marshes—which remains a continuing feature of Maritime land use.

The German (Hanoverian) settlement of Lunenburg, established in 1753 at the invitation of the British government, was a community which from its inception had a certain flair. The settlers embellished their simple frame buildings with colourful scroll decorations, elaborating a folk idiom on their frames, windows, doors, fascias and porches; and they placed their homes on a rugged coastal terrain with an unerring eye for the right site and prospect. Today a town of about five thousand people in the Halifax—South shore region, it retains a special interest as a place in which landscape, plan and architecture achieve an uncommon harmony.

The pre- and post-revolutionary New England settlers transplanted to the Maritimes a land and settlement system which features the rectangular rural enclosure as well as the gridiron town plan (for example, at the settlement of Shelburne) of which the basic subdivision unit was a square block made up of sixteen 60 foot × 120 foot lots. The Nova Scotia Yankees also established the balance between freehold and public land (for church and school and courthouse, gaol, orphanage, and government wharfs) that we have come to consider commonplace. And there is more than a suggestion that with these systems there was also transplanted a value system, stemming from the ancestral Massachusetts model, that had its original impulse from Cromwellian Puritans who regarded private property as a bastion against the interfering tyranny of the state. One of the Loyalist settlements, Sydney, on what was then called Spanish Bay, is of interest for what did not happen; when Cape Breton was separated from Nova Scotia in 1784, the first British governor was the celebrated cartographer, Colonel J.W.F. des Barres, who prepared an elaborate plan for the town. It included the concept of a major centre, connected to five satellite communities on an axial road pattern, the core of each centre being circular and including commercial plazas and an inner common. But for reasons not entirely understood the pattern of development in Sydney reverted to the prevailing Loyalist mode.

The beautiful but more forbidding northern part of Nova Scotia was settled by Scotsmen, who were induced to migrate by the late eighteenth-century policy of the British government to hold and consolidate its North American position. One can still observe the faded glory of at least one such settlement (Pictou, on the north shore of Nova Scotia) in the stately homes, originally built as registry offices, banks, and public buildings in the 1860s and 1870s when Pictou was an important shipbuilding centre.

These various streams of settlement resulted in a substantial level of urbanization. Canada's foremost urban demographer has observed: "The Maritimes comprise one of the two oldest of the major regions of Canada (the other is Quebec) in regard to a history of considerable European settlement, and this region may have been the most highly urbanized of the major regions some time in the eighteenth century."[12]

The Rural Centre and Resource Towns

In viewing Canadian development from the perspective of its urban dimension, several broad patterns stand out. One is the centralization of its growth. The original predominance of a trading city like Montreal was perpetuated, and as settlement spread from east to west, a few big places have concentrated the capital and manufactured goods and the services required by hinterland populations. The towns established close to rural settlement remain comparatively small, scaled to the day-to-day necessities of a limited service area. Another characteristic is hierarchy: towns and cities are not isolated phenomena, but form a network of regional sub-systems in which constituent communities are differentiated in function and size, and all are linked by economic and social ties to a major centre. And still another pattern is one of geographical specialization and character: the prairie town, the northern mining town, and so on.

Whichever of these views is invoked, there are two types of urban community that have deep roots in Canadian conditions: the towns serving agricultural settlement, and the centre that is based on extracting the wealth of mine and forest.

The emergence of the rural centre is associated with the successive opening up of arable regions. Broadly speaking this occurred first in Ontario through the clearing of the lowlands hardwood forest, mainly between the twenties and eighties of the last century. It was followed by several waves of settlement on the prairie grasslands and parkbelt beginning in the 1870s in Manitoba and extending throughout the region until World War One, and continuing today on the last

13

of the unsettled black soil lands, in the Peace River region of Northern Alberta.

In the last quarter of the twentieth century, the original rural centres of southern Ontario are increasingly associated with and are affected by a highly industrialized and urbanized belt, and have overlaid on them either manufacturing or service functions (for example, Whitby, Midland, Nanticoke), or overspill dormitory functions (Georgetown and Aurora in the Toronto area; Elmira, New Hamburg—Kitchener in the Waterloo area; Strathroy, Lambeth in the London area). It is therefore mainly on the prairies that the rural centre survives, as a place primarily concerned with providing goods and services to an agricultural community.

Accounts of the origins of prairie towns read very much like a real-live model of the classical dissection of the "country towns" by Thorstein Veblen (1887-1929), the persuasive institutional economist who emphasized the spirit of speculation and the warping of civic life by the collective urge to boost real estate values and amass windfall gains. There is a certain typical prairie town life cycle: it is precipitated by the rather explosive concurrence of the railway, rural settlement on cheap homestead land, and Red Fife grain which, because of a short maturation period, eludes the bite of prairie frost. The town is designated a railway divisional point, there is a sudden increase in homestead entries in the region, and it takes off. From a virtual construction camp of a few hundred people, the settlement mushrooms into a town of several thousand almost overnight. The growth ethic takes over.

"A good city is a small city that's certain to grow into a big city; that is where all the easiest fortunes are made," declared a prominent early booster of Moose Jaw, Saskatchewan. Some places like Moose Jaw almost made it as "one of the greatest cities on the plains," then experienced a severe decline in the process of trying to cope with a crushing burden of municipal debt during the Great Depression. Others had a fate like Biggar, Saskatchewan, about sixty miles west of Saskatoon. It went through a typical early life cycle, complete with a phony land promotion in a slough (which sent its mayor to jail), but its great expectations were not fulfilled. Today Biggar is described as being "all squished together, tiny Victorian frame bungalows . . . on - 25-foot lots . . . crowded and claustrophobic as if its population were two million instead of 2,600." And this "niggardliness about land" in the midst of endless acres of grassland is attributed to "an urban tradition which equates land with wealth."[13]

It was the excesses of land specualtion in western development which most impressed Thomas Adams, the British town and country

Prairie Landscape, Manitoba
The form of the prairie town shows very strongly the close relationship between settlement and the land in western Canada. The railway, which went through in the last quarter of the nineteenth century, is the town's lifeline. It provides the spur, sites for grain elevators and links to major terminals and world markets. In this sense it is the by-product of the country's first major planning concept — the relating of transportation, tariffs and land settlement in the National Policy.

"The Dominion of Canada represented a planned society. Canada was never the negative laisser-faire state of the individualist doctrinaires but a positive state from the beginning, a semi-socialist state, the top layer of whose society was the beneficiary rather than the bottom." Arthur R.M. Lower, Colony To Nation, (1946).

15

planner who participated in the first major national review of the use and abuse of Canadian natural resources. "In a new country," he wrote in 1917, "a certain amount of speculation is inevitable, and is not an unmixed blessing. It draws out and stimulates energy and enterprise that might otherwise lie dormant. . . . But, when the pioneer stage is over and the building up of the social life of a new community begins, speculation takes on new and injurious forms. Socially created values are inflated and exploited and monopolies in natural resources are established. It is in this latter form that specualtion in Canada in recent years had produced deplorable moral and financial results, in rural as well as urban areas." And he went on to recommend, as at least a partial remedy for the associated problem of inflated land values and misused productive land, "a well organized, carefully planned and economically sound system of land development."[14]

As it later turned out, there were other elements in western Canadian society which were to lead to a positive response to Adams' plea. The vicissitudes of prairie existence in both climate and world markets, together with the openness and pragmatism of the frontier heritage, provided a basis for cooperative systems and innovative politics. This was expressed in somewhat extreme form in the rural utopia proposed in 1925 by E.A. Partridge, the organizer of the cooperative Grain Growers' Company. His ideal settlement would be in the form of self-sufficient and self-governing communes of thirty-five hundred and seven thousand residents, without private property, rent, taxes or lawyers. And this counter-tradition was expressed in the system of land development which, ironically, was built out of the ruins of the Depression. The many thousands of acres of tax-delinquent land, much of it subdivided but not developed during previous speculative sprees, provided a basis in regional centres like Saskatoon, Red Deer and Edmonton for the planned development of new residential districts on publicly owned land.[15]

While the establishment of the rural centre is based on east-west forces — the railway, the path of migration and settlement — the emergence of the other types of resource-based towns is a south-north phenomenon. Most of these urban places, like Schefferville or Sturgeon Falls, Flin Flon or Kitimat, are the by-product of investments by metropolitan-based corporations in the iron and other base metals of the Canadian Shield, in the pulp resources of the boreal forest or the power resources of the Shield or Cordilleran Coast Mountain area. They have a number of features in common with agriculturally-based rural centres: dependence on railway access for production, both to get supplies in and bulky goods out (although in

Chemainus, Vancouver Island, British Columbia
Pulp Town, Lumber Port, Sawmill Centre

Single-industry towns located near the resources of mine or forest, a power supply and the means of moving primary products to market are one of the characteristic forms of urban development in Canada. These were recently estimated to include over six hundred communities of less than 30,000 people, representing a total population of about one million.

These places offer a unique challenge to community planning and building. Their residents exhibit to a degree more than people in other types of urban places a preoccupation with their isolation from outside communities, and with opportunities foregone. This is intensified by another feature of such towns: the high level of observability. "All citizens have an ongoing account of the activities of many people in the community." There is social pressure to conform in ideas and behaviour and "the isolation of the majority of one-industry communities literally seals them off from other alternatives for great periods of time." Quoted by Rex Lucas in Minetown, Milltown, Railtown *(1971)*

17

more remote centres air travel now supplants rail traffic); and service to a working population where jobs are subject to the whims of an international staple market.

The major differences, however, are that the resource base is extractive and not renewable and hence sometimes precarious and unstable, and the economy of these towns is not based on independent employment, but on wage labour in mine, mill and processing plant, often operated by a single predominant company; nor is it based on extensive settlement. As a consequence such areas tend not to have highly developed urban systems, with trading centres of varying size and economic reach, as in the prairies. And, as an aspect of this, the largely unsettled countryside accentuates the feeling of isolation from the main stream of development around the big cities, whose head offices are perceived, rightly or wrongly, as the manipulators of the life of the hinterland.

Altogether the single-enterprise resource towns represent an important feature of urbanization in Canada, for there are over six hundred such communities, with populations generally less than thirty thousand, which are home to over a million people. Recent research has drawn attention to the special social climate of these places. Their residents exhibit, to a degree more than people in other types of urban places, a preoccupation with their isolation from outside communities, and with opportunities foregone. In a 1970 Manitoba study on the quality of life in resource frontier communities, the residents of such places ranked "access to cities in the south" and "communications" as the services most in need of improvement in their own communities. The factor of isolation is intensified by another feature of such towns: the high level of observability. "All citizens have an ongoing account of the activities of many people in the community." Given the hierarchial social structure of these communities, there is social pressure to conform in ideas and behaviour and "the isolation of the majority of one-industry communities literally seals them off from other alternatives for great periods of time." These are some of the features of resource communities that present a unique challenge to community planning and building. [16]

Urbanization: Challenge and Response

From a certain point of view, Canadian history since the turn of the century can be seen as an evolution from primary resources to secondary industrial production, from rural to urban settlement, and from scattered regional development to an integrated but highly centralized national economic structure. The demographer, Leroy Stone, has pointed out how "the expansion of wheat production for export became a major force in promoting the integration and inter-dependence of Canadian regions (with a particularly notable impulse to manufacturing in Central Canada), and this expansion had an important *multiplier effect* upon employment opportunities in the centres where non-primary activities were concentrated—that is, in the urban area."

These transformations are reflected in population statistics. Within a century, from 1851, Canada's urban population (urban centres over 1,000) had increased from 13 per cent to 70 per cent of the total population. Canada's current rate of annual increase in urban population, 4.1 per cent, is the highest amongst the advanced countries.[17] The pattern of urbanization is uneven across the country: as reported in the 1971 census, the central provinces, Ontario and Quebec are respectively 82 per cent and 81 per cent urban, while British Columbia is 76 per cent, the prairies, 67 per cent, and the Atlantic region, 56 per cent.

The response to urbanization in Canada has been similar to the experience of all industrialized countries, with certain special accents arising from the association of growth with two phenomena: large-scale European immigration and the opening up of settlement and development frontiers in the western plains and the mineral and forestry hinterlands of the Precambrian Shield. In this context, our typical environmental responses have assumed the characteristics of a series of expedient and not quite effective adjustments to rapid, technologically induced change. Paradox and contradiction are the essence of the industrial city and each adaptation contains the seeds of a dilemma.

Urban Development and Urban Form

To meet the needs of expanding urban populations, the rectangular layout of towns provided a handy form of cellular growth at a time when sophisticated design expertise was scarce. There were a few exceptions in eastern Canada; for example, Rosedale was Victorian Toronto's major expression of the Garden City Movement. But gen-

Urban Growth Rates, 1951-61*
Industrial Countries

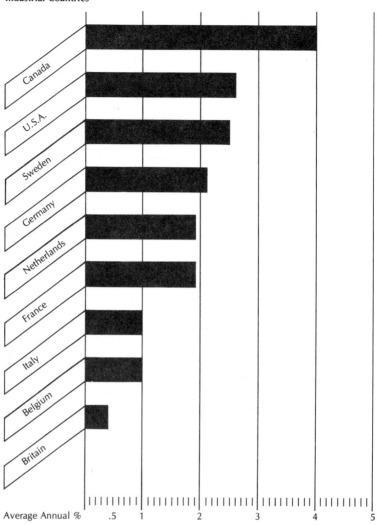

Canada		
U.S.A.		
Sweden		
Germany		
Netherlands		
France		
Italy		
Belgium		
Britain		

Average Annual %   .5   1   2   3   4   5

Note: Actual period for specific countries were as follows: 1951-61, Britain, Italy, Canada; 1950-60 U.S.A., Sweden; 1950-61, Germany (F.R.); 1947-61 Belgium; 1947-60, Netherlands; 1946-62, France.

Source: Fourth Annual Review, Economic Council of Canada, Queen's Printers, 1967.

erally the gridiron pattern of development left a legacy of monotony, and of functional disorder in the form of street patterns which invited ubiquitous traffic flows and frustrated the organization of efficient transportation systems. As early as 1914, when streetcars were being introduced to Canadian cities, Mr. Frank Beer, head of one of the first private-public efforts to build "decent cheap housing for wage-earners," reported to the fifth annual meeting of the Commission of Conservation that "the checker-board plan of city subdivision, unbroken by diagonal thoroughfares and with too little provision for rapid transport, entails an excessive waste of time upon citizens going to and from their work . . . masons and carpenters are required to travel for over an hour after leaving their homes in order to reach their work."[18]

It is perhaps easy to forget under today's circumstances that much of the early interest in community planning in Canada arose in response to the poor health conditions of the most industrialized cities. When Montreal had a population of 500,000 and Toronto 400,000, at about 1912, they had a death rate attributable to typhoid fever of 10.4 and 20.5 per 100,000 respectively, compared to the current rate for Canada of .4. Those were the days when a contemporary report on "Necessity of Uniform Laws for Sanitary Plumbing" noted the following about inner city factories: "Some of their so-called sanitary conveniences become so repulsive through lack of attention to requirements and cleanliness, that they are a menace to public health. It is a standing disgrace, that in some factories the sanitary equipment does service for both sexes. Sometimes the water closets are used as urinals, which is liable to cause filthiness, and by such use they become a danger instead of a benefit." About rooming houses: "It is not an uncommon thing to find one water-closet, without bath or lavatory accommodation, serving the needs of the occupants of whole flats." And about systems of sanitary plumbing: "The bad conditions prevailing in some of our industrial cities is a very serious matter. The City of Hamilton, with a population of over

---

Comparative Urban Growth Rates

Comparing Canada's international position on rate of urbanization underlines strongly the surge of urban development in this country. This can be translated into terms of investments required in housing, transportation and other services, and into the demand for intelligent planning and management. The pace of development gives a special accent to the Canadian urban experience. We inherit the results of city-building under pressure: some shoddy, thoughtless development, the squandering of productive land, environmental abuses and financial stress. But we also inherit the zest for tackling anew each decade the task of creating man's city. It is still an open question whether we can mobilize the management skills, imagination, individual restraint and social conscience to create really humane cities in Canada.

80,000 people, without any recognized system, may be cited as an example, and also towns like London, Guelph, Kingston, Galt and Windsor in Ontario, Quebec and Three Rivers in Quebec, Brandon and Portage la Prairie in Manitoba, Fernie and Kamloops in British Columbia, Amherst and Truro in Nova Scotia."

These were the kinds of conditions that made the central city a place to escape from for those Canadians who could buy convenient access to the countryside. Central city pollution induced a flight, aided in turn by the horse-drawn train, commuter rail, electrified streetcar and automobile, to the more salubrious conditions of the suburb. The Canadian urbanite's vividly recalled rural background, whether in this country or in Europe, gave this tendency impetus and had something to do with its low density, liberally gardened form. The Arcadian dream dies hard! But out of such innocent aspirations came the rigid separation of house from work, the dormitory suburb, restrictive zoning, the erection of "municipal fences," and the weakening of integration between the parts of the city. This complex of consequences is one of the major sources of the current struggle, under the banner of regional government, to spatially reintegrate our urban areas and restore both the sense and fact of community.

From the beginning the industrial city in Canada produced a dominant core, based on the concentration of the industrial power source and the centralization at a downtown hub of inter- and intra-urban transport. While there has been a succession of displacements of specific uses from the centre, the core remains as the focal point for those amenities, such as a concert hall or an employment office, which need optimum accessiblity to the entire urban area, and those institutions, like brokerage houses and the stock market, which require close day-to-day contact. The advantages of the centre have made it the peak of land values, which has further intensified development in the core. These centripetal forces produced one of the major features of the industrial city: the central skyscraper cluster. This type of pyramid building is still very much going on in Canada, not only in the biggest cities, but in the medium-sized cities like Edmonton, where a virtual explosion of office buildings and high-rise apartments has within twenty years produced characteristic attributes: the strong central symbol, the intensity and vitality arising from the jostling of people, functions, and traffic. But behind these virtues is the vice of congestion. As the largest concentration of employment in the area, the business centre attracts the daily tidal waves of traffic, from and to dispersed residential areas. A recent survey of urban transportation indicates that in Canada the pressures of this phenomenon apply equally to small municipalities with less

The Central Skyscraper Cluster

One has a certain awe—and anxiety—in the face of the irresistible urges to build to the sky in places like downtown Toronto. The pressure of business growth and population and escalating land values is supposed to be behind it; but an objective analysis will show that the existing and announced floor space far exceeds any reasonable forecast of need. What drives the process? Where will it lead?

Half a century ago, Louis Henry Sullivan, the Chicago architect who had most to do with the fostering of the skyscraper, made the following penetrating observations:

> "The lofty steel frame makes a powerful appeal to the architectural imagination where there is any... The appeal and the inspiration lie, of course, in the element of loftiness, in the suggestion of slenderness and aspiration, the soaring quality as of a thing rising from the earth as a unitary utterance, Dionysian in beauty.
>
> The tall steel frame structure may have its aspects of beneficience; but so long as a man say: 'I shall do as I please with my own,' it presents opposite aspects social menace and danger. For such is the complexity, the complication, the intricacy of modern feudal society: such is its neurasthenia, its hyperesthesia, its precarious instability, that not a move may be made in any one of its manifold activities, according to its code, without creating risk and danger in its wake."

The Autobiography of an Idea (1924).

than 50,000 people as they do to the large metropolitan areas. Perhaps the greatest challenge posed by the contemporary business centre is to prevent its dehumanization as its functions become more specialized and its form increasingly monumental.[19]

Immigration, Settlement and Social Distress

Historian Arthur Lower has succinctly described the role of immigrant labour in the development of Canada: "All great staples have thrown up high-coloured exploitive socieites like wildfire, and have rapidly subjugated all the country fit for producing them. Wheat was to be no exception to the rule. It called for men and for railroads, and it soon got both." Between 1896 and 1930, about five million immigrants came to Canada, representing a score of countries and ethnic groups in Europe. "Winnipeg and other western towns had become veritable Towers of Babel. . . . " By the mid-thirties, net migration had stabilized at a point where about a fifth of the population was made up of "new Canadians, who settled in agricultural colonies or formed ethnic enclaves in the cities, many in the older deteriorating districts.[20]

At the peak of this immigration in 1913 when it reached half a million, Mrs. Plumptre, speaking on behalf of the National Council of Women, identified the relationship between immigration and urban social problems. "The difficulties in connection with public health and housing," she declared, "are very largely due to the enormous influx of persons, some of whom are not accustomed to city life. . . . We invite people to come to Canada, and then fail to make provision for homes for them."

While ethnic communities were better than no communities at all, immigrant groups added a new word to the urban lexicon: "alienation." This problem had been anticipated a few years earlier in Chicago (in the last decade of the nineteenth century) by a brilliant social worker, Jane Addams, and by a young protégé who later became a specialist in labour-management relations and eventually prime minister of Canada, William Lyon Mackenzie King. The nature of her solution, Hull House, a settlement house providing an oasis of brotherhood in a disintegrating and somewhat hostile urban community, was indicative of what had become a general problem in northern American cities. In Canada, there were added dimensions arising from the relationship of the extractive hinterland to the established cities. These included the drift of the unskilled, seasonally unemployed miner or lumberjack, often unattached and homeless, to the city for the winter; the flow of vice between the two poles ("vice suppression in the cities intensified the moral problems of the hinterland, while suppression in the hinterland intensified the problems of the cities"); and the brutalization and cultural poverty of life in disproportionately male populations in the mining and lumbering settlements established in Northern Ontario, Quebec, and interior British Columbia. The major expression of immigrant alienation, however, was in the large cities. Here high rates of desertion, illegitimacy and prostitution reflected the difficulties of rapidly growing cities, which were incapable of providing enough jobs, housing and services. Also, the real estate market, protecting the values of the established well-to-do, inadvertently fostered the ghettoizing of the Canadian city. In many ways, and in spite of our impressive humanitarian reformation, we are still fighting a rearguard action against the conditions of the early industrial city.[21]

The Pressure of Land Costs

The preoccupation with land—land settlement, use, trading, speculation and cost—has been a continuing motif in Canadian development. The real estate market, the prevailing mode of buying and selling land as a commodity subject to the price system like any other commodity, has had far-reaching repercussions on the urban habitat. It has coloured all aspects of urban development, as well as having a number of very specific effects. While the gross level of land prices has taken some violent swings in Canadian history, there is increasing evidence of a rising trend in urban land prices. From 1951 to 1966, when housing construction costs per square foot increased by 40 per cent, residential land costs increased by 200 per cent. Land costs which for the country as a whole averaged 10 per cent of the total cost of a new house in 1951, were 17 per cent in 1967. This trend continues unabated. It is particularly striking in the metropolitan areas with the highest growth rates, namely Calgary and Edmonton, where land costs as a percentage of total dwelling cost rose from the 19 to 21 per cent level in 1965 to 26 per cent in 1973. The development response to this situation in specific urban regions, particularly in areas like Vancouver, Edmonton and Toronto experiencing rapid population increase, is to push out towards lower, rurally oriented land costs and, as indicated above, in towards intensification of uses near the centre. While these tendencies have the effect of widening environmental choice, they have contributed to both the fission of the urban community (integration of the parts is achieved with increasing strain and cost) and to the problems of overdevelopment in the city core.[22]

Volatile land prices on the urban fringe are an important part of complex forces that create the "urban shadow," an extensive area around the city, subject to indirect urban pressures, which is gradually pushed out of production. This area, which on average is over twice the built-up urban area, contains the land bank for private development; but the size of the area and its indiscriminate impact on productive land and on recreational and landscape resources leads to a degree of waste that we can ill afford.

The Inner City: Urban Decay and Renewal

The kinds of expedient adjustment to rapid change here described have had a far-reaching impact on the industrial city. The vertical expansion of the centre and its concomitant lateral contraction, the flight of population from the centre of the area of transition around it, and the expansion of housing and industry on the urban periphery— the combined impact of these forces has produced a big gap in the urban structure, an area of intensifying and expanding deterioration around the centre. While some of the underlying tendencies have changed, the phenomenon of the inner city problem area remains a part of the contemporary urban scene. The inability of the market mechanism to "correct" the situation has led to massive intervention under the banner of urban renewal: a traumatic experience which, through its failures more than its successes, has demonstrated compellingly the need for an urban policy that places man much closer to centre stage. Such a policy would be founded on a diagnosis of the conditions of the inner city, in the total sense of understanding what contributes to, or detracts from, human welfare. We are now in a position to offer only a tentative analysis.

Whatever the causes, the larger Canadian cities are still characterized by areas around the business-civic core in which there is a concentration of old and sometimes deteriorated buildings, mixed land uses, people of diverse ethnic origins, poverty, high land prices, and a lot of push for change. Understanding the inner city, and doing something about its problems, requires that three different types of inner city areas be recognized.[23]

There are areas, like St. Henri in Montreal and North Point Douglas in Winnipeg, which appear to be caught in a cycle of decline and decay. These are areas in which population has been steadily decreasing during the last decade, as commercial and institutional buildings, parking lots and arterial roads eat away at their residential edges. It is still these areas of Canadian cities which receive successive waves of the disadvantaged: people displaced by redevelopment in the central business district; people migrating from rural areas, such as the Indian and Métis in Winnipeg; or immigrants from abroad, such as the Asiatics in Vancouver. The young and occupationally mobile people in the 15-24 age group tend to leave these areas, as well as others on the way up, leaving a disproportionate number of older people over 65 and of the very young. The people who live in these areas are mainly tenants (with the conspicuous exception of North Point Douglas, Winnipeg) in meagerly maintained buildings put up before 1920, working in service jobs or unskilled and semi-skilled industrial jobs. Many are unemployed or earning low incomes.

Then there are areas which are subtly but significantly different, in which living standards are not dramatically better, but morale is higher and such places take on the characteristics of stable residential communities. Kensington Market, just north and west of the Toronto business core, typifies this inner city phenomenon. A young, economically virile but slowly assimilating immigrant group, the Portuguese, have made the area their home since the mid-fifties. Their stake in the area as it is—the low-rise, red brick, semi-detached and row house streets — has been given expression by a small but articulate and well-established Canadian middle-class leadership. The result is a determined, almost militant, opposition to the invading pressures of downtown business, expressways, high-rise housing, hospitals and the University of Toronto.

A third type of inner city experience is represented by those areas like Fairview and the West End in Vancouver, which are undergoing rapid change. Young people in single-person households, not rich but on the make and mainly Anglo-Saxon in origin, push out a remnant poor population to the fringe areas of the central business district, such as Strathcona in Vancouver, or Allan Gardens in Toronto. Offices, high-rise apartments and land-consuming transportation facilities drastically alter established living patterns. Population declines and is transformed, with a strong bias towards the young, towards middle-income white-collar employment and away from a domestic to a cosmopolitan focus. And the rising aspirations of these areas are reflected in a rising spiral of land prices.

This complex inner city mosaic raises a number of difficult questions for policy-makers: How can declining areas be improved without pushing out the resident, and often-disadvantaged population? Can stable residential communities be maintained within the inner city in the face of invading development pressures from without, and rising land prices within? What is the best way to manage the development of areas in transition so as to minimize disruption and

28

Immigrants in the Canadian City

There are places in the larger Canadian cities which immigrants from many streams, mainly European, have made their own: Winnipeg's North End, Kensington Market in Toronto, Montreal's Main Street, and so on. These are often areas of poverty and some despair, sometimes in the path of the big developer, but always important in the adjustment of special groups of people to a new world.

A Winnipeg novelist has captured one of the vital transactions of an old street market. "From the inside, I got a good close look at the life of anxiety bordering on anguish that is lived by the marginal traders of the perishable goods of the earth. With profit so small, with wastage so high, with the goods he is selling deteriorating by the minute before his very eyes, no wonder the storekeeper gives way sometimes to his gnawing wrath when customer after customer reaches out a greedy hand and in a few short hours a firm, nubile little tomato is turned into a bruised old pro. Every leaf to be discarded was a loss; every fruit or vegetable that a customer criticized was to be defended with peevish and despairing eloquence." Adele Wiseman in Old Markets, New World *(1964).*

29

preserve features of intrinsic value, such as a fine building, street or park, or simply features which give continuity to the human experience in cities?

The Metropolitan Phase: What Is the City?

Urban Canada is now in its metropolitan phase. The distinguishing mark of the metropolis is its size, in population and area. Statistically the metropolitan drift is dramatic: at Confederation, one city with over 100,000 people; at the 1971 census, twenty-two (and, of these, seven contained half a million people or more). At the turn of the century, about one-quarter of the population lived in the "principal regions of metropolitan development;" and today, about half. If present trends continue to the end of this century—and this may turn out to be a big if—it is estimated that over half the population will be in the twelve largest metropolitan areas, and Montreal and Toronto together will contain one-third of the total population of Canada.

The metropolis may seem to be no more than the industrial city writ large. But it is quite clear that much more is involved; increased size is associated with certain qualitative changes in urban structure, institutions and morale. In the main we are disturbed and disoriented by the disappearance of certain characteristic urban traits — a clear physical identity, relatively high density sharply distinguished from the countryside, unique social diversity, centrality in trade and communications, and a single unified government, providing a high degree of local self-determination. The activities of the metropolis are so widely dispersed that it has become in its vital functions and land uses a mixture of city and country; and the same centrifugal thrust has destroyed its corporate unity. With a few exceptions metropolitan areas are municipally balkanized. A mood of confidence in technological and administrative powers alternates with a mood of despair, a palpable fear of losing control over the urban behemoth and over our lives. Paradoxically, as society becomes urbanized, the city itself is in jeopardy. And we are forced back to first principles: what is the city?

The answers that come back from some of the best minds do not, by comparison with reality, offer much comfort. Weber's institutional theory of the city established a kind of benchmark: emphasis was placed on the institutions — political and legal, economic and military — that create an autonomous, self-regulating community. This is confirmed by Toynbee, although he would minimize institutional form and emphasize the substance of social relationships. The sense of community is the touchstone of urbanism. There have also

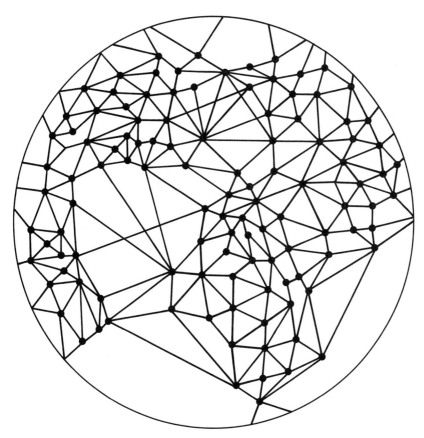

What Is the City?

"The City of the future will form a world-wide network consisting of centres of several orders interconnected by settled parts of various importance". Constantinos A. Doxiadis.

"We have defined it as being an association of human beings who have a feeling that they constitute a community, and who have succeeded in translating this feeling into the terms of a practical corporate life.... The question is whether the physical Megalopolis can ever be made into a city in the social sense. During the last two centuries there has been a race between the proliferation of Megalopolis and the humanization of the conditions of life in it; and, so far, we do not know whether, in this grim race, it is brute matter or humanizing form that is going to come out the winner. This still undecided question is putting a premium on the art of town-planning." Arnold Toynbee.

been social-psychological concepts such as Louis Wirth's concern with the psychic effects and behaviour patterns associated with the rapid increase, high density and heterogeneity of population. Mumford has emphasized the social humanizing function of the city ("the city fosters art and is art"); it is the setting which, through its multitude of opportunities and pitfalls, challenges man, individually and collectively, to his highest achievement.[24]

All of these concepts of the city have one common denominator: an assertion that the city is more than the huddling together of a group of people, with their buildings, who must produce and trade for food to survive. And it is this understanding, highly articulated by some and intuitively felt by many, which underlies the current unease about the city. The hydrogen bomb, as metaphor if not fact, is seen as the technological Frankenstein that delivers the final death blow. With joyless irony it completes the circle from the days when the city defended by wall and citadel (Weber's medieval model) provided maximum physical security, to the present, when the city where people congregate is the most vulnerable form of human settlement. Canada between two colossi has reason to appreciate this point.

From City to Metropolis to Megalopolis
"What is this world-encompassing city going to do to human life in the course of the two thousand million years during which it is said this planet will remain habitable for human beings if, in our time, we refrain from liquidating mankind . . .?

Los Angeles may swell physically to the size of a sub-continent, but the tropical luxuriance of its physical growth may never succeed in making a city of it. In order to become a city, it would have also to evolve at least the rudiments of a soul. This is the essence of cityhood." Arnold Toynbee in Cities of Destiny (1967).

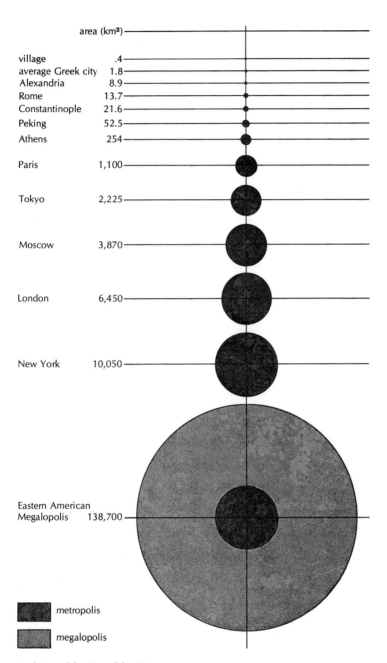

area (km²)

village	.4
average Greek city	1.8
Alexandria	8.9
Rome	13.7
Constantinople	21.6
Peking	52.5
Athens	254
Paris	1,100
Tokyo	2,225
Moscow	3,870
London	6,450
New York	10,050
Eastern American Megalopolis	138,700

metropolis

megalopolis

Evolution of the Size of the City.

2 Transportation: Symptom of Urban Disorder

"Machines are made to serve man, not man to serve machines, regardless of whether the machine is an automobile or a computer. Surely democracy does not dictate that an expressway must be cut through quiet development in a city . . . "[1] The origin of these words, in the prosaic setting of a report of the Ontario Municipal Board, tells us something about the nature of urban problems. The problems of the cities are the problems of society in general, and a decision on transportation in a city raises basic questions about our scale of values, and our environmental priorities. In fact, this is the time in Canadian urban development when such awareness has received explicit recognition at the national level. The federally sponsored overview, *Urban Canada*, demonstrates that the problems in our cities are not exclusive to cities, but have their origins in broader forces. In seeking both understanding and solutions, we must go beyond the city itself.[2]

Urban Canada, the report prepared by Professor Harvey Lithwick for the Minister responsible for Housing in 1970, sets the stage for an attack on the problems of Canadian cities. Lithwick demonstrates that urban patterns are the by-product of an urban process which is closely bound up with the centralist tendency of our economic development. At the national scale it has produced an urban system in which people and jobs are increasingly concentrated in a dozen big cities, at the top of a hierarchy of towns and lesser cities. At the local level, the urban pattern is shaped by the struggle for space; activities are located and related through a series of trade-offs between accessibility and quantity of space. And the problems that emerge in the urban system — poverty, housing, transportation — are all conditioned by the overall urban problem, which is the imbalanced emphasis on economic criteria, to the neglect of total human requirements, in national development. Our cities show the strain.[3]

Transportation Conditions in Canadian Cities

If the city is a system, then any flaws in the functioning of its parts may be a clue to its general state of health. In the spirit of a physician testing blood pressure, it is natural to turn to the most conspicuous aspect of urban life: its transportation. The diagnosis is not good. In October 1971, a study released by the Science Council of Canada reported that in most cities with a population of more than fifty thousand, the following conditions prevailed:

  −automobile and truck traffic congestion during peak periods of travel
  −severe and rising accident rates
  −increasing levels of noise and air pollution, and neighbour-hood blight associated with automobile traffic and parking
  −destruction of developed areas by road expansions
  −declining quality, and rising costs, of public transit.[4]

These conditions are strongly associated with the automobile; more than 80 per cent of total daily urban trips are made by car. Cars are increasing twice as fast as population. The annual rate of growth of automobiles in Canada between 1945 and 1965 was close to 8 per cent. Although truck movements accounted for about 20 per cent of urban traffic, the way we cope with the movement of people in our cities is decisive.

Transportation and the Form of Urban Growth

There are few aspects of the city that reflect so clearly the legacy of nineteenth-century history, as transportation. The major intra-city traffic movements have their origins in the conditions of the industrial city: the segregation of functions, concentration of activities in the centre, reliance on technological solutions, the daily trip to work, the massive denuding of the natural environment, and the pervasiveness of the real estate market. These conditions underlie the predomi-nance of the urban travel trinity: the journey-to-work, the journey-to-centres within the city, and the journey-to-recreation outside the city to satisfy man's "biological hunger."

While the development of inter-urban transportation in the nineteenth century made possible the concentration of production and people in big cities, the later development of intra-urban transportation—from horse-drawn and electric streetcars to the subway and motor car—created the metropolitan form of settlement as we know it. There is now a flow of population to the suburb limited only by what is considered a comfortable commuting distance from home to work. This process is still highly active in Canada, as

City and Urban Fringe Growth, Five Metropolitan Areas Per Cent Changes, 1956-66

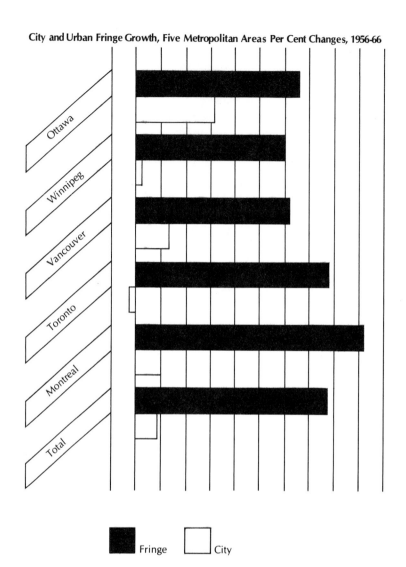

Fringe ☐ City

Source: N.H. Lithwick, Urban Canada, Ottawa: Central Mortgage and Housing Corporation, 1970, p. 102.

City and Urban Fringe Growth

The graph above demonstrates the dominant fact of growth within urban regions: the increasing spatial spread of our city. This process of metropolitanizing both expresses the mobility of the car, and the increasing strain on the urban structure, as development moves to the margin of comfortable commuting distance from the work and leisure and shopping opportunities of the metropolis.

suggested by the accompanying figures on the split of growth from 1956 to 1966, between the city and the urban fringe in our five largest metropolitan areas: Montreal, Toronto, Vancouver, Winnipeg and Ottawa.

Urban Growth, Five Major Metropolitan Areas, City and Urban Fringe 1956–1966

| | Metropolitan Area Population | | | | | | |
	Montreal	Toronto	Vancouver	Winnipeg	Ottawa	Total	%Change
CITY/FRINGE							
City proper							
1956	1,109,439	667,706	365,844	255,093	222,129	2,619,211	
1966	1,222,255	664,584	410,375	257,005	290,741	2,844,960	
% Change	+10%	−1%	+12%	+1%	+31%		8.6
Fringe area							
1956	636,461	834,582	299,173	157,439	123,340	2,050,995	
1966	1,214,562	1,493,912	481,911	251,754	203,794	3,645,933	
% Change	+91%	+79%	+61%	+60%	+65%		77.7

SOURCE: N.H. Lithwick, *Urban Canada* (Ottawa: Central Mortgage and Housing Corporation, 1970), p. 102.

The general distribution of growth is quite clear: while the city proper had a population increase of about 8 per cent, the fringe area increased by over 77 per cent. The metropolis has been spreading out.[5]

The General Theory of Urban Transportation

In response to metropolitan conditions, a general theory of urban transportation has evolved, which assigns to each mode of travel its appropriate role, based on such performance characteristics as capacity, speed, cost and convenience. According to the theory, forms of transportation may be ideally assigned along two axes — of space and of time — in accordance with the concentration of trips along those axes. Recommended modes range from rail rapid transit with a capacity of forty thousand passengers per hour to cars on streets and freeways with hourly capacities, depending on circumstances, from nine hundred to nine thousand passengers. And if many things "are kept equal," it is possible to demonstrate that transportation service, in terms of capacity and cost, can in this manner be optimized.[6]

The ideal model that emerges from the application of this theory is a system of nicely modulated facilities, from cars in the buffered

37

**The Highway in the City — Macdonald-Cartier Freeway —
Avenue Road — Bathurst Street exit**

The urban highway, or expressway, has in the age of the motor car become an indispensable feature of the modern city. Accessibility, the supreme virtue of cities, depends on the expressway. But, paradoxically, the expressway has come to symbolize our failure to come to grips with transportation in our cities. In practice, we appear to be caught in a rather gloomy parody of Parkinson's Law: traffic expands to fill the available road capacity. The tortoise of supply can never overtake the hare of demand. Increasingly, we are forced to ask ourselves: what price private mobility?

streets in the low-density suburbs, to small local buses or other forms of public transportation along collector roads, leading to rapid transit stations or mainline bus stops; and finally to the major trunk service itself (subway or surface depending on the size of the city) through the high-density core of the city to its business and civic heart. In the largest metropolitan areas, commuter railroad lines are plugged into the system both at rapid transit transfer points and the downtown area. In off-peak hours, the car is ubiquitous.

There is nothing wrong with this theory except that it does not work. Other things do not remain "equal." The city is subject to near cataclysmic shifts, arising from changes in the form, distribution, amounts and areal spread of the activities that are the generators of travel — like the dramatic shift that occurred after 1966 in Canada's major cities from low-rise single-family detached residences to high-rise multiple-family apartments. Such changes create imbalances in the urban circulatory system. As the pendulum swings between forms of development with vastly different impacts on travel patterns (e.g., the spread-out suburb compared to the concentrated apartment district), transportation policy and programs are characteristically preoccupied with solving yesterday's problems. This built-in difficulty is accentuated when a city's transportation capability is not well balanced: that is, when it cannot organize delivery of service from several candidate transportation modes with more or less equal effectiveness. And this problem is aggravated further when the transportation function is treated in isolation, as a species of engineering, and is not coordinated with the planning system for the environment at large. Not surprisingly, the real world of urban transportation is full of trouble. And the most conspicuous manifestation of this is our inability to cope with the private automobile, notwithstanding that we make our heaviest financial commitment to accommodating it. Investment in major roads within the eleven largest urban areas, ranging in size from Thunder Bay to Montreal, has been running at a per capita level which is about five times the investment in public transit.[7]

Canada's slight technological lag behind the United States makes the American experience both a disturbing and edifying foretaste of present trends. From this we can see that a large-scale road-building program, massively supported by the federal government, still leaves the transportation system of most American cities in a state of incipient crisis. Experience suggests a rather gloomy parody of Parkinson's law: private traffic expands to fill the available road capacity.

39

A striking example of this is the widening of the Macdonald-Cartier Freeway (Highway 401) north of the Metropolitan Toronto area from six to twelve lanes. Since the start of the project in 1961, there has been an approximate doubling of annual average daily traffic to about 90,000 vehicles in 1969, with a peak of 152,000 in that year in a central 1.2 mile stretch. This is a rate of growth that far exceeds any metopolitan, provincial or national population growth rates.[8] The spread of pavement in response to this kind of apparently insatiable demand creates extreme tension and increasing opposition from the communities along the way.

Economic Diagnosis

While the problems that are inherent in an auto-dominated system are serious enough, a sound appreciation of transportation within cities requires consideration of overspill effects. At present, urban transportation unfortunately provides an almost perfect demonstration of the economic concept of external diseconomies: the situation that arises when the provision of goods or services results in damages being inflicted on other groups of people or on the public at large. For a service like road-based transportation this means that the value of its imputed benefits would be reduced by the aggregate value of the damages. Amongst the damages must be counted traffic accidents; all forms of pollution; the inefficient use of energy, i.e. fossil fuel; the rate of land consumption relative to other modes; junkyards; and various repercussions on urban structure and the built environment, including the disruption of established communities and the incremental costs of developing in a low-density spread-out pattern. Many of these adverse consequences are difficult to compute but conceptually it is not far-fetched to imagine that the social value of the service, after all damages are taken into account, may be negative.[9]

An Ecological View

Beyond the economist's model, there are implications of the motorized environment that are more far-reaching and disturbing. The headlong drive to urbanization, the expansion psychology, the rise of the metropolis (or clusters of metropolises) as the predominant form of human settlement, the dependence on the private car and the social trauma produced by its mass use constitutes a chain of conditions that raise the most fundamental questions about the fate of the human community. The car becomes the symbol of urban man's precarious adjustment to the environment. This is illustrated by the

The Car Cemetery

As a blot on the landscape, this kind of junkyard must be counted as one of the external costs or diseconomies of the automobile. It is a symptom of changes in the technology of steel production, the more efficient oxygen furnace, which uses less scrap steel and has less tolerance for impurities such as copper and aluminum, which are in car bodies. And it is an unlovely symbol of the industrial system's inability to complete the recycling of its wastes. New waste-handling techniques — hydraulic crushers, car-eating machines which sort component materials, non-polluting incineration — strongly suggest a need for regional collectional and processing centres. Who will be responsible to make this happen?

41

contrast between the cultural sequence of technological society and the natural energy-food sequence.

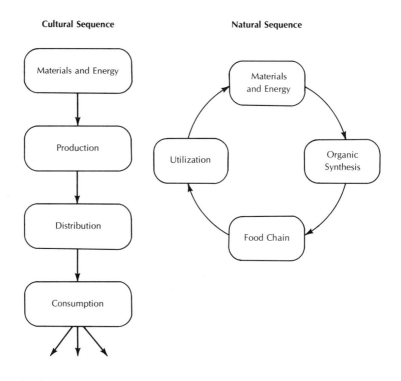

Cultural Sequence

Materials and Energy

Production

Distribution

Consumption

Natural Sequence

Materials and Energy

Organic Synthesis

Food Chain

Utilization

The human production system in society is basically linear; it produces large volumes of waste which are not recycled. By contrast, processes in nature are basically cyclical. In "living communities" an open, steady state is approximated. "Green plants utilize solar energy to build carbon compounds that sustain themselves and animals as well, while complementary processes return material for re-use."[10] The components of the system remain in balance. In the energy-production cycle of the contemporary human community, the final critical phase of re-use is highly deficient. As a consequence, crises of energy supply and waste disposal are built in.

The car only too dramatically exemplifies the fatal flaw in the cultural sequence. The internal combustion engine is a massive consumer of fossil fuels at a time when a limit to supplies is in sight, and it is a relatively inefficient user of fuel — thermal efficiency does not exceed 10 per cent to 25 per cent. From the point of view of gallons per passenger mile, the bus is five times more efficient than the car, and the train twelve times.[11]

The very design feature which underlies the engine's thermal qualities—high compression requiring a fuel air ratio of about 12 to 1 —accounts for the major source of automobile air pollution, which is the emission through the tailpipe of the incompletely burned hydrocarbons. In an urban situation in which traffic moves in peaks and is frequently stalled and left to idle, the air is filled with the danger of the "seven deadly" pollutants: lead, organic compounds, carbon monoxide, nitrogen oxides, particulates, sulphur oxides, and carbon dioxide. The motorized environment of our time is loaded with a high hazard for respiratory damage: bronchitis, bronchial asthma, emphysema and lung cancer.

Is the Car Obsolete?

It is tempting for the technological mind to see a way out of the automobile syndrome by the discovery and application of new devices. The Science Council of Canada, with its thirty-three "transportation improvement projects," yielded a little to this temptation in its statement on the application of science and technology to urban development. It is of critical importance, however, not to oversimplify the problem. The car may kill us, but we cling to it because it has become a "necessity." One is reminded of the observation of the philosopher Herbert Marcuse: "At this stage, the question is no longer: how can the individual satisfy his needs without hurting others, but rather how can he satisfy his needs without hurting himself." Other viewpoints confirm the depth of the problem. "The passiveness of man in industrial society today," writes the psychiatrist Erich Fromm, "is one of the most characteristic and pathological features." And John Kenneth Galbraith, the prominent economist, exploding the myth that "the consumer is king," has demonstrated how the corporate structure manages and creates its own market. Innovations that do not conform to entrenched production prototypes make very little progress: for example, hybrid fuel-burning or electric cars with drastically lower emission but with maximum speeds of 55 m.p.h. are not being actively developed and promoted. The car as we know it is still, in spite of the bicycle revolution, firmly entrenched as part of the Canadian way of life.[12]

Are we caught in an urban transportation trap? At this stage we need the perspective of history. Hans Blumenfeld, writing on the "theory of city form" has demonstrated that every new means of intra-urban transportation promotes horizontal growth.[13] He traces this path in the development of the North American city from pioneer days to the present. Within the contemporary metropolitan area we

43

Man's Love Affair With The Car. From romance . . . to stark reality . . . to romance?
*"Cars are clearly the most popular of all consumer durables. They are containers as
well as movers, for shopping, for children, for the whole family on holiday. They
appear in the wake of affluence as man's first technological love. They will thus not
easily be banished. Can anything be done to make them rather less lethal?"*

*"The worst pressures from automobiles both in terms of air pollution, congestion,
and disruption occur in cities and certainly no commuter pays the full economic cost
of bringing his car — often a single driver in a station wagon — into the scarcest real
estate in the world, the center city." From Only One Earth by Barbara Ward and René
Dubos.*

44

seem to have reached, by means of auto-mobility, the final form of growth: the phase of interstitial growth. The space between the suburbs, established along radial transportation lines, has filled in, creating a solid, densely built-up area. At this stage of urban evolution, we have gone through several cycles of establishing new urban nuclei on the fringes of cities, followed by the filling-in process, and further suburban leaps followed by more filling-in, and so on.

This historical scenario begs a critical question: Have we reached a stage in the most heavily urbanized parts of Canada where the car is obsolete? Given the time-distance tolerances of the journey-to-work, have we attained the limits of the automobile's range as an agent of urban transportation? If the answer is in the affirmative, we will have to increasingly turn our attention to creating a new kind of city, and with it new modes of transportation, consistent with the expanded scale of settlement.

The features of this new urban form can be drawn out from our diagnosis of the city's ills. We still suffer the consequences of the paradoxical forces unleashed by full-scale industrialization. The city as a production machine and as a real estate market is not yet reconciled with the city as a place to live. The very solutions we have contrived for coping with these forces, such as the car and the expressway, bring us into still deeper trouble: a disintegrating urban form and a polluted urban habitat. The answer to this does not lie in some kind of Luddite abandonment of technology, but in the socially responsible use of technology, and in planning that is ecological — based on the widest view of human requirements and of the capacity of the environmental system to meet them.

This approach, for example, would lead us to prefer transportation facilities which have lower toxic emissions and which absorb less energy per unit of service and to the deliberate shaping of the elements of human settlement towards agreed ends. In practice, this produces a bias away from the internal combustion engine towards, for example, the electrical linear induction motor (used in trains), and other low-polluting forms of motive power; towards cars with low compression ratios rather than high ones, as at present; and towards the movement of goods by trains rather than trucks because the former use only one-sixth the energy of the latter per ton-mile.[14]

As far as the form of cities is concerned, the key is to change the prevailing structure, the distribution of activities and their linkages, in accordance with collective preferences. For example, these days we seem to want both the economies of bigness and the joys of community, both anonymity and a personal environment. These seemingly contradictory wishes are attainable — at a price. We would have to build (or rebuild) our city on the spine of a fast, low-polluting, mass transportation service. By reversing the present role of mass transit and the private car for the journey-to-work, more people would have more choice in types of living environments. The radius from a major centre to residential communities might, under present technology, be quite readily doubled without any increase in the time of travel. Labour would become accessible to places of work throughout the system, and hence a substantial part of employment, except certain high-order functions with strong centralizing affinities, would be decentralized. Pleasure could be pursued throughout the urban region. A new form of settlement assuming the form of a regional city would gradually emerge.

Land: The
All-Pervading
Problem

The land has entered deeply into the Canadian consciousness. It was a conspicuous ingredient of John A. Macdonald's National Policy. Harold Innis, our most eminent economic historian, has built an impressive theory of Canadian growth around the concept of staple production from the forests, mines and farmland. The land's grandeur—and delicacy—has been immortalized by the Group of Seven, and it is a brooding presence in our literature from Frederick Philip Grove and Malcolm Lowry to Margaret Laurence and Yves Thériault.

During most of this time it has been a symbol of the superabundance of our natural resources, of the pioneer's struggle to render it productive, and of a certain awareness of man's fragile fate in the face of eternal and unyielding nature. To a degree, Thériault speaks for all of us when in the words of Ashini, the Montagnais Indian hunter, he says " . . . man in the old time . . . took the time to stoop and study the bare living earth. He climbed the trees to watch the living sky. And if he heard the voices of animals or of the wind, of water, and of trees, he listened until he knew them. I think that today the good of man is his solitude, and that he loses all balance when he joins himself to other men."[1]

And join ourselves we certainly have, with far-reaching consequences that we are only beginning to acknowledge. This country is well advanced in the metropolitan phase of urbanization, but has not yet fully adjusted to the concomitant development pressure on land in the major urban-centred regions. The resultant conditions, characteristically expressed in rising land prices, are manifested in particular in those regions like the Lower Fraser in British Columbia and southern peninsular Ontario, which have high urban growth rates and a limited regional land base. Both provinces have intervened to moderate prices and protect their good land: Ontario with a 50 per cent tax (1974) on speculative gains, and British Columbia with the establishment of a Land Commission (1973) empowered to designate agricultural reserves and to acquire lands for open space and a land bank. It will be interesting to observe such different measures applied to two of the three Canadian regions (the other is Montreal) that most

47

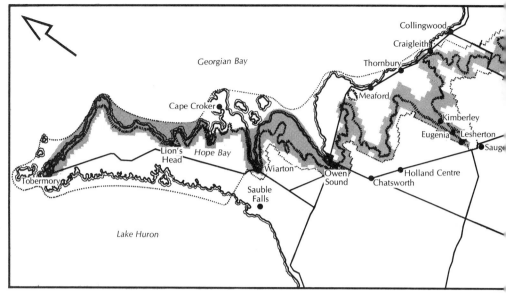

Niagara Escarpment, Environmental Corridor

"No amount of 'cosmetic surgery' during or after production can hide the fact that a pit or quarry is incompatible with the accepted policy of preserving the Niagara Escarpment." Development Planning in Ontario: The Niagara Escarpment *(1973).*

The policy challenge posed by the Niagara Escarpment is one that Canadians increasingly face: how to preserve an area of unique natural parkland in a region of heavy urbanization and resource use conflicts? Ontario proposes a three-pronged approach: the restriction of quarrying in the belt of prime recreational land; the acquisition of key areas; and development control. A Niagara Escarpment Commission has been established to supervise the planning and control process.

---

severely experience urbanization pressures.

The situation is particularly acute in Ontario, which has 35 per cent of Canada's population, and about 9 per cent of the improved arable land—most of it along the Great Lakes transportation corridor. There are no more than about 13,500 square miles of crop land within the province, and possible rates of attrition, even without urban encroachment, look alarmingly high in the light of projected medium-range urban population levels of over eight million in 1981 and twelve and three-quarter million by 2001.[2] It is no wonder that in announcing a joint federal-provincial land study early in 1972, the responsible minister, Jean Marchand, declared: "Plans must be instituted now to preserve agricultural land required for future food production."

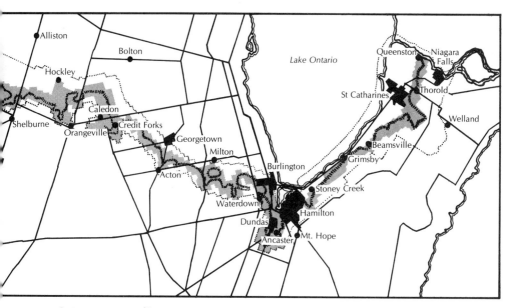

Land Costs as a Policy Issue

Against this background the scenario of a particularly critical policy issue, focused on land, is unfolding in the Ontario of the early seventies, which might well become of general national concern. In recent years there have been two new departures in environmental policy at the provincial level. One has been to identify and conserve certain unique and strategic natural resources; and the other has been to get ahead of the development game by formulating and implementing desirable patterns of settlement for entire regions. The program for the Niagara Escarpment is an example of the first; and the concept of the Toronto-Centred Region, as put forward in the government's revised *Design for Development* in 1970, of the second. The first of these has had a lot of public exposure, and the issues involved are quite widely appreciated. The second has not so far enjoyed the benefits of imaginative presentation but, details apart, it represents an entirely new policy departure: an attempt to shape and structure the framework of a regional city. Both these programs have in common the fact that control of land is critical to their fulfilment.

The Escarpment program involves the preservation of a minimal environmental corridor of 390,000 acres, of which more than one-quarter—the backbone of the park system—must be tied down by purchase or easement. Approximately 40,000 acres of this consists of unique Escarpment features and of areas of high recreational capability which need to be acquired almost immediately if they are

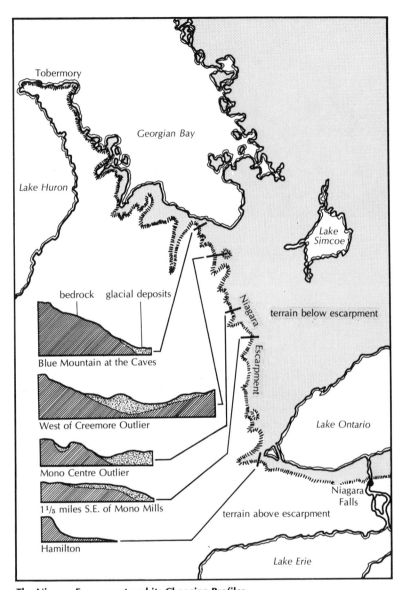

The Niagara Escarpment and its Changing Profiles

The Escarpment has been carved from a succession of rocks that were laid down on the floors of ancient seas. The main cause for the formation of the Escarpment is the fact that the stratigraphic succession—the layers of sedimentary rock, varies in hardness, with the harder rocks being near the top. Rocks near the base erode faster and an escarpment can form, retreat and maintain a vertical face by a series of rock falls. This action, plus the legacy of glacial deposits, typically in the form of hummocky ridges of clays and sands known as moraines, account for the topographic features of the Escarpment landscape.

Cape Crocker — Bruce Peninsula

This is some of the legendary scenery of the Bruce, the peninsular section of the Escarpment, facing Georgian Bay. The Cape is part of an Indian Reserve with a high recreational potential.

52

to be saved from conversion to urban and/or extractive industrial use. The Toronto-Centred Region concept involved amongst other things the establishment of a parkway belt, extending for about one hundred miles, from Hamilton to Oshawa and broad enough to serve as a transportation and utility corridor, an urban limiter or separator, an environmental buffer, and as the site for low-intensity institutional uses. This TCR concept also involves the assembly of sites for five to seven new communities, ranging in size from 25,000 to 200,000 people.[3]

The key point is that, whether we move to conserve unique natural resources or to creatively shape the cities of tomorrow, public control of land is critical. It is the base on which the whole enterprise rests. And this is where our trouble begins. When a public agency moves into the land market it is confronted by high and rising prices. This is a general condition, not localized and not confined to public purchases. In his 1970 government report, Harvey Lithwick demonstrated convincingly that competition for scarce urban space is one of the mainsprings of the urban process, as well as a major determinant, of the form and structure of human settlement. He states: "Urbanization [thus] has a unique effect on the city: it creates ever-increasing space needs that continually raise the price of land throughout the urban space."[4] It is this general situation that conditions the large-scale public purchase of land, induces a play of forces that causes the escalation of prices, and erects a barrier to our environmental programs.

Illustrations of this land-cost syndrome are all too common. During the legislative debates leading to the Commission of Enquiry on the Niagara Escarpment Study (summer 1971), the costs of acquiring Escarpment land were brought dramatically to public attention. The Department of Public Works reported the highest increments at

---

Features in a Natural Park System

a. The Bruce Trail woods to walk in
b. Webster's Falls, near Hamilton spectacles to enjoy
c. Mountain Mill, Ancaster history to contemplate
d. Eugenia Falls a forest to preserve
e. Hockley Valley inspiration for the artist
f. Talisman, Beaver Valley skiing in a scenic valley

The Niagara Escarpment Study recommended that this unique land form be preserved, planned and developed as a single park network. The parks system concept calls for the knitting together, by trail and scenic road, of eight major parks, with such features as waterfalls, viewpoints, rock formations and the scarp itself.

fifteen and thirty times on two Escarpment transactions within a turn-over period of five and six and a half years respectively. In August 1971, the Status Report on the Toronto-Centred Region drew attention to the problem: "Land prices are escalating so rapidly that an increasing number of people are facing great difficulty in financing a home of their own; or alternatively, are having to live long distances away from their place of work, and must commute for several hours a day."[5] Such land market conditions prevail within the Toronto-Centred Region. A good example is North Oakville, west of Toronto, which is the site of a proposed new community of 180,000. In Ward 1 — the area which contains the proposed site — the following conditions were found in the fall of 1969:

(a)   61 per cent of the land is in the "investment" category, i.e., it is absentee-owned farm and residential land;

(b)   real estate transactions have increased three times in the five-year period 1964-69;

(c)   land prices have risen five times (from an average of about $500 to $2,600 per acre), in the same period; and

(d)   titles to land are considerably fragmented; about 64 per cent of the acreage is in parcels of less than 100 acres; of these, about one-quarter are in parcels of less than 50 acres.

The area in question is zoned agricultural, but it is quite clear that the assembly of land in the Oakville area — about 14,000 acres will be required — will have to contend with a market already heavily influenced by speculative forces.[6]

There is a tradition in North America that links land speculation with sinister forces. This had its root in pioneer society; the arch villain is usually the mortgage collector. In our Canadian mythology the honest tiller of the soil confronts the fast-buck operator, usually from the city, who gambles with land as if it were just so much paper stock. We have been registering our concern for a long time, beginning most conspicuously with the Commission of Conservation established in 1911, which inveighed against "the paralyzing fever of speculation," and which took pains to establish that speculatively boosted land prices were tantamount to a tax on industry.[7] This tradition goes marching on. It turned up in a 1971 report on "Power and Land in California," prepared by a Ralph Nader study group. According to the *New York Times*, the report charged "that a massive interlocking economic and political power structure governs California's land and water resources and threatens to plunder the state of its basic wealth." And it turned up in the summer and fall of 1971, in the Legislature of Ontario, around the issue of Escarpment lands. In a sense the debate on the public cost of acquiring these lands took a turn which led away from the key issue. The dramatization of a conspiracy theory of land speculation robbed us of an enquiry into the fundamental issues which might have provided the foundation for a land policy. The land-price syndrome has much deeper, although admittedly less colourful, roots in our society. It is a symptom of the classical dilemma that arises when public land is acquired in a market society under conditions of a relatively fixed or inelastic supply of land. On the one hand, land values increase above "existing use" value as a result of the growth of the community, but the increment accrues to the individual owner. On the other hand, the community as land purchaser must pay a substantial premium when it acquires land for a public purpose.

Charles Abrams' Man's Struggle for Shelter in an Urbanizing World shows this to be an almost universal dilemma. His global overview yields two intriguing observations on the Canadian position on the land issue. We belong to that category of society in which land held by the state (for example, crown lands) has been progressively desocialized, in contrast to those states, such as the Soviet Union, in which private land has been nationalized. Accordingly, we still experience a certain amount of trauma when employing the public power of compulsory purchase. Countries in this category, when faced with the need for direct control of extensive areas of land, have apparently resorted to a strategy of gradually accumulating public land reserves.[8]

The Stockholm Approach

Stockholm provides an important example of an urban region in which public land reserves play a major role. The municipal ownership of land emerges as a critical factor in the ability of the city to achieve both detailed design concepts and standards, and a broad pattern of development in the form of urban units, each with its own centre, and with some degree of inner balance of activities. This has had three important consequences: (i) it has given the initiative to the city in deciding where the next step will be in the sequence of development; (ii) it has enabled the city to assume the primary planning role for new development (that is, the role of preparing the comprehensive layout for each unit of residential development); and (iii) it has brought the developer to the doorstep of City Hall, putting the city in a good position to negotiate detailed design and establish

55

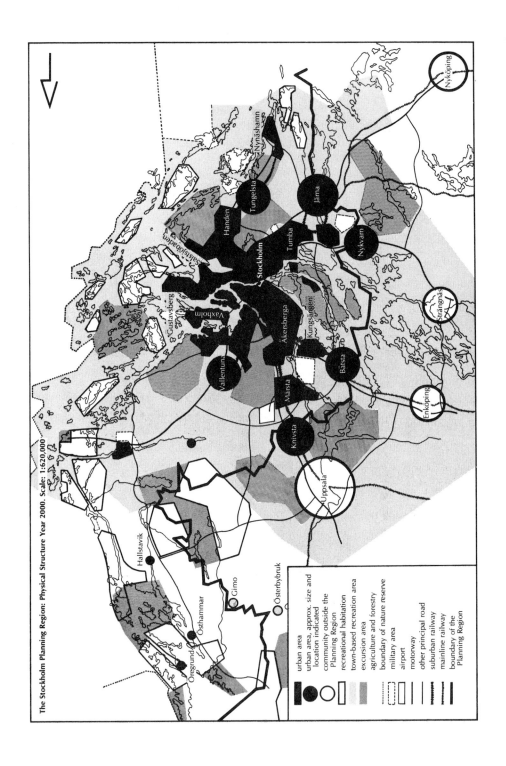

The Stockholm Planning Region: Physical Structure Year 2000. Scale: 1:620,000

urban area
urban area, approx. size and
location indicated
community outside the
Planning Region
recreational habitation
town-based recreation area
excursion area
agriculture and forestry
boundary of nature reserve
military area
airport
motorway
other principal road
suburban railway
mainline railway
boundary of the
Planning Region

Nyköping
Nynäshamn
Tungelsta
Järna
Handen
Stockholm
Tumba
Nykvarn
Saltsjöbaden
Vaxholm
Åkersberga
Kungsängen
Strängnäs
Gustavsberg
Vallentuna
Bålsta
Enköping
Märsta
Knivsta
Uppsala
Hallstavik
Gimo
Östhammar
Öregrund
Österbybruk

conditions of development.

Public land ownership will continue to be a major force because as of 1969 the City of Stockholm holds over 80,000 acres, of which 60,000 are undeveloped, including park reserves. This acquisition is not all a heritage of the past. While it started at the beginning of the century, almost half was acquired in the sixties.

The city planner of Stockholm is unequivocal concerning the critical role of public land in the planning process, considering it a sine qua non. The importance of this public prerogative is indicated by state law, permitting a public authority to intervene before a private sale is consummated, and to take the land in question at the price of the prospective sale. This had been used by the city on three or four occasions in the 1960s where it was necessary to prevent the thwarting of development plans.

The British Experience

It is becoming increasingly clear that the new environmental strategies require that we make a frontal attack on the land-cost syndrome, and move the issue of land policy to centre stage. In doing so, we will be wise to learn from the jurisdictions that have attempted to deal with this problem, and in this respect the British experience is particularly relevant. The search for a sound land policy has received the most assiduous attention during the past thirty years and has been the bête noire of a series of British governments.

In 1941 the Wartime Coalition Government established a Committee on the land problem, under Mr. Justice Uthwatt. Reporting in 1942, the committee coined the term "floating value" to dramatize the observation that "development value" — the difference between existing use and market value — spreads over many more acres than are ever likely to be developed; it recommended as an essential minimum the transfer to the state of all development rights and development values on un-built-on land; prescribed a

---

Stockholm: The Municipality as Planner and Owner

"Stockholm is one of the most interesting and successful examples of city growth in the world. . . . Stockholm now owns an area greater than the administrative area of the city. . . . Where the city wishes to have a greenbelt or forest reserve the land can be protected from development without paying ransom to speculators. . . . The cluster satellites are built where it is judged best to build them, in accordance with the master plan. . . . The whole procedure is so infinitely more effective in producing an agreeable and convenient environment than is common in North America, that it deserves careful study, as a model; and municipal ownership is the key." R.W.G. Bryant, in Land, Private Property, Public Control *(1972).*

57

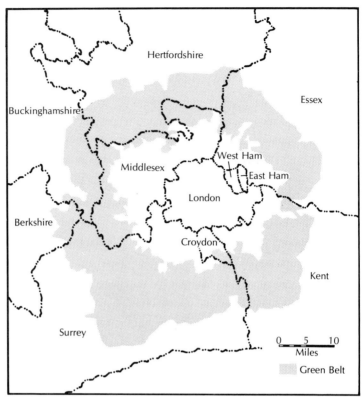

London Green Belt Prior to Extension. Note: All of the area inside the green belt runs together as one continuous city.

What is a Greenbelt?

A greenbelt is a ring of land around cities in which urban development is not to be permitted. The concept has been most fully developed in the United Kingdom, where such belts are typically five to ten miles broad and encompass about 6 per cent of the land surface of England. Their purpose is to preserve amenity, protect agricultural land and to regulate the advance of urban growth. Implementation of a greenbelt zone is not always smooth sailing.

Writing on this problem in circumstances characterized by a free land market, which has prevailed since 1970; Daniel Mandelker pinpoints some of the administrative difficulties: "Planning power may simply not be capable of implementing a permanently restrictive green-belt policy under the present assumptions underlying English planning law. With the development charge abolished, any landowner is left free to realize the full development value of his land, if he can. In the green-belt, however, a landowner who is denied permission to build will be left with a compensation claim worth much less than the market value of his property. No wonder the Minister has given way slowly in green-belt areas." Greenbelts and Urban Growth (1966).

somewhat intricate mechanism which would permit public purchase at "existing use value"; and generally produced what has become a kind of bible for urban land reformers.[9]

In 1947, two years after coming to power, the Labour government passed the Town and Country Planning Act. Some of the major provisions of this Act were:

(a)   Development rights were nationalized.
(b)   Landowners retained a right to "existing use" value only. To compensate for this, landowners were entitled to a once-for-all payment for the loss of any development value that had accrued up to one year after the act.
(c)   When permission to develop was granted, a developer had to pay the Central Land Board (the body administering the policy), a development charge equal to the development value; this was called "betterment."
(d)   When land was acquired compulsorily for public purposes, the purchase price was based on existing use value.

This ingenious scheme boomeranged. Real market prices failed to approximate existing use value because in a seller's market, purchasers were obliged to pay development value twice, once to the Central Land Board and once to the vendor. The policy was turned on its head, and instead of restoring a reasonable level of land prices, its impact was inflationary. When the Conservatives came to power in 1951 they gradually dismantled the Labour government's land policy.

The result has been characterized by a British commentator as "a curious mixture of doctrinaire opposition to public land ownership and a concern to secure some of the benefits of public land planning."[11] Under this policy, owners who obtained permission for private development were able to reap the full, tax-free development value. Owners selling for public development were still compensated, as provided in the 1947 act for "existing use" value only. And owners who were refused planning permission often obtained no compensation whatsoever.

This "relative injustice" was supposed to have been corrected by the 1959 Town and Country Planning Act which re-established open market values as the basis of compensation for compulsory public purchase. But this led to other problems. By that date comprehensive planning policies and controls were established, making so-called "open-market values" heavily dependent on what development would be permitted. If land was needed for a regional park where planning policy would have permitted a shopping centre, the owner, by obtaining "a certificate of alternative development" from the planning authority, stood to gain substantially. But if planning permission on the land across the road was for agriculture only, compensation would be dramatically less. The tying of compensation to planning permission resulted in a wide disparity of treatment, making paupers of some and lords of others. All that the new policy appeared to achieve was a fearsome boom in urban land prices. The 1959 policy became untenable and political pressure for change mounted steadily.

In 1967, therefore, a Labour government passed the Land Commission Act, which did two things: it drew off some of the heavy windfall gains, by imposing a 40 to 50 per cent levy on development values; and it gave the Land Commission power of compulsory purchase at a price reduced by the amount of the levy. This had the effect of restoring some of the benefits as well as some of the pitfalls of the 1974 Act.[12] But with the accession of the Heath Conservative Government in 1970, one of its first acts was to scrap this policy and abolish the Land Commission. The clock has been turned back at least thirty years, and land prices are spiralling upwards again.

The British experience has not been all negative, however. A notable exception is the land policy for new towns. This policy, initiated in 1959, provided that any increases or decreases attributable to the carrying out of new town development were to be disregarded in compulsory purchase. Further legislation in 1966 excluded from compensation the new town values, where extension of the designated area into the surrounding greenbelt were made after the specified date of 13 December 1966. On balance this policy appears to be both politically acceptable and administratively successful, but whether this is because of the demonstrable benefits of the new towns it is hard to say. The new towns mechanism has apparently been so effective that the Ministry of Housing embarked, in 1969, on a new program of applying the new towns formula to the fringes of such established areas as the Portsmouth-Southampton conurbation.[13]

A Canadian Response

What do we in Canada learn from the Swedish and British experiences? The Stockholm experiment provides an edifying case, but does not in itself represent a solution to the challenge we face: the strategic acquisition of relatively large amounts of land to fulfil public policies, under conditions of congenital price escalations.

In Canada, we appear to be caught happily in the imperatives of the democratic planning process, which is given a special bite and irresistibility in this participatory age. We inform and consult the public before we implement and when we do so, we excite the land market and erect a formidable barrier to our plans. At the scale of action required by the new environmental strategies, to rely exclusively on the public ownership of land, we run the risk of either beggaring the Treasury and distorting the overall pattern of expenditures or building in a structure of high costs and debts for which the consumer ultimately pays, both monetarily and in a distorted environmental pattern.

If we are to embark on development policies that will involve the control of land by public agencies on a large scale, we will need to add a land strategy to our repertoire of policies; and, in Canada, this will be primarily at the provincial level. Such a policy would have the general aim of preventing both undue speculative gain and undue costs of public acquisition without provoking the inflationary and discriminatory effects that were the undoing of the British initiatives.

As a direct response to this requirement, a study by Ian C. Bender is of particular interest.[14] Mr. Bender reviewed the relevant theory and practice concerning the problem of land costs, related these to conditions in the Toronto-Centred Region, and then worked out an approach in terms of Ontario conditions and institutions. This prescribes that:

(a) The Province of Ontario should pass legislation defining a land policy, administered by a semi-autonomous body, the Ontario Land Board (OLB).

(b) The OLB should establish a ceiling price on the sale of undeveloped land for the entire province at a level that approximates the maximum value of rural land in Ontario; this should apply to all sales, private and public, including expropriation.

(c) The ceiling price should be adjusted annually in response to the cost-of-living index.

(d) At the same time, a market value should be established by the OLB for all undeveloped land, representing the full development value, accrued say to 1970, and adjusted at five-year intervals.

(e) For a period of twenty years following the establishment of the ceiling price, full development value would be guaranteed to each vendor of land, with the difference between the ceiling price and the development value being paid by the OLB, through a special fund established by the provincial government for this purpose.

(f) After the twenty-year period, development value would cease to be paid.

This rather idealistic, long-range proposal is dictated by the need for trading off private and public interests in the land. If it works, there is a presumption that it would ultimately lead towards a tenable solution in which land prices for all purposes will be indefinitely dampened.

Consider, for example, its advantages in implementing a "new cities" policy within the Toronto-Centred Region. If the Bender strategy were invoked, new communities would not be saddled with disproportionate debts and a high structure of costs. In addition, market values would be held in check by the establishment of land prices by the OLB, and by the psychic impact, increasing year by year, of the prospective rurally oriented ceiling price at the target date.

As the end of the twenty-year period is approached the risks of speculative investment would increase, and speculation would have to be restrained. The diseconomies of the market would be minimized, and we would move unhampered towards the building of the New Jerusalem — maybe!

Policy Approaches at the National Level

In emphasizing action at the provincial level, it is not suggested that Ontario, or any province, can solve its problem in isolation from the rest of the country. We realize we are dealing with an urban process which is national in scope and in which the elements of development, policy and geography are interdependent. It is essential, therefore, to give some attention to the policy requirements at the national level.

The setting up of the Task Force on Housing, under Paul Hellyer, in 1968, provoked considerable discussion of our urban problems. Several submissions presented to the task force should be mentioned. For example, two proposals on the land issue were made.[15] One was to initiate a far-reaching enquiry as a basis for formulating land policies nationally. The enquiry would be independent and possibly financed under a National Housing Act grant, administered by an autonomous body. Its terms of reference would include the following: documentation of past trends in land prices in Canada; consideration of the effects of land prices on the pattern and quality of urban development, and on the conservation and use of agricultural, forestry and recreational land; and recommendation of a comprehensive land policy for the regions of Canada, geared to both development and conservation objectives.

The second proposal was of a more short-run nature. It was argued that the pressure of high land prices would produce distortions in the development pattern, forcing inordinately high densities in some areas, and in other localities precipitating the costly scatter and sprawl of the urban tissue, as developers reach out for cheaper land beyond the rural-urban fringe. To deal with this situation, it was suggested that the device of senior government land assembly, which has been on the statute books for some time, be used more vigorously to assure the availability of land for the next stage of urban development in those major urban centres that have planned their regional growth patterns. These areas would include such major centres as Vancouver, Winnipeg, Hamilton, Toronto, Ottawa, Montreal and Halifax, where there has been an on-going, professionally aided planning process for a number of years and where the metropolitan governments were in a good position to delineate the lands that would be critical to their next stage of development. In elaborating the idea at the time, it was stated:

> The program will make sense only if it can be carried out quickly, before the rise of the next tide of real estate inflation. In most provinces, recently formed provincial housing corporations probably provide the best vehicle for this purpose. Such organizations would administer federal and provincial capital funds, and select sites in consultation with city, metropolitan and regional planning authorites. To be effective, housing corporations should be prepared to relate re-sale or lease values of assembled land to the economic returns that can be expected from the different urban activities set out in area plans. In some parts of assembled areas, this will justify an appreciation in land prices, and in others the price may have to be written down. If turn-over is rapid enough, the costs may be self-liquidating. The foregoing is not proposed as a basic, long-range land policy, but as an essential "holding action" while a searching enquiry is preparing the way for a more fundamental and forthright attack on the land problems in our city regions.[16]

In the early summer of 1972 legislation was brought before Parliament and passed in the 1973 winter session, which offers some promise that land assembly could be used to greater effect along the lines suggested. The National Housing Act has been amended with a view to encouraging the more vigorous use by provinces and municipalities of loans for the acquisition and servicing of land. The program makes it absolutely clear that land required for activities that are an integral part of a *residential community* is eligible for assistance, and not just land required for "housing purposes" in the strict sense. The amortization period is extended from fifteen to twenty-five years and, perhaps taking a leaf out of Swedish experience, no principal repayment is required until the assembled land is made available for development and begins to bear revenue. Further inducement is provided by the stipulation that a land assembly loan can be secured by a first mortgage held by Central Mortgage and Housing Corporation, or other suitable assets such as debentures.

Whether these amendments will become a vehicle for making public land assembly a truly significant instrument in the strategy of urban development depends on the scale of the federal financial commitment, and on the initiative of provincial and municipal governments and authorized agencies.

What Kind of Strategy?

The problems to which these measures were addressed are still very much with us. The total strategy of which they are a part may be summarized as follows: The goal of positive environmental planning involves the public control of land on an unprecedented scale, either to protect certain key areas for their recreation and landscape features, or to assure the desired location, timing and sequence of new development. These unprecedented policy initiatives are confronted by a barrier of high land acquisition costs which are a by-product of the urban process, but are accentuated by the prospect of substantial public purchases. In consequence, public ownership of land and easements needs to be extended selectively; however, in the face of high costs, it cannot be relied upon exclusively to achieve the aims of public policy. In addition a policy will have to be formulated to control the escalation of land prices, based on four guidelines:

(i) the discouragement of speculation in undeveloped land;
(ii) equality of treatment to owners of land involved in a private or public transaction, including expropriation;
(iii) the acquisition of land for public purposes at prices exclusive of increments induced by public action;
(iv) the protection of existing owners from undue loss or hardship as a by-product of the imposition of a new land policy.

This leads to an approach which will guarantee a fair market value for a sufficient period to work off present land investments. This is judged to be about twenty years, after which land would exchange hands at a price which would not exceed an established ceiling price.

Action at the provincial level needs to be backed up by national initiatives. Two are suggested here: an independent national enquiry on the land problem; and the immediate building up of land banks to meet the most urgent needs of our cities.

4 The New Community in the Regional City

As we move into the last quarter of the twentieth century, the Canadian city is faced with a dilemma that characterizes urban development in its metropolitan phase. Growth brings many benefits: the classical "agglomeration economies" in jobs, markets and the pursuit of pleasure. But growth also forces the lateral spread of the city, placing strain on its transportation system and other major service systems, and tends to weaken, if not destroy, its sense of community. These physical and social changes have their counterpart politically in the rise of big government at the regional scale, and in the deep, almost instinctual urge to retain a sense of the communal and the human at the local level.

During the past quarter-century a response to this dilemma has slowly emerged which takes the form of creating new communities within the orbit of metropolitan areas. One of the earliest postwar experiments was on the south shore of the St. Lawrence opposite Montreal, where the enlightened urbanists Harold Spence-Sales and Jacques Simard combined creative imagination, a seigniorial heritage and plain old enterprise to establish the dormitory community of Préville, which was outstanding for its sensitive, albeit unpretentious, design standards.

The decade of the fifties saw the initiation of three other new communities within metropolitan areas, each of which added something to our understanding of the urban process. Don Mills, a suburb of Metropolitan Toronto, was conceived as a planned suburb of 35,000 people. Built by private enterprise on land assembled by a single company, the project contained a broad socio-economic mix in population, its own centre, substantial local employment and a high degree of community identity and self-sufficiency. Today the development retains a relatively strong sense of community and its individuality is preserved by its fortuitous location within two wooded arms of the Don River. But Don Mills is indistinguishable in its relationship to the metropolis from any other middle-class suburb; the bias of the builders and lenders and of the real estate market has pushed up the level of shelter prices. The area features some high-quality industrial and commercial development, but only about 10 per cent of the residents are actually employed in Don Mills.[1]

Kanata, on the western edge of the Ottawa greenbelt, promoted and designed by William Teron, was a shrewd anticipation of the urban form implicit in the greenbelt concept: compact growth up to the greenbelt and concentrated urban nodes beyond the greenbelt linked to the capital centre by rapid transportation facilities. The plan, which accommodates a population of about 70,000, places considerable emphasis on the development of its own sub-regional centre and employment base; of the more than seventeen thousand jobs created about 20 per cent are filled by Kanata residents. Staging of the development has placed emphasis on housing and minimal services, which gives the place a somewhat truncated quality, while the attainment of the employment objective depends almost entirely on the accident of federal office location.[2]

The third case, St. Albert, a few miles northwest of Edmonton, was conspicuously different from the other two. It was publicly initiated by the Edmonton Regional Planning Commission, applying the Alberta New Towns Act, with its provisions for planning, administration and finance. From the start it was designed to fulfil an aspect of the urban strategy for the region. St. Albert is well on its way to achieving its planned target population of 25,000.[3]

This Canadian experience, limited as it is, illustrates the possiblity of a growth pattern that breaks out of the dilemma of monolithic metropolitan growth. While all of the developments are interesting in themselves as efforts to attain a communal form of growth, there are some vastly different lessons to be inferred from an urban strategy viewpoint. All of the cases suggest the importance of assembling a large tract of land and of unified project management. The Montreal and Ottawa cases were ad hoc and cannot be readily replicated. The Alberta case is particularly instructive because it reflects both a policy and a mechanism for creating new communities. At present the new city of Mill Woods, planned for a population of 120,000, is being built on a site of over seven thousand acres, mainly publicly owned, and situated beyond a buffer zone south of Edmonton along a major transportation route.[4]

In the Toronto region, the Don Mills project remains an artifact of the real estate market and an important model for comprehensive private development. The mastery of the building process it demonstrated played some part in the evolution of Ontario's Toronto-Centred Region (TCR) concept, which was developed in the mid-sixties and launched as a provincial policy in May 1970. The TCR concept represents the first systematic effort to back up the dual challenge of the contemporary metropolis: to retain the advantages of agglomeration without a loss of accessiblity and the sense of community.[5] The objective which is sought has been well stated and with great precision by Harvey Lithwick: "The economic dynamic of

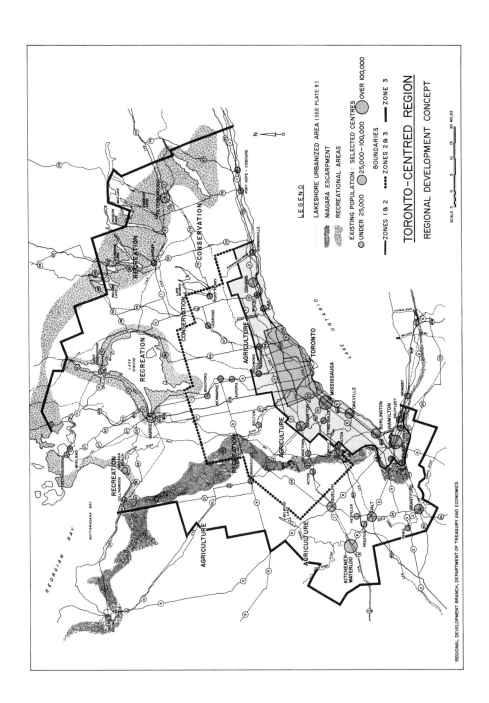

TORONTO-CENTRED REGION

REGIONAL DEVELOPMENT CONCEPT

LEGEND

LAKESHORE URBANIZED AREA (SEE PLATE 5)

NIAGARA ESCARPMENT

RECREATIONAL AREAS

EXISTING POPULATION : SELECTED CENTRES
UNDER 25,000   25,000-100,000   OVER 100,000

BOUNDARIES
ZONES 1 & 2   •••• ZONES 2 & 3   ——— ZONE 3

SCALE 5   0   5   10   15   20 MILES

Toronto — Centred Region — Regional Development Concept

The Official View

The key points of future development policy are:

Develop a well-structured urbanized zone from Bowmanville to Hamilton for a population of approximately 5.7 million by the year 2000, the structure to be basically a two-tiered arrangement of cities separated by a parkway belt of open space with mainly non-urban uses, but containing high performance interurban transportation and other trunk services. Stimulate the eastern corridor to a higher growth rate.

Encourage growth in key places to the north (such as Barrie and Midland) and the east (such as Port Hope and Cobourg) where there already exists an unused potential for development.

Reserve sizeable districts northeast and northwest of Metropolitan Toronto for open space, conservation areas, recreation and agriculture.

Design For Development: The Toronto-Centred Region. Toronto: The Government of Ontario, May 1970.

"We will have a hierarchy of plans — that of the Province, the regional municipality, and the local municipality. As we go down this hierarchy, each level of planning will be more detailed than the plan prepared above. There should be collaboration in the process of preparing these plans and of course consistency between them." Hon. W. Darcy McKeough, Minister of Municipal Affairs, "Presentation of Design for Development Toronto-Centred Region," May, 1970.)

Some Critics

"We are concerned with the lack of specific statements clarifying the difference between a concept and a plan, and on the degree of flexibility of the proposals. We are particularly concerned with the dichotomy between the frequent references to a 'flexible concept' and the apparent intention of the Government to implement this concept as a precise plan." (Town Planning Institute of Canada, Ontario Branch.)

"It is submitted that this is a complete reversal of the procedure of planning as developed in any of the democratic countries of Western Europe and of North America, and is for the first time an introduction of a totalitarian form of planning where the authority appears to have sprung from the small group of civil servants directed to make the initial study and appraisal." (Township of Chinguacousy.)

"To implement the concept will require financial expenditures of hitherto unknown proportions in the Province and will, therefore, need extremely careful planning and co-ordination. Without these, the concept is most likely to remain in limbo of guidelines incapable of being implemented to any material degree and very probably unable to influence and change the present trends and patterns of urban growth in the region." Wojciech Wronski, Commissioner of Planning, Metropolitan Toronto.

All of the above criticisms were reported in the Globe and Mail, December 29, 1970.

69

presently large centres must not be destroyed, the labour force and markets must remain accessible. Thus future expansion must be integrated into the urban system. At the same time, it must not add to the land-use problems of the large metropolitan areas. This requires the siting of new development beyond the urbanized area. These two superficially conflicting requirements — of integration yet spatial divorce—lead to only one solution; the sequential development of new communities."[6]

The Toronto-Centred Region concept is an approximation of this strategy. It is concerned with the restructuring of the urban settlement pattern on a regional scale. It involves the deflection of substantial growth away from the Metropolitan Toronto core, and its coalescing into a network of closely interacting new cities, distributed in two tiers on major transportation routes along one hundred miles of the Lake Ontario shoreline. In addition, development will be encouraged within a peripheral zone in two local axes. Barrie— Midland and Port Hope—Coburg. This concept represents, in a sense, a conceptual watershed between a period of orderly filling in of urban development within metropolitan service limits by numerous projects, and a period of purposeful shaping of the structure of regional development by influencing the location, size, function and sequence of entire urban communities.

A development strategy of this nature presents an unprecedented challenge to our administrative structures and planning and development processes. It is a new ball game. It requires the working out, in terms of structures and processes, of an approach which will be effective in a dynamic, highly urbanized region like Toronto (and other regions like it), taking into account the province's economic conditions as well as political structures and traditions.

The New Community, Integrated with its Region

One of the strongest and most articulate expressions of the new community concept in our time has come from Finland. Its stage has been the region of Helsinki, its major creation the new town of Tapiola, and its philosopher, Heikki von Hertzen, head of the country's Housing Foundation.

"The New town idea proposes that the large metropolis be built as a series of succinct but interrelated and possibly interwoven pieces, each of much richer texture and activity than any portion of an "unplanned" metropolis. Most frequently designs for a series of new towns are a pattern of built-up and open land. The built-up lands are the new towns, and they are separated from each other by open space. The open spaces, while essential, can be employed to link as well as demarcate the separate new towns. . . . The new town then is really a social, functional, physical and developmental entity, the basic component unit of an urbanized region." Heikki von Hertzen and Paul. D. Spreiregen, in Building a New Town *(1971).*

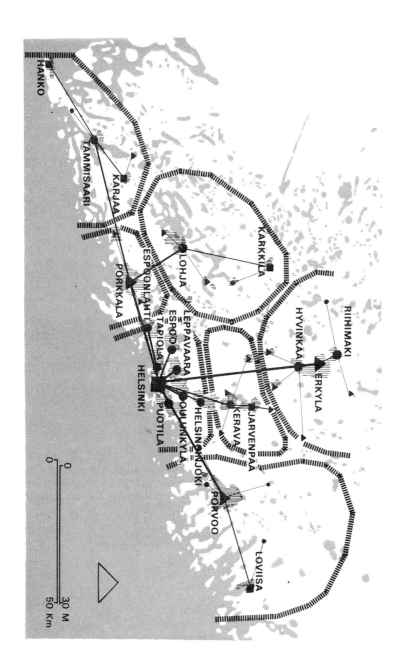

The New Integrated City

The term "community" has been used in this chapter in the ordinary, non-specialized sense of a group of people living together. The term "city" and "new city" is used in the TCR concept in a special sense which needs to be clearly understood, for it has both theoretical and practical consequences that are important.

This concept has its roots in the three traditions of city building — the British, the Scandanavian and the American. The British new town in its classical formulation is a self-contained community. It is large enough to ensure a high quality of services, developed on public land, independent in employment, having its own inner balance between urban activities, with business and leisure time links to other new towns and a metropolitan centre. It is usually conceived as an element in the urban development strategy of metropolitan-based regions, and has been elevated to an instrument of national policy. The administrative mechanism for carrying out the new towns policy is a development corporation, appointed by the responsible minister and empowered to plan, to acquire land compulsorily, to finance and to develop.

The Scandanavian tradition has in common with the British model a comprehensive approach to design, and the public ownership of land. It differs, however, in its sponsorship, planning and management, and in the role of the new city within the urban-centred region. The Stockholm communities are very much the product of bottom-up, citizen-based action led by social democratic regimes of the city government. The city administration plans, designs, finances, provides utilities and sometimes takes on the developers' role through a city-owned development company. There is no attempt to make the new communities self-sufficient in employment. Their regional position, located not more than thirty minutes by subway from central Stockholm, assures a high degree of integration with the metropolitan area.

The development of new cities in the United States has been mainly undertaken by private enterprise. They tend to be planned for a population of at least 100,000, to be located within the orbit of major metropolitan centres, and to aspire to a high degree of employment independence. They are conspicuously different from either the British or Scandanavian counterparts in one very critical respect. Because they are "unique events," developing at the opportune moment when financial and market conditions are right, they do not constitute a part of a wider system of cities. Under present legislation, they do not hold out much promise of becoming a major

Urbanity and the Environment of the New Community: The Tapiola Model

"The test of success . . .is to see Tapiola on the ground and to consider again what the objectives were. The basic intent was to build a modern cross-section community, biologically healthful, rich in opportunity and choice, and close to nature."

"One issue is that the garden city is antiurban, that the new town is an anomaly in urbanizing societies. On this point — the matter of urbanity or nonurbanity of the garden city — it might be useful to consider what in fact the term "urbanity" means."
Building a New Town

alternative to prevailing patterns of growth. While the best of the private developers have stressed the coincidence of public benefit and private gain, they have not yet met a decisive test. In the 1969 annual report of the Rouse Company, developers of Columbia, Maryland, the following objectives are found side by side:

> "To create, by superior planning, a higher quality of life for man and his family.
> To make an outstanding profit."

Within the Toronto-Centred Region formulation there is the prospect of developing a type of new city which borrows and carries to a logical conclusion some of the elements of the British, Scandinavian and American traditions. It would be conceived, like the British example, as part of a strategy for directing the growth forces of a metropolitan-based region, and would have a distinct role and community identity within the region. It would not, however, be self-sufficient in employment. The Scandinavian reliance on a public commuter system, backed up by a highway network, would be emulated by the facilities of the parkway belt. Following the Stockholm pattern, regional integration of communities is the aim. Emphasis would be on the city in the region, on creating cities along a transportation corridor that forms, not only a single labour market, but a single leisure market. To develop sub-regional centres with a wide range of high-quality services, the new cities in the TCR concept must, as in the American case, reach for a substantial population level, say in the 100,000 to 250,000 range. The skill exhibited by the best of the American new city developers suggests a unique challenge to the Canadian process: to harness private enterprise in new city development in a manner which is sufficiently sustained and precise in timing, function and location, to make the new city not an accident of the market nor, as William Alonso and Paul Hellyer suggest, merely a laboratory for urban experiment, but, as part of a

---

The Town Centre

"Urbanity is not a matter of how much exists in gross but of how well things blend in daily experience."

Top. A model of the town center showing the church, the proposed hotel in the foreground, the proposed theater to the right of the tower, and the recently completed Heikintori department store above and to the west of the shopping plaza.

Bottom. Model of the fourteen-storey tower alongside the pool. The theater is to the right. Behind the tower is the shopping plaza. The information pavilion (not shown) is to the left.

ng

75

The Town Center and the Approach to the Town

Clockwise beginning from top left. The town center, looking westward.
The town center at night, with the tower penthouse illuminated as a beacon. The fountain is also illuminated.
The approach to the town center on a winter night, at Christmas season.
The approach to the town center. The stairs are very carefully proportioned for an easy ascent. Their breadth and elegance establishes a sense of occasion.

system of cities, a genuine alternative to prevailing patterns of growth.

Having defined "new city" in a somewhat special way the question arises whether the term "city" is appropriate, and "borough" has been suggested as an alternative. According to the dictionary, borough is associated in some way with an area of local government, and that does not quite fit. The word "city" is preferred because it is a word of great historical depth, with strong spiritual overtones. The new areas of urban concentration in the Toronto-Centred Region must be more than undifferentiated slices of urban tissue. Such areas may be distinguished from the traditional self-contained city by being called the "integrated city," to give emphasis both to its communal integrity and its links of all kinds to the metropolis and the other cities in the region.

The Planning and Development Challenge

In responding to this challenge of new city planning and development, it is possible to distill out of our own experience and that of other countries a certain set of problems which constitute the special requirements of new city development. These are:

(i) to find the capital for acquiring substantial amounts of land and financing the basic utilities, transportation networks and social services (e.g., hospitals and schools) before a tax base has been created;

(ii) to suppress the tendency of a large urban development to produce, by raising expectations, a level of land prices that is prohibitive;

(iii) to initiate, before development, and sustain throughout a lengthy development period, an effective planning process;

(iv) to create by skilful design the best qualities of spontaneous growth, e.g., diversity and responsiveness to many needs, while attaining a high standard of functional efficiency;

(v) to find a way of administering the development of the on-going affairs of the city which is effective in a technical sense, and responsive to residents, without unduly discounting the future; and

(vi) to divert powerful growth forces from accustomed to new patterns of development.

Responding to these requirements and building a sound mechanism for new city planning and building is, whenever the process has been launched, a matter of some urgency. For example, meeting the year 2000 growth target, in the sub-regional centres of the lakeshore urbanized area in the TCR concept will require the attainment of an annual growth rate of 4 per cent, or about twice the Metro Toronto average. This will be necessary to avoid massive urban development immediately contiguous to metropolitan limits. Indeed, one more commitment of that nature might foreclose forever the opportunity of developing a decentralized form of growth in the Toronto region. The problems of the first two of the cited requirements — the high start-up costs for land and basic facilities, and holding the lid on land prices — are at centre stage in the development of the North Pickering New Town, jointly announced and endorsed by the federal and Ontario governments early in March 1972. If the development proceeds as indicated, 18,000 acres will be assembled for Toronto's second airport, and 25,000 acres for the new city and related service corridor and parkland. Price control on affected land was established by the province by regulations under the Expropriations Act. Prices to be paid by the province for the new community site and the service lands are not to include an escalation attributable to the presence of the airport itself.

These measures taken together represented a policy initiative of some daring and foresight. Attaining this kind of regional strategy requires the creation of an effective mechanism to deal with the whole train of circumstances set in motion by a new city development strategy. Based on the cumulative western experience and relating that to the conditions of Ontario for purposes of illustration, the main features of the mechanism can be sketched out.

To meet the challenge of a concept like the Toronto-Centred Region design, a New Cities Act for Ontario is needed which would define the responsibilities and powers and relationships of each agency in the new city structure of administration. The broad provincial interest would reside (a) in determining the general framework of development — the location, size, function and development sequence of new cities; (b) in establishing a land policy that prevents the inflation of land prices becoming a barrier to desirable urban patterns; (c) in making available some of the loan capital required to overcome the initial hump of public investment; (d) in assuring that the new cities through their various phases of planning and development have a sound administrative base; and (e) in rendering technical assistance, particularly on land and financial aspects, where it may be required.

The top of the pyramid within the provincial administration is seen as a senior advisory committee to the cabinet on urban and regional planning performing a central coordinating role on development matters in the province. The main executive arm of the province is seen as a new agency, the Office of New City Planning and Development, within the Ministry of Treasury, Economics and Intergovernmental Affairs. This should be a new function with a staff assembled for its special knowledge and expertise in the problems of large-scale urban development.

The central principle of the proposed structure is that the locus of responsibility be placed in a new city administration within an existing unit of regional administration, preferably a regional government. Its board would represent the interests most directly involved: the regional government itself; constituent local governments, if they exist; special agencies like a Conservation Authority; representative citizens' associations; private developers and the residents of the new city. The direct representation of residents on the board is important, because for many years as a small minority within the region there would be a risk of their submergence and alienation if they were not provided the opportunity to play a part in the management of the affairs of the new city.

Emphasis on the regional role arises out of the opportunities opened up by the emerging framework of regional government. If that reform is to mean more than simply raising present local governments, with all their limitations, to a larger unit of activity, it will require that the new regional regimes become the means for the people of these areas to positively shape their own environments. This role will call for a new order of maturity. It is not at all consistent with narrow parochial politics — "you scratch my back and I will scratch yours"; but the consequences of not assuming this role, which would unquestionably be a more centralist solution along the lines of the British development corporations, ought to carry conviction in any province with strong local government traditions. In the western world, the example of Stockholm indicates the potential for achieving both entrepreneurial skill and imagination through a municipal organization. To encourage this possibility in the Ontario context, it is suggested that the new city administration have a high degree of executive autonomy within broad policies of Planning and Finance established by the Regional Council.

The functions assigned to Ottawa are in line with its place in the federal structure. Inherently, the federal government must take the broadest view of development in the country. As such it has a part to play, in a consultative process with the province, in working out broad policy parameters with respect to the location, function, and timing of new city development.

At this broad level of policy-making, new community policy merges with urban policy, as well as federal regional development policy and industrial strategies. As questions of inter-regional disparities, the national pattern of cities, the distribution of population across Canada, the size of cities and their environmental impact and so on — as these questions rise to the top of national concerns, the federal role will become increasingly important, as will the process of three-level consultation on the major objectives and strategies of urban growth.

While this kind of federal involvement would be important, its main operational role would be financial. It is not suggested, however, that financial support be used as a basis for adding yet another layer to the new city planning process. To avoid this kind of federal posture, and to mobilize new sources of capital, there are grounds for giving serious consideration to the establishment of a Canadian Urban Development Bank. Such an organization would assemble both public and private institutional capital to support the infrastructure (roads, utilities and services) of large-scale urban development. The basis for the participation of banks, trust and insurance companies is the change in the character of investment requirements in the urban economy. Concepts such as the Toronto-Centred policy are symptomatic of a new phase of urban development in Canada, in which communities through their public agencies are attempting to assume control of those major elements of urban development that affect the character and quality of urban life. Accordingly, there is a need for our financial institutions to supplement the established forms of participation in the urban process (such as mortgage financing and bond purchases) with a more direct commitment to improving the quality of our urban performance. The investments of the Urban Development Bank would be in the nature of foundation investments that underpin the security of all other private investments in the urban economy.

This three-level mechanism for the planning and development of new cities will have to accommodate a process that answers directly to the noted requirements of new city development. And that process, partly political and partly administrative, will have to encompass the entire life cycle of a community from its initial concept of the good urban life, through its broad planning, design and financing, to the acquisition and servicing of land and the staging of its construction, to its emergence as a place with its own political institutions and style.

The Regional City: A Humane City?

A concept like the Toronto-Centred plan is a species of a theoretical notion called the "regional city." This construct needs to be understood on several levels. One is in terms of function and structure. Lewis Mumford, in *The City in History,* likened it to an electric power grid, characterized by a combination of units of varying capacity and type into a flexible efficient system.[7] The analogy is rough but pregnantly suggestive. The regional city defined in contemporary terms has the following elements: a regional centre; sub-regional centres; high-speed transportation between the centres; and fully developed information/telecommunication systems. These elements together make possible the association of a number of physically separated, functionally distinct urban communities in one interacting network, operating as a single labour market and a single leisure market. Functionally this facilitates:

(a) concentration of high order unique activities in the regional centre;

(b) decentralization of general urban services into sub-regional centres, both within the established urban fabric and at new locations;

(c) specialization of sub-regional centres on the basis of lcoation, local resources, special skills or community initiative;

(d) certain economies of scale: each centre can enjoy the benefits of the entire system; and

(e) certain advantages, environmental as well as economic, of living in places which are much smaller than the regional centre.

Looking at the regional city in terms of another dimension—as a physical structure — the following features are salient:

(a) the growth of the regional centre is limited by the accommodation of growth in a series of new (or accelerated) urban nodes;

(b) sub-regional centres need to grow only to the point where an adequate level of general urban services can be supported;

(c) each end of the system is within practical commuting range of the regional centre;

(d) the settlement pattern fosters a transportation dynamics, such as well-balanced, two-directional passenger load patterns, which are supportive of a regional mass transportation system;

The Design of Centres as Community Focal Points

"These are places that give shape and focus and purpose to the urban environment. They are strategically important in offsetting the sense of alienation which people suffer when their environment seems purposeless and meaningless."

Trois-Rivières, a successful centre

"Surely something excellent has happened when the young people of a town enjoy sitting on the steps of the city hall, feeling that this is their place?" Humphrey Carver, in Habitat *(1972).*

(e)   present transportation capacities and time-distance tolerances favour a linear regional form, contained within a distance of about one hundred miles; and

(f)   the internal regional pattern of land use is characterized by a network of urban communities concentrated around express transportation stops, and physically separated by open country.

Administratively, the theory of the regional city makes two inferences: that the boundaries of the regional are defined by the pragmatic limits of the interactive system (for example, a tolerable round trip in a single evening); and that each major unit, regional and subregional, has a distinctive interest in and community base for participation in both local and regional decision-making processes and structures.

But the touchstone of the regional city is the quality of life it accommodates: what does it offer urban man? The striking feature of the regional concept lies in the opportunity it provides for *choice* and *diversity:* in where a person lives and to a degree *how* he lives, in his work, in where he finds leisure, and in the kind of environment he chooses to cultivate his sensibilities or talents.

To say this much is to assert that the regional city retains — indeed fosters and enlarges—one of the historic attributes of the city; that is to provide, by the scope, complexity and richness of its facilities and interests, the stimulus for human fulfilment and creative power. But this is only one side of the urban coin. The other side is the sense and reality of community. Lawrence Haworth, author of *The Good City,* has observed that specialization cuts two ways: it enhances opportunity and erodes community—"the sense of living a common life and having common concerns." The "good city" is attained by the effective combination of opportunity and community.[8]

While it would be extravagant in the extreme to attribute these qualities to any existing enterprise for organizing settlement on a regional basis, the regional city concept holds out this promise. For it is central to the concept in two respects. The regional centre can be sustained as the symbolic focus of the entire region precisely because it is the locale of region-wide services: the great concert hall, the big department stores, the boutiques and the bars. In a similar fashion, the sub-regional centre is the focus of the component areas of the region, forming a point of reference for the patterns of human association and acknowledged common interest that we call community.

This relationship between city and the quality of life raises certain social-psychological issues, which are of particular interest to

The Quality of Life: The Touchstone of the Regional City

The combined effect of psychological density and population potential is explosive. It has much to do with the galvanizing of human energy associated with city life as celebrated in our literature by Callaghan and Richler. This same energy can be the source of social pathology and violence; or it can in the right setting provide the fuel for the good urban life.

85

dynamic, heavily populated and urbanized regions like southern Ontario. The consequences of "pscyhological density" and population potential have been extensively studied by John B. Calhoun, who is noted for his studies of crowding amongst mammals.[9] Liberally paraphrased, his thesis runs something like this: urbanization is accompanied by a general rise in the level of educational experience, which heightens the individual's consciousness of the world about him, thereby increasing his psychological mass. Urbanization also means higher population densities, which increase the possibilities for interaction between individuals. This is expressed by the formula that every individual is affected by every other individual in proportion to the reciprocal of the distances separating them. The potential of the individual living at an average density of about eight thousand per square mile in Metropolitan Toronto is many times greater than that of the farmer living in an agricultural area settled at a density of about fifteen to twenty per square mile.

The combined effect of these two forces—psychological density and population potential — is explosive and demands a precise institutional and environmental response. It has much to do with the galvanizing of human energy associated with city life, as celebrated in our literature by Callaghan and Richler. This same energy can be the source of social-pathology and violence; or it can in the right setting provide the fuel for the good urban life. "Every level and every centre of organization," says Calhoun, "should have free and easy communication with every other level or centre."[10] Only an environment which is organized to achieve this kind of unfettered communication can provide for the full scope and diversity of society and human personality. Viewing the quality of urban life in this way suggests both the potential of the regional city concept, as it is being developed in Ontario, as well as the criteria by which people will ultimately judge it.

The Strategy Restated

This review of the new city in Canadian urban development may be stated in summary in five observations:

>—The new "integrated city" constitutes an element in a new regional growth form which offers an alternative to the centralized monolithic metropolis.
> — New city development should be an aspect of provincial policy. The broad framework questions of where? when? how big? and what purposes? should be dealt with at the provincial

level. Where federal involvement is important, functionally or financially, these questions should be considered jointly by the provincial and the federal governments within the context of national urban objectives, arrived at consensually through a three-level consultative process. The federal role will be critical in sustaining that process, and in providing back-up legislation affording the opportunity to utilize the "new community" alternative in the management of urban growth.

— The planning and building of new cities should be integrated with the evolving structure of regional government, wherever a process of local government reform towards a regional orientation is under way; hence, executive responsiblity for the process should be placed in an agency of that kind of government.

— Within the structure of regional government, recognition must be given to the special needs of the new city planning and development process.

— The new city planning process is an intergovernmental process requiring participation from the local to the federal level. The federal role is important but it should not take a direct administrative form.

Two of the beneficial by-products of the operation of these four principles are that new "integrated cities" will not be isolated experiments and become, as Blumenfeld fears, the road to utopian escape; and secondly, at the stage when a new city becomes well established, a region will not be left with a bureaucratic residue in the form of obsolete agencies, that becomes a problem, an expense and an embarrassment after it has outlived its usefulness. The new city development process would become absorbed in the on-going regional municipal process.

This concept of new city and of the regional city with which it is associated, must ultimately meet the test of its impact on the quality of life. It must satisfy the requirements, deceptively contradictory of "opportunity" and "community." And, in the special social-psychological conditions of massed urban populations, it must foster the release of the creative powers of its residents.

5 Regional Planning and National Urban Policy: The Alberta Case

Basis for a National Urban Policy

The relatively recent emergence of urban-regional issues as a matter of national policy concern raises the important question of how the urban regions of this country will be related to the policy process. The acknowledged turning point in policy thinking was the publication in December 1970 of N.H. Lithwick's advisory report, *Urban Canada: Problems and Prospects*.

The central thesis of the report was that we have failed to cope adequately with urban problems because we have dealt with each— housing, transportation, poverty, social unrest, environmental quality, and the fiscal squeeze—largely in isolation. In doing so we have gone up a dead-end road dealing with symptoms instead of causes, because each of these has its roots and is inextricably intertwined in what Lithwick calls the urban process. This process is closely bound up with the economic development of the country which, insofar as the urban pattern is concerned, has been increasingly expressed in the concentration of population in a dozen large cities. Within each city the struggle for urban space has been a major determinant of the form and structure of cities, and of many of their problems.

A number of points are made in the report that illuminate the urban process, as well as the requirements of national urban policies. There are four implications that are particularly noteworthy.

The first is the interdependence of urban problems and the associated need in seeking solutions to be aware of these relationships. For example, our preference in the recent past for single detached dwellings results in a high level of urban space consumption, in low density, the lateral spread of cities, high travel costs from homes to other places, and rising land prices. We will be wise in seeking to deal with any of these issues to understand how each is locked into a chain of relationships within the urban process.

The second implication concerns the relationship between towns and cities. As the report expressed it: "Urbanization determines not only the growth of individual urban units, but the evolution of the whole urban system, ... An approach that fails to appreciate the totality of this urban network, that fails to see the impact of city A on city B, and through it the feedback into the whole urbanization process ultimately will be unable to cope meaningfully with urban reality."

Thirdly, in the growth of this country there has been a "line of influence," going from economic development to the growth of the urban system, to the rise of the individual town and city. Looking at the urban system in this way, it is concluded that in attempting to solve their problems, individual cities are not self-sufficient and autonomous, and are subject to major forces that do not lie within their control.

Finally, the interdependence of all the elements of the urban system (functionally and geographically) requires that we find a new policy-making mechanism that would permit all of the major groups to struggle towards coordination and consensus, which is essential if they are not to conflict and confound each other and ultimately waste scarce resources. To make this possible a national urban council is suggested. Since this is constitutionally a sensitive area, Lithwick carefully picks his words on the concept and composition of the proposed urban council:

> It would be a forum where the interests of the various groups involved in the urban policy system could be presented, where objectives could be reconciled, and where feasible plans could be drawn up—strong regional differences and the unique role of the provinces must be recognized. One alternative would be to have a two-tier system. Regional councils would develop regional plans. The membership on these would consist of local federal officials, relevant provincial authorities, and representatives of the relevant urban communities, both at the higher level and including particular local interest groups, which will necessarily vary in the different regions. Above these councils would be the National Council, where regional and national objectives could be harmonized and integrated.

Since the publication of *Urban Canada*, events have moved towards the establishment of a tri-level process of policy consultation between the federal government, the provinces and the municipalities. This is in part a reflection of one of the key principles in the mandate of the Ministry of State for Urban Affairs: "the fostering of co-operative relationships in respect of urban affairs with the provinces and, through them, their municipalities, and with the public and with private organizations."[1] The major result of the first tri-level conference, held in November 1972, was an agreement to initiate three-level meetings, province by province, or by groups of provinces, and to hold a second national tri-level conference in 1973. This 1973 conference, held in Edmonton, initiated a tri-level study of urban finance.

Regional Planning in Alberta

At the juncture of what is apparently a new chapter in policy-making on human settlement in Canada, it is important to understand the evolution of sub-provincial and regional policy-making structures and processes. This is best illustrated by the case of Alberta which has been since 1950 the leading edge of regionalism in Canada, at least for the basic framework function of regional planning. It owes this distinction to the application of the principle of collective action by municipalities sharing common concerns within a common region. The principle was invoked within a planning system which has the following features:

1.   The planning regions, administered by regional planning commissions, are delineated by the province, in consultation with the municipalities, in a way which recognizes the inter-dependence of town and country.

2.   The regional planning process is seen as a mechanism for rural and urban municipalities to reach a measure of consensus on the central issues of urban and regional growth — the direction, sequence and extent of urban development, the overall pattern of communities, and the relationship of these to natural resources.

3.   The province is a direct participant in this process, both as a substantial contributor to regional budgets and as a member, through the relevant departments, of the various commissions.

4.   The method of adopting regional plans acknowledges the validity of the region as a unit of planning administration; a regional plan is confirmed by the affirmative vote of two-thirds of the members present and voting on the resolution.

5.   Financing of the commissions, which has always been on a shared basis between the province and the municipalities, involves the principles of provincial-municipal partnership and the collective responsibility of municipalities within each region. Amendments to the Planning Act in 1971 established an Alberta Planning Fund, providing for contributions by municipalities by a regular tax levy, with the mill rate set on a sliding scale, in proportion to population. The province contributes 1.5 of the total amount of the municipal contributions.

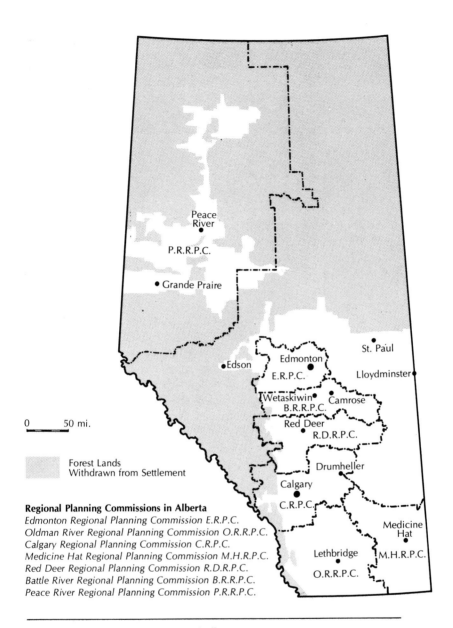

Regional Planning Commissions in Alberta
Edmonton Regional Planning Commission E.R.P.C.
Oldman River Regional Planning Commission O.R.R.P.C.
Calgary Regional Planning Commission C.R.P.C.
Medicine Hat Regional Planning Commission M.H.R.P.C.
Red Deer Regional Planning Commission R.D.R.P.C.
Battle River Regional Planning Commission B.R.R.P.C.
Peace River Regional Planning Commission P.R.R.P.C.

The Regional Planning Commission of Alberta

Taken together the Alberta commissions represent a system of regional planning, concerned with the integrated development of town and country within regions and the coordination of land use, environment and development between regions. The system which has been evolving since 1950 is now well established. Its financial base is secured by a provincial tax levy on constituent municipalities, and by a direct provincial contribution. The commission's membership is made up mainly of municipalities, which in the various regions work together on problems of the urban regional environment. The question is: how can this on-going process of interaction around the natural regional associations of the province be plugged into the emerging consultative process between the three levels of government?

91

6. The Planning Commission assumes an active role in the development process by (a) its exercise of the subdivision approval function, delegated from the province; (b) its technical planning services to member municipalities; and (c) its planning-management role in the development of new communities under the New Towns Act (1956), in resource-based and urban-centred regions.

By 1972 this pattern of regional planning administration extended from the American border to the Peace River region, and included seven commissions, centred on the major cities of Alberta: Medicine Hat, Lethbridge, Calgary, Red Deer, Weatskiwin/Camrose, Edmonton and Grande Prairie/Peace River. These covered about 58 per cent of the area of the province and 86 per cent of its population.

In the context of the intergovernmental process of policy consultation, the Alberta case deserves more than cursory treatment, because it is so inseparably a part of the government system in that province, and because it represents a tendency expressed in different forms in the other provinces of the country — for example, the regional district in British Columbia, the regional government in Ontario, and the regional administration in Quebec.

The Oldman River Region: Building the Region into the Nation

The kind of regional evolution, exemplified by Alberta, should be a source of great strength to the tri-level process. This can perhaps be best appreciated by considering how one urban-centred region might be related to the evolving intergovernmental mechanism. The region in question is the Oldman River region in southwestern Alberta, a vast area of over 10,000 square miles, containing about 8.5 per cent of the Alberta population (116,491 in 1971) and centred on the city of Lethbridge. In most respects it is a regional analogue of Lithwick's observations on the urban system.[2]

The region is highly diversified, including such towns as Taber (population 4,590 in 1966), thirty miles east of Lethbridge, a service centre for an irrigated district farmed intensively on the sugar beet, mixed farming pattern; Pincher Creek (population 3,220 in 1966), based on ranching country near the foothills and in the vicinity of important natural gas discoveries; Cardston, the centre of Mormon settlement, on the edge of the Blood Indian Reserve about fifteen miles north of the United States border; and Vulcan in the northern part of the region, an important grain elevator terminal serving a rich wheat-growing area. All of these diverse elements, together with

92

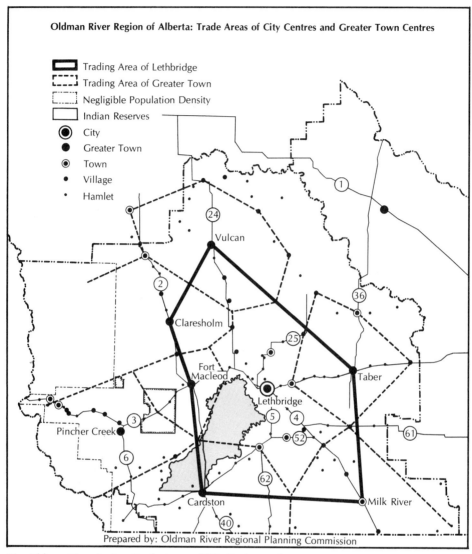

Oldman River Region of Alberta: Trade Areas of City Centres and Greater Town Centres

- Trading Area of Lethbridge
- Trading Area of Greater Town
- Negligible Population Density
- Indian Reserves
- ◉ City
- ● Greater Town
- ◉ Town
- • Village
- · Hamlet

Vulcan
Claresholm
Fort Macleod
Lethbridge
Taber
Pincher Creek
Cardston
Milk River

Prepared by: Oldman River Regional Planning Commission

The Oldman River Region: Trade Areas of City Centres and Greater Town Centres

Underlying the institutional fact, the Oldman River Regional Planning Commission, is a functional fact: the interdependence of the community within the region. Lethbridge, the principal city, is at the top of a hierarchy linked to a network of "greater towns," offering fifty-six to a hundred services, which in turn are linked to towns and villages with respectively thirty-one to fifty-five and eleven to thirty services, and so on. Two major urban issues that arise at this time are (a), the relationship between investment in public services and selective town growth within the region, and (b), the future economic base of Lethbridge as it reaches steady state as a wholesaling centre.

93

other towns, villages and hamlets, form part of an urban system focused on Lethbridge (population 46,620 in 1966). As a 1970 study shows, it is a system in three ways: (1) the component urban centres form a service hierarchy that meets the requirements of the regional population; (2) Lethbridge serves as the distribution centre for the entire region; and (3) the rate and quality of its economic development has a significant impact on the development of the region as a whole.[3]

It follows that none of the communities are "self-sufficient and autonomous." Their roles as service centres are dependent on a complex web of related variables, the most important of which are location and transportation/communication facilities, range of services, trade areas, threshhold levels (the minimum amount of purchasing power necessary to support the supply of a good from a central place), and economic reach (the maximum distance that consumers are willing to travel to a centre to obtain services of that centre). A change in any one of these variables for any one centre can upset the entire system.[4]

Since 1955 this functional interdependence has been expressed in a form of institutional interdependence through the Oldman River Regional Planning Commission. Under the provisions of the Planning Act of Alberta, the twenty-eight municipalities and improvement districts of the region have been developing an integrated approach to the problems of land use, industrial development, population distribution, transportation, recreation, public services generally, and the "financing and programming of public development projects and capital works."[5] This is a prolonged and difficult process; in 1971 it was reported that the commission had partially completed a "preliminary regional plan."

From the point of view of developing a cooperative approach to policy thinking in Canada, it is important to note some of the policy issues that emerge in the Oldman region. One of them is the relationship of the service structure and the urban hierarchy to public investment, federal, provincial and municipal, in roads, public works, health services, housing, education, welfare, not to mention jails, Treasury branches and liquor stores. Even in a province where wealth comes pouring out of the ground, financial resources are not unlimited, priorities have to be set and choices made. The location and maintenance of public facilities reinforce the roles of the selected towns. It is important that the allocation of public investment be related to urban development policy worked out regionally with a view to optimizing the accessiblity, range and quality of offered services.[6]

Another issue is the future development of Lethbridge as a regional centre. Commission work suggests that the city is at a turning point, having reached an approximate steady state in employment on the basis of its role as a regional wholesaling centre. Manufacturing, particularly food processing and beverages, are mentioned, as well as the impetus of the Univeristy of Lethbridge, as possible new sources of growth.[7] This is a lively public concern. The 1971 annual conference of the commission adopted as its theme: "To grow or not to grow." Factors that need to be considered in responding to this issue include the question of size: Lethbridge is a compact community with a strong sense of identity, "large enough to have the amenities one expects in a city, but still small enough to retain a sense of community, and to allow free movement between social classes;"[8] the question of *growth rate,* from the viewpoint of socio-economic and environmental assimilation; and the *opportunities* opened up by the city's *regional role.*

For example, education is a regional service which has made an impressive start in the form of a community college and the new University, which in its dramatic central location on the coulees of the river valley is already a local landmark. The full unfolding of a University of Southwestern Alberta, which in its landscape and human background is so distinctive, offers some fascinating opportunities for giving a regional emphasis to studies in georgraphy, economics, sociology, anthropology, art and archeology, and history. It is not difficult to imagine a genuine flowering of creative work around the expression of a regional culture. The strong emphasis on continuing education in both the college and the university is an augury of this potential.

These policy issues have local, regional, provincial and national dimensions; for example, Lethbridge is eligible for DREE's manufacturing incentives program. However they may be settled, the foregoing suggests one indispensable prerequisite in this Lithwickian world, and that is that the interdependence acknowledged and institutionalized and so carefully cultivated by the people of the Oldman region be plugged into the consultative process being developed between governments. For its area, the Oldman Commission already represents "a forum where the interests of the various groups involved in the urban policy system could be presented, where objectives could be reconciled, and where feasible plans could be drawn up." We need to build upon this organic process of regionalization wherever it occurs. Should this not be done in the Oldman case, then it is very likely that the policy issues of concern to the region will not find their place on the conference agenda; and the intergovernmental process itself will not build from established strength.

While the case for regional involvement in the tri-level process has been made for one region in Alberta, it applies with equal force to the six other regional planning districts in that province, as well as to the regional governments of Ontario, the districts of British Columbia, the administrative regions of the province of Quebec, and so on.

Education for Planning and Action

Canadian urban problems are complex, interconnected, historically rooted but changing, fraught with value choices and conflicts, difficult to deal with separately — pressures released in one problem area, such as transportation, will show up in another, like land or housing; and a high degree of public responsiblity must be assumed for their solution.

These are circumstances in which individuals, groups and governments require a way of sorting and integrating an avalanche of urban information in the light of preferred urban goals. For the facts themselves are neutral: a slum is a slum is a slum. What is needed is a holistic view of the world, a philosophy which first, permits us to organize a confusing array of information, and secondly, provides a basis for making a judgement on the facts: What is good? bad? and what should be done about what we do not like?

This philosophic search is the most difficult task of all. While it will be conducted wherever men and women are confronted with choices and decisions on the environment, one of the major centres for its development should be in the universities and colleges that lay claim to responsibility for the education of planners. In this setting, a philosophy of planning: what do we do about our environment? and by what means? becomes an integral part of a philosophy of planning education, for it answers the classic question—education for what?

Environmental Planning: The Historical Context

To begin at the beginning, the presumption is made that some understanding of the place of planning in society is a necessary precedent to stating a philosophy of Planning Education. The historian, W.H. McNeill, has shown that the rise of western society, the global cosmopolitanism that has become dominant in this past century, is characterized by two major themes: "(i) the growth of human control over inanimate forms of energy; and (ii) an increasing readiness to tinker with social institutions and customs in the hope of attaining desired goals." The first of these is the province of science and the second, while not wholly the preserve of planning, is the area in which it occupies a significant place. The "manipulation" of inanimate and social energies has become the master theme of our epoch and planning is deeply rooted in this theme.[1]

This common root of science and planning has implications for the method of planning. It has been argued that in viewing man's situation in the perspective of biological time, we have moved from an era of problem-solving by the genetic method (the method of survival by the species), to the method of problem-solving by the individual (through the development of a sensitive nervous system and brain, permitting the individual organism to learn the hard way by danger and experience), to problem-solving by science (the method of study and anticipation, reaching its highest pitch in our time by means of feedback or cybernetic anticipation).[2]

This is the method which makes it possible, through the laws of physics, to put a spacecraft in orbit, or through the laws of economics to anticipate and avoid a recession. The method of problem-solving by anticipation, which has been so fruitful in the physical and life sciences, is the very same method required "for large-scale human organization and control."[3] It constitutes a large part of the method of planning—if it is understood to include both the exercise of forethought, and the implementing of such forethought in dealing with society's problems, and to be tempered by an appreciation of the complexity of human personality and growth.

The concern in this statement is specifically with society's environmental problems. Environment is conceived broadly to include natural, biological, communal and urban-regional components. Thus, in speaking of environmental planning, we mean an activity concerned with inventorying the economic and aesthetic resources of a region; with understanding the ecosystems of an area's unique plant and animal life and of the peculiarities of its watersheds and airsheds; with knowing the community life of an area, both subjectively and objectively in terms of functions, relationships and flows of all kinds between communities of different sizes and purposes; and with the integration of these environmental elements into a form of settlement, an urban-regional environment, that satisfies consensual goals to the highest possible degree. For purposes of policy application, this concept will have spatial limits: a city, region, province or country. And it will make people — their needs and perceptions, values and institutions — the focus of its concern.

In Canada we are, of course, inheritors of other western traditions, such as those of individualism, from the English, French and American bourgeois revolutions, not to mention our own nineteenth-century eruptions. It is a little startling to read in William Lyon Mackenzie's Navy Island Proclamation of 1837 such earth-shaking objectives as "Freedom of Trade—every man to be allowed to buy at the cheapest market and sell at the dearest," and "the distribution of the wild lands of the country to the industry, capital, skill and enterprise of worthy men of all nations."[4]

The further elaboration of this aspect of the liberal-democratic tradition is a matter of record. One of its high marks was the social impact of the concept of biological evolution. Darwin, who recorded so humanely his horror at the oppression he saw in South America during the voyage of the *Beagle,* lived to see his concepts of natural selection and survival of the fittest employed to "justify both a rugged individualism at home and a ruthless collective imperialism abroad."[5] Vestiges of these attitudes have tended to flare up in Canada during times of change or stress, as in the first quarter of this century: "To healthy Britons of good behaviour our welcome is everlasting: but to make this country a dumping ground for the scum and dregs of the old world means transplanting the evils and vices that they may flourish in a new soil. ... "

In North America the challenges of pioneer existence gave us from the beginning a split personality. On the one hand, the opportunity to own land under the homestead policy nourished all the individualist tendencies towards fierce self-reliance and independence. On the other hand, the special hazards of the pioneer life, including the vicissitudes of the grain market, and the urge to build rapidly the entire superstructure of a modern technological society, drove men towards cooperation and government intervention.

These different strands in the Canadian and general western background are cited because they represent living forces which condition the purposes, style and impact of environmental planning.

The evolution of contemporary planning is inextricably bound up with three types of breakdown in societal arrangements: the breakdown of the auto-regulative process known as the market; the breakdown in the use and management of natural resources; and the breakdown of the urban environment, including certain aspects of the property system. From the first has come national economic planning, with emphasis on the manipulation of the critical aggregates — employment, income, savings and investment — to keep the economy on even keel. From the second has come the interest in conservation and natural resources planning. And from the third breakdown has come the bottom-up planning tradition with its emphasis on the protection of property values through zoning, on the City Beautiful, on humanitarian reform, and on urban-centred regional planning. Each of these requires some brief interpretation.

The Market: Economic Disparities and Regionalism

One of the striking features of national economic planning in Canada and the United States is that it has been accompanied by a heightening of interest in regional issues and regional planning. The reason is not far to seek; in times of recession some areas which were dependent on highly vulnerable staple products were hit much harder than others. However, in both theory and practice, the idea of purposive planned intervention to overcome social crises was coupled with the idea of decentralization of some responsiblity and some power to the constituent regions of the country.

One of the seminal experiences in regional planning, both in North America and internationally, has been the work of the Tennessee Valley Authority (TVA), initiated by the government of Franklin Delano Roosevelt in 1933. The boldness of its concept and its conspicuous early success against great odds have made a deep impression. The journals of David Lilienthal, its second chairman provide the most vivid expression of the governing concepts of the TVA approach. One of the key principles was the integrated development of the Valley's resources: "TVA isn't (just) a power project . . . it is small industries coming to towns . . . better navigation and recreation . . . reforestation and communities becoming strong." Another was the decentralization of administration, which took the form of a struggle against co-ordination" by the Department of the Interior in Washington. And a third major concept, related to the decentralization theme, is participation. "What the technical developments will mean in terms of the values of human life," Lilienthal wrote, "is what will determine the final answer: is it good or not? And since it is the end result in these terms that we must have constantly in mind, I . . . lay great emphasis on the ways and means adapted to secure the participation of people in the work that has been carried on, the efforts to utilize and release and stimulate human energies and creativeness. . . . "[6]

In Canada the regional fact has come to be expressed in national and provincial policies designed to close the gap in living standards between regions. "Balanced regional development" has become one of the commandments of the Economic Council of Canada.[7] This is as much a political and social as an economic concern. Greater equality between regions has become a national priority because many Canadians wish to enjoy the distinctive features of their own region without being forced by circumstances to migrate to greener pastures.

Roosevelt and Lilienthal and the Planning Concept

The development of the concept of regional planning in Canada owes something to the compelling example of the Tennessee Valley Authority and its articulate spokesmen, Franklin D. Roosevelt and David E. Lilienthal. In Lilienthal's Journals, there is an entry (April 22, 1942) referring to a discussion with President Roosevelt in which the President made reference to his initiation of broad land use planning in the State of New York, and which brought the following response: "Mention of his work in New York on the planning idea gave me the opportunity to say something to him that I had long wanted to. "Occasionally people will ask," I said, "where did the regional planning idea of the TVA come from? We know that Musele Shoals and Senator Norris account for the power part of TVA. But what about planning, and how come? What you have said about your beginning the land-use study idea in New York suggests the answer that I give: the regional planning idea of the TVA is a direct outgrowth of the experience and thinking of Franklin D. Roosevelt."

101

Conservation and the Emergence of Planning

For insight into the resources element of Canadian planning, attention is directed towards a 1970 paper, *Conservation, Resources and Environment,* by C. Ray Smith and David R. Witty. There is a link between the Commission of Conservation of fifty years ago, the Resources of Tomorrow Conference of 1961, the contemporary conservation agencies and our present efforts to more closely align Ecology and Planning.[8] The root of much of the environmental philosophy of the 1970s is to be found in the emphasis of these earlier conferences on a comprehensive approach, on the interdependence of different resource uses, on the need for better research, planning and resource management. The commission shared even the present concern for the quality of life, but with a somewhat different and less existential twist: "Conservation of life . . . counts most largely in increasing production."

It has been a long road from the follies of the Palliser Triangle—the misguided plowing up of dry western grasslands—to the goals of Environment Canada: "The focus is on major changes in land and water use. . . . The requirement is to ensure that the costs and benefits of all consequences to the environment are taken into account before commitments are made and plans completed. . . . Pollution is to be controlled for the protection and benefit of men and all living things."

The Urban Environment

The surge of urbanization in Canada early in this century at first evoked a response that was influenced by the City Beautiful movement associated with the Chicago Exposition of 1893 and Daniel Burnham, who conceived that city's celebrated lakefront park system. This influence showed up in Canada in the Civic Guild of Toronto, in a competition for the Vancouver Civic Centre and in the 1915 plan for Ottawa prepared by Sir Herbert Holt.[9]

This concern for the sensory environment, however, was soon to give way to a less heroic tradition. In a book on city planning. published in 1916, which reviewed both American and Canadian legislation and practice, Frank Backus Williams, a lawyer of some distinction who drafted the first city planning law of the State of New York, gave articulate expression to the gospel of planning for property. "Government," he wrote, "has . . . the main function of regulating and adjusting the actions and property interests of its inhabitants. . . . " And "districting," which was the contemporary term for zoning, had a twofold objective: "first, to discover differences in different parts of cities and adapt regulations to them ... , secondly, to protect, accentuate or create character in a district. ... " He further asserted that "the result of the systems should be to increase land values, and prevent fluctuations in them." These views were echoed by Naulon Cauchon, president of the Town Planning Institute of Canada from 1923 to 1928, who laid it on the line: "Town Planning, properly understood, means obtaining the most for our money. ... " He was referring to the benefits of greater efficiency in the physical organization of cities as well as the stabilizing effect of zoning on property values.[10]

In Canadian planning's formative period there were, of course, other responses to the problems of our cities which were contemporarily described as "housing conditions which shame our civilization ... thousands of families occupy(ing) but one room each ... ," etc. "Our boast should be," wrote the humanitarian reformer, Mr. Frank Beer, "not how many fine houses there are in our cities, but how few poor, unsanitary and unworthy ones." And, as has already been noted, a major force fifty and sixty years ago was the Commission of Conservation which laid the foundation for the present concept of urban-centred regional planning, in which there is a coalescence of economic, resource conservation and environmental themes, and in which the guiding idea is to achieve the mastery required to shape the environment towards consensual images of "the good life."[11] The "bottom-up" environmental concerns and the "top-down" concerns of economic development meet and coalesce, into the new discipline of regional planning. In this concept, the region becomes the place where local notions of the good life are reconciled with provincial and national policies of economic development.

The Post-Industrial Perspective

There is also a very strong presumption in current theories of social development that structural changes in our society are making us increasingly a planning society. The new industrial model propounded by such writers as John Kenneth Galbraith and Daniel Bell has emphasized that planning has its roots in increasing complexity, accelerating rates of social change and massive technology. It is further characterized by an enlarged scale of capital investment, expansion of social capital, intensified environmental vulnerability, increased capacity to manipulate and analyse information, and a new highly sensitized, highly educated political constituency. Planning, under these conditions, becomes embedded in society, not only to help solve its technical problems that lend themselves to systematic analysis and rational solution, but as a means of achieving consensus and decisive action on basic issues.

Criteria for Planning Education

With this view of the societal role of planning as background, a number of criteria for education in planning will be attempted.

Social Concept   The first criterion is that the critical place of planning in contemporary society be understood. It is hoped that the foregoing observations, at the very least, suggest that we are not dealing with some narrow technical process, but with an essential social technique related to the fundamental issues of our time. It follows that everyone involved in the educational process should come to conceive of their tasks with a creative imagination which is commensurate with the challenge.

Planning as Process   The second criterion is that planning be understood as a continuing process which to be effective must be rooted in our social and political institutions. From this point of departure, research, policy-making, action and feedback are seen as part of a single indivisible struggle or process and our studies must give due weight to each. To be effective in any phase, we must know something about the requirements of each and their interrelationships. For example, the inescapable complexity of contemporary data and analysis and the need to anticipate the impact of one action on another sometimes lead us to the tools of systems analysis as an aid in decision-making. But it is in the nature of systems analysis that it is dependent on an explicit statement of goals as a basis for explicit evaluation criteria. In this sense, the quality of the planner's advice will depend on the sophistication he develops in formulating policy goals. He must add to his repertoire the essential "software" skills, which might include the capacity to analyse problems in a deep historical and ecological sense,[12] social surveys, determining interest group consensus, and formulating value issues for policy-makers.

Elements of the Planning Process, Goals/Achievement Approach

This is an outline of the elements of the planning process conceived in goals-achievement terms. In this concept of planning method philosophical issues: what to do and why? are joined with plans of action: how to do it? and vigorous analysis of choices, the ordering of programmes: when to carry out actions? and the evaluation of their effect: who benefits or loses? and how much?

The Planning Process

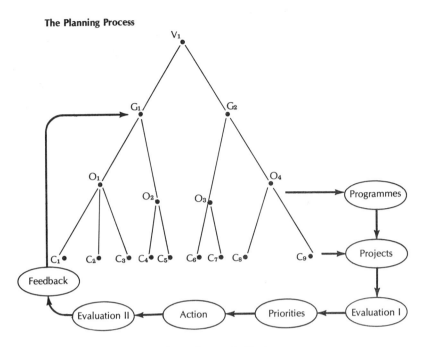

Values (V)	*a patterned set of general attitudes*
Goals (G)	*idealized end states expressed in terms of real world processes and conditions*
Objectives (O)	*a specific aim, conforming to and fulfilling goals, and obtainable*
Priorities	*the ordering of objectives, programmes and projects in the light of techniques of anticipatory evaluation, such as cost-benefit analysis and/or societal and political urgencies.*
Programmes	*sets of proposed actions to implement objectives*
Criteria (C)	*operational definitions arising from particular objectives, that is the conditions that must be satisfied, which form the basis for the design and evaluation of programmes and projects*
Projects	*specific actions undertaken as part of a programme and fulfilling specific criteria*
Monitoring and Feedback	*the systematic recording, documentation and communication of programme and project experience*
Evaluation	*the judgment of the programme/project experience on the basis of specified criteria, and the drawing of policy inferences concerning goals, objectives, programmes and projects, i.e. their relative soundness or need for change and improvement. This takes place before (Evaluation 1)—as an input to setting priorities, and during and after action (Evaluation 2), as a basis for change and improvement in programmes and projects*

105

The Commitment Criterion   The third criterion follows from the foregoing. A Planning scholar is not a passive and detached observer of a process. He is preparing himself to be an active participant. To be effective he will require a high degree of commitment to what will often be a combative role. To those who may be discouraged by this, remember the assertion of Jean Paul Sartre that commitment is the corollary of freedom, the ability to choose one's life work or mission.

Regional Focus   The fourth criterion is that, in any planning society, a particular program of Planning Education must identify its own area of concern with a view to achieving a substantial degree of concentration, internal unity and focus. There are many options of equal validity as long as they respond to the conditions and needs of the environment in which we work. For example, at Waterloo we responded to the need to develop the discipline of regional planning in a way that is sensitive to the great regional diversity in Canada, which contains both highly "advanced" industrialized areas as well as totally undeveloped regions. Thus the program relates to both urban-centred regions and developing regions; it encompasses development resources and environmental issues, with the issue emphasis shifting within the spectrum from highly developed to developing regions.

In the elaboration of the regional approach, for education or action, there is need to be wary of the thin line between regionalism, a celebration of an area's innate life potentials, and sectionalism, the parochial preoccupation with defending and aggrandizing one's own turf. This distinction is very clearly expressed in the school of thought led by Howard W. Odum, sociologist and planner. Regional planning is a social instrument for reconciling and achieving a balance between technology and indigenous culture, between regional individuality and the forces of standardization, and between the region and the nation. Canadian curricula will ignore these nuances at their own peril.[13]

The Discipline Mix   The selection of this focus leads to the fifth criterion: a planning program must include a discipline mix that is as broad as its prototypical units of study. In the case of regional planning, the disciplines suggest themselves: geography and economics for the analysis of structural and functional features (the impact of labour markets as well as soil patterns); ecology for the observation of biotic ecosystems and man's relationship to them and as a link to human ecology; sociology for an understanding of the context of values and social institutions; political science for a grasp of statutory frameworks and decision-making processes; urban design to reveal the aesthetic potentials of different environments; and regional planning to draw out the insights and implications of these and other fields and develop strategies for their application in an integrated fashion to society's problems. This approach avoids the pitfall of an imbalanced emphasis on one stream, such as the traditional emphasis on design; it also requires a high degree of flowing together of the various streams. Achieving this is a subtle matter, but it is facilitated by a faculty which includes "specialists" as well as "mainstream" planners, and by fostering interaction and a reasonable degree of conceptual rapport internally. This introduces a constraint on the size of the faculty group because, beyond a certain point (perhaps the point where it is no longer possible to sit around a big table), such cohesion is extremely elusive. And this approach also introduces an obligation to minimize the old-style single virtuoso project, and to develop in its place broad studies of regions or major problem areas requiring the orchestration of a diversity of talents and expertise.

An Experimental Approach   The sixth criterion arises, in a sense, out of the preceding five. A philosophy which emphasizes process and an inter-disciplinary approach must discover learning forms that are appropriate. By definition it must be experimental. The Waterloo approach may again serve as an illustration. Emphasis has been placed on group projects or working teams to simulate planning field experience; on contact with outside environments, developments and events; and on the opportunity for research, giving scope for the student to find himself as a scholar, to develop his own working methods and hopefully nourish his or her potentials for making a more than perfunctory dent on planning theory and practice. The ultimate aim of the Waterloo approach is to dissolve classroom walls. An inflexible commitment to a single approach is to be avoided as relevant experience is limited and we have very few models to go by. In our working style we must remain good pragmatists.

Man: The Centre   The seventh criterion is the most difficult of all because it responds directly in an ideological sense to the societal role of planning. Since planning is a social and political process, it is deeply involved in the battleground of ideas and human values. While the planner as a professional individual must respect the political context in which he works, planning as a method and an institutional approach cannot escape philosophical judgments. The

107

point is made cogently by Erich Fromm in his observations on planning and computer technology:

> What is the procedure of humanistic planning? Computers should become a functional part in a life-oriented social system and not a cancer which begins to play havoc and eventually kills the system. . . . The values which determine the selection of facts and which influence the programming of the computer must be gained on the basis of human nature, its various possible manifestations, its optimal forms of development and the real needs conducive to this development. That is to say man, not technique, must become the ultimate source of values; optimal human development and not maximal production the criterion for all planning.[14]

Accepting planning's creative social role — in fact, Fromm's criterion of "optimum human development" — suggests that there is a particular tradition which deserves a special place in the program of studies. The line of thought leading from Emerson to Thoreau to Benton Mackaye to Patrick Geddes to Lewis Mumford and Howard Odum (and recently given vigorous expression by John Friedmann) has contributed greatly not only to philosophy, literature and social criticism but, indirectly through its contemporary reinterpretation, to the development of a philosophy of regional planning. In the Canadian literature on the environment and the city, it is reflected in the writing of such authors as Hans Blumenfeld, Pierre Dansereau and Lawrence Haworth.

Historically, this philosophy has assumed the role of critic of the early industrialism of North America in which environmental values played little part. Thoreau observed, "If a man walks in the woods for love of them half each day, he is in danger of being regarded as a loafer; but if he spends his whole day as a speculator shearing off those woods and making earth bald before her time, he is esteemed an industrious and enterprising citizen." The positive ideas of this philosophy have tended to be a blend of utopianism which Emerson immortalized, and a shrewd response to contemporary development issues. Benton Mackaye, who acknowledged his debt to Thoreau, calling him the "philosopher of environment," was perhaps the first to advance the idea of a regional city, combining both urban and rural elements in a single interacting system. His broad interests and curiosity about new experiments led him in 1918 to visit the Clay Belt community of northern Ontario, Kapuskasing, which was developed on crown land for World War One veterans by the Ontario government. While he had some praise for the initiative of public policy, he

Preserving Amenities in Stratford, Ontario — Thomas Adam's Concern

This illustration from Thomas Adams' book Rural Development *(1917) reflects one of the preoccupations of early planning thought in Canada: the linking of town and country. Thus, the original caption stated: "The making of small towns more attractive is one of the best means of securing the healthy combination of urban and rural development in Canada." This was a point of view which was to be submerged in the avalanche of urbanization in Canada only to re-emerge very recently in our attempt to fashion — out of dire necessity — a more holistic concept of planning.*

identified the Achilles heel of Canadian frontier development: "three vital things that are not provided for — a thorough-going system of land classification, town planning, and land tenure based squarely upon use."[15]

Patrick Geddes, a Scottish biologist and a student of T.H. Huxley, is widely regarded as the progenitor of environmental planning in the western world.[16] Geddes' thought was characterized by a central dichotomy: one side of it was the grimy coal and steel Victorian environment, formed by that process described by Bernard Shaw as "calculated on the cubic foot of space . . . that you can get higher rents letting by the room than you can get for a mansion in Park Lane." The other part of the paradox had its seeds in the new technology of hydro power and light metals, and in the inescapable backlash against environmental squalor. Reading Geddes again today makes a community planner appreciate how providential is the tradition he represents for the development of contemporary planning theory and practice. For he was one of the first to draw attention to the ecological constraints that surround the human community, and by the same token to point the way towards a valid planning methodology summed up in the injunction "let diagnosis precede treatment." Geddes' work is of special interest because of his influence on Thomas Adams, the British planner, who spent seven years in Canada, from 1914 to 1921, as an adviser to the Commission of Conservation.

In our time, this vital tradition has given us, through Lewis Mumford, a humanist view of the city:

> One may describe the city in its social aspect as a special framework directed toward the creation of differentiated opportunities for a common life and a significant collective drama . . . from habit to choice, from a fixed mold to a dynamic equilibrium of forces, from taking life as it comes to comprehending it and redesigning it—that is the path of both human and civic development.
>
> This transfer of emphasis from the uniformities and common acceptances of the primary groups to the critical choices, the purposive associations, and the rational ends of the secondary group is one of main functions of the city.
>
> The city is in fact the physical form of the highest and most complex types of associative life.[17]

A Philosophy's Defence

Mumford has been quoted at length because he and the whole tradition he represents has in recent years become the target of attack from a new criticism, descending from the lofty heights of Harvard University. This is of interest to our theme because this critique, which is presented in the fascinating book of the philosophers Morton and Lucia White, *The Intellectual Versus The City,* takes the form of a comparison of two philosophical streams. The one to which we refer here is identified as transcendentalist, anti-scientific, anti-technological, and anti-urban; and the tradition of pragmatism, identified mainly with C.S. Pierce and William James, is considered pro-scientific, pro-technological, and by inference, pro-urban.[18]

In this critique Mumford emerges as the arch-villain: "even more antipathetic to the American city than Henry James . . . and the most thorough, unrelenting, contemporary expression of the tradition under consideration." It is not necessary to labour the contrast between these epithets and Mumford's own vivid concept of the city. But it is necessary to register some rebuttal to the White thesis. It seems to be based on a profound lack of rapport with contemporary humanist thought, and to betray an extremely weak historical perspective. For example, it leaves no basis for understanding why the New England transcendentalists, who were known as the Party of the Future, were in the vanguard of social reform and of the abolitionist movement in the nineteenth Century; and it certainly misses the point of their philosophical thrust which is perhaps best represented by Emerson's essay on Education: "Our culture has truckled to the times. . . . We teach boys to be such men as we are. We do not teach them to aspire to be all they can. . . . We aim to make accountants, attorneys, engineers, but not to make able, earnest, great-hearted men. The great object of Education should be commensurate with the object of life . . . to inspire the youthful man with an interest in himself; with a curiosity touching his own nature; to acquaint him with the resources of his mind . . . to make us brave and free."

It is strange, if not tragic, that some of the best philosophical minds in American academia, and certainly two of its most effective communicators, should feel obliged to attack a critic of the urban condition whose assertion of human values, and deep historical vision, is so directly needed in troubled cities that can command every resource except the one indispensable: a sense of community.

In summary, the philosophy of planning education as outlined here can be expressed in seven words: Social, Process, Commitment, Regional, Interdisciplinary, Experimental, Humanist. It is presented

in the spirit of having to start somewhere and with not a little appreciation of the hazards and booby traps along the way.

There is a link between the education of a certain kind of specialist called a Planner, and our ultimate capacity to create good cities. This is an aspect of the relationship between university and society. Pierre Dansereau makes the point: "The aim of higher education in Canada as elsewhere is cultural. . . . Positive achievement in all fields of science and art, new realizations in social structure, economic endeavour and political strategy are the only things that really count. . . . Such a blossoming of hopeful originality, such an implementation of our natural vitality, such an escape from our congenital timidity and dullness will be possible only through a well-directed increase in specialized training and research, with an unreserved enthusiasm for creative endeavours."[19]

From this point of view, in speaking of the education of the environmental planner, we speak only of a beginning. What is important is what follows in the streets of Moose Jaw and Montreal. The future of our living places is in the hands of you, the reader.

Notes — Chapter 1

1. Thomas Adams, *Rural Planning and Development* (Ottawa: Commission of Conservation, Canada, 1917), pp. 45-71.

2. Kenneth Clark, *Civilisation* (London: BBC and John Murray, 1969), p. 177.

3. The term "baroque" is used here in the sense that it has been defined by Lewis Mumford: "The concept of baroque, as it shaped itself in the seventeenth century, is particularly useful because it holds in itself the two contradictory elements of the age. First: the mathematical and mercantile and methodical side, expressed to perfection in its rigorous street plans, its formal city layouts, and its geometrically ordered landscaped designs. And at the same time, in the painting and sculpture of the period, it embraces the sensuous, rebellious, anticlassical, anti-mechanical side, expressed in its clothes and its sexual life and its religious fanaticism and its crazy statecraft. Between the sixteenth and nineteenth century these two elements existed together; sometimes acting separately, sometimes held in tension within a larger whole." *The Culture of Cities* (New York: Harcourt, Brace and Co., 1948), chapter 2.

4. Kenneth McNaught, *The Pelican History of Canada* (Harmondsworth: Penguin Books Ltd., 1969), p. 20.

5. Michael Hugo-Brunt, *The History of City Planning* (Montreal: Harvest House, 1972), p. 257; and Frances Moore Brooke, *The History of Emily Montague*, as quoted in A.J.M. Smith, ed., *The Canadian Experience* (Toronto: Gage Publishing Co., 1974), p. 10.

6. McNaught, *History of Canada*, pp. 80-81.

7. Harold A. Innis, "Unused Capacity as a Factor in Canadian Economic History," in *Political Economy in the Modern State* (Toronto: Ryerson Press, 1946), pp. 206, 207; and Jack A. Blyth, *The Canadian Social Inheritance* (Toronto: Copp Clark, 1972), pp. 14, 15.

8. *The Report and Despatches of the Earl of Durham* (London: Ridgeways, 1939), pp. 87, 188.

9. McNaught, *History of Canada*, pp. 76-78; and Leroy O. Stone, *Urban Development in Canada* (Ottawa: Dominion Bureau of Statistics, 1967), p. 20.

10. *Montréal Economique* (Montréal: Ecole des Hautes Etudes Commerciales, Université de Montréal, 1943), pp. 28, 30, 193.

11. In this section on the Maritimes I have drawn considerably on Michael Hugo-Brunt's article, "The Origin of Colonial Settlements in the Maritimes," *Plan Canada*, Vol. 1, No. 2, 1960.

12. Stone, *Urban Development*, pp. 19, 20.

13. Heather Robertson, *Grass Roots* (Toronto: James Lewis and Samuel, 1973).

14. Adams, *Rural Planning*, pp. 102-103.

15. P.J. Smith, ed., *The Prairie Provinces,* Studies in Urban Geography (Toronto: University of Toronto Press, 1972); and Robertson, *Grass Roots.*

16. Rex A. Lucas, *Minetown, Milltown, Railtown* (Toronto: University of Toronto Press, 1971).

17. *The Canadian Economy from the 1960's to the 1970's*: Fourth Annual Review (Ottawa: Economic Council of Canada), pp. 177-179. The cited rate, 4.1 per cent, was for the period 1951-1961.

18. *Report of the Fifth Annual Meeting,* Commission of Conservation (Ottawa: Government of Canada, 1914).

19. Hans Blumenfeld, *The Modern Metropolis* (Montreal: Harvest House, 1967), pp. 54, 55; *Plan for Downtown Toronto* (Toronto: City of Toronto Planning Board, 1963), p. 11; and *A Survey of Urban Transportation Problems and Priorities in Canadian Municipalities*: a study prepared for the Canadian Federation of Mayors and Municipalities by Kates, Peat, Marwick and Co. (Toronto, 1970), II, pp. 11-15.

20. A.R.M. Lower, *Colony to Nation* (Toronto: Longmans, 1947), pp. 422-425.

21. Morton and Lucia White, *The Intellectual Versus the City* (Toronto: Mentor, The American Library of Canada, 1964), pp. 150-158; and S.D. Clark, *The Developing Canadian Community* (Toronto: University of Toronto Press, 1962), pp. 120-127.

22. Wolfgang M. Illing, "The Rising Cost of Housing and Problem of Financing," in Michael Wheeler, ed., *The Right to Housing* (Montreal: Harvest House, 1969), pp. 145-146; and Roman Herchak Acres Consulting Services Ltd., et al., *Urban Residential Land Development* (Edmonton: Alberta Land Use Forum, 1974).

23. See R. Mclemore et al., *Inventory of Conditions and Trends in the Inner City* (Ottawa: Discussion paper, MSUA, 1973).

24. Max Weber, *The City* (New York: Collier Books, 1958), pp. 30-33, 41-45, 54-57. (Note the prefatory remarks, "The Theory of the City," by Don Martindale); Arnold Toynbee, *Cities of Destiny* (New York: McGraw-Hill, 1967), pp. 13-14; and Mumford, *The Culture of Cities,* pp. 480-482.

Notes — Chapter 2

1. The Ontario Municipal Board, *Decision of the Board,* Spadina Expressway, 17 February 1971, p. 13.

2. Lithwick, *Urban Canada,* pp. 17-36.

3. Ibid., pp. 17, 25, 29-32, 25, 45, 49, 50, 57.

4. Science Council of Canada, *Cities for Tomorrow* (Ottawa: Information Canada, 1971), p. 33.l

5. Hans Blumenfeld, "Transportation in the Modern Metropolis," in Larry S. Bourne, ed., *Internal Structure of the City* (New York: Oxford University Press, 1971), pp. 231, 232.

6. Ibid, pp. 236-239. See also, John F. Kain, "Transportation In Metropolitan Areas," in Simon Miles, ed., *Metropolitan Problems* (Toronto: Methuen, 1970), pp. 79-87; and *Capacities and Limitations of Urban Transportation Modes*, Institute of Traffic Engineers (Washington, D.C., 1965), Table 7, p. 20.

7. N.D. Lea and Associates, *Urban Transportation Developments in Eleven Canadian Metropolitan Areas* (Ottawa: Canadian Good Roads Association, 1966), p. 83.

8. *A.A.D.T. Traffic Volumes 1955-1969 and Traffic Collision Data 1967-1969, On the King's Highway* and *Secondary Highways* (Toronto: Department of Highways, 1969), pp. 8, 9.

9. Ezra J. Mishan, *The Costs of Economic Growth* (New York: Frederick A. Praeger, 1967), pp. 53-55; and Kenneth P. Cantor, "Warning: The Automobile is Dangerous to Earth, Air, Fire, Water, Mind and Body," *The Environmental Handbook* (New York: Ballantine Books, 1970), pp. 200, 201.

10. Paul B. Sears, "Ethics, Aesthetics and the Balance of Nature." This quote and other ecological references are from Sears, *The Ecology of Man* (Eugene, Oregon: Oregon State Systems of Higher Education, 1957).

11. C. Starr, "Energy and Power," *Scientific American,* Volume 224, No. 3, September 1971, pp. 42, 43; and Cantor, "Warning: the Automobile Is Dangerous," p. 206.

12. Science Council, *Cities for Tomorrow,* pp. 35-38; Herbert Marcuse, *An Essay on Liberation* (Boston: Beacon Press, 1969), p. 4; Erich Fromm, *The Revolution of Hope* (Toronto: Bantam Books, 1968), p. 40; and J.K. Galbraith, *The New Industrial State* (New York: Signet Books, 1967), pp. 208-220. For reference to the Sterling electric car see Frank Morgan, *Pollution, Canada's Critical Challenge* (Toronto: The Ryerson Press, 1970), pp. 78, 79.

13. Hans Blumenfeld, "Theory of City Form, Past and Present," *The Modern Metropolis* (Montreal: Harvest House, 1971).

14. Barry Commoner, *The Closing Circle* (New York: Bantam Books, 1971).

Notes — Chapter 3

1. Yves Thériault, *Ashini* (Montreal: Harvest House, 1971), p. 13.

2. Dominion Bureau of Statistics, *Canada Year Book 1970-71* (Ottawa: Information Canada, 1971), p. 544; and J.W. MacNeill, *Environmental Management* (Ottawa: Information Canada, 1971), pp. 188, 189.

3. L.O. Gertler (Coordinator), *Niagara Escarpment Study* (Toronto: Regional Development Branch, Treasury Department, Finance and Economics, 1969), pp. 3-9; and Government of Ontario, *Design for Development: The Toronto-Centred Region* (Toronto: The Queen's Printer, 1970), pp. 15-19.

4. H.N. Lithwick, *Urban Canada* (Ottawa: Central Mortgage and Housing Corporation, 1970), p. 58.

5. Government of Ontario, *Design for Development: A Status Report on the Toronto-Centred Region* (Toronto: Queen's Printer, 1971), p.1.

6. L.O. Gertler, *The Process of New City Planning and Building* (Waterloo: The School of Urban and Regional Planning, 1971), pp. 32-36.

7. Thomas Adams, *Rural Planning and Development* (Ottawa: Commission of Conservation, 1917), p. 140 and pp. 102-124, 140-141.

8. Charles Abrams, *Man's Struggle for Shelter in an Urbanizing World* (Cambridge, Mass.: MIT Press, 1966), pp. 274, 292.

9. Frank Schaffer, *The New Town Story* (London: MacGibbon and Kee, 1970), pp. 62-72.

10. Ibid, pp. 72-77.

11. Wyndham Thomas, *Land Planning and Development Values in Postwar Britain* (Chicago: American Society of Planning Officials, 1967).

12. Schaffer, *The New Town Story*, pp. 76, 77.

13. Ibid., pp. 75-77; and Lloyd Rodwin, "Economic Problems in Developing New Towns and Expanded Towns," in *Planning of Metropolitan Areas and New Towns* (New York: United Nations, 1967).

14. Ian C. Bender, *Land Issues in the Process of New Town Building* (MA thesis, University of Waterloo, 1970), pp. 164-175.

15. "Statement to the Task Force on Housing and Urban Development" (Toronto: The Town Planning Institute of Canada, 1968).

16. Ibid.

Notes — Chapter 4

1. P. Keilhoffer and J.W. Parlour, "New Towns: The Canadian Experience," Ministry of State for Urban Affairs, discussion paper prepared for OECD, 1972, pp. 12-15. Dr. Albert Rose asserts that "the people who live in Don Mills believe they are part of a recognizable community." Albert Rose, *Social and Physical Aspects of User Requirements: A Report on Housing* (Ottawa: Science Council of Canada, 1970), pp. 67, 68.

2. Keilhoffer and Parlour, "New Towns," pp. 16 and 17.

3. Ibid, pp. 16 and 23-24.

4. Ibid, pp. 19-20.

5. *Design for Development: The Toronto-Centred Region* (Government of Ontario, Queen's Printer, 1970), pp. 10-11.

6. Lithwick, *Urban Canada,* p. 230.

7. Lewis Mumford, *The City in History* (New York: Harcourt, Brace & World), 1961, pp. 540, 541.

8. Lawrence Haworth, *The Good City* (Bloomington and London: Indiana University Press, 1966).

9. John B. Calhoun, "Psycho-Ecological Aspects of Population," *Unit for Research on Behavioural Systems, National Institute of Mental Health,* ORBS DOC No. 62, rev., 1966.

10. Ibid, p. 124.

Notes — Chapter 5

1. These words are from the proclamation in Parliament setting up the Ministry of State for Urban Affairs.

2. Government of Alberta, *The Role of Regional Planning,* Task Force on Urbanization and the Future (Edmonton, 1971), pp. 10. 11.

3. *Service Centre Study, Oldman River Region* (Lethbridge: Oldman River Regional Planning Commission, 1970), pp. 18-21, 30, 31.

4. Ibid., pp. 24, 25.

5. *Alberta Planning Act,* Section 69, a, b, c, d. Note eleven of these twenty-eight are not active members, although they contribute to the budget of the commission through the Alberta Planning Fund, and subdivisions in their areas are administered by the commission; *Regional Planning,* pp. 6, 11.

6. *Service Centre Study,* p. 31.

7. Ibid., p. 30.

8. Herb Johnson, "To Grow Or Not To Grow, That is the Question," *Lethbridge Herald,* April 1971.

Notes — Chapter 6

1. William H. McNeill, *The Rise of the West* (Chicago and London: The University of Chicago Press, 1963), pp. 729, 730.

2. J.R. Platt, "Life Where Science Flows", in William R. Ewald Jr., ed., *Environment and Change,* 1968, pp. 77-80.

3. Ibid., p. 79.

4. Margaret Fairley, *Spirit of Canadian Democracy* (Toronto: Progress Publishing Co.) pp. 33, 34.

5. McNeill, *Rise of the West,* p. 760.

6. David Lilienthal, *The Journals of David Lilienthal,* Vol. I (New York: Harper and Row, 1964), pp. 606, 660.

7. Economic Council of Canada, Second Annual Review, *Towards Sustained and Balanced Economic Growth* (Ottawa: Queen's Printer, 1965), pp. 8, 97-143.

8. C. Ray Smith and David R. Witty, "Conservation, Resources and Environment," *Plan Canada,* Vol. II, Nos. 1 and 3 (December 1970, May 1972); and *Environment Canada, Its Organization and Objectives* (Ottawa: Information Canada, 1971).

9. Michael Hugo-Brunt, *The History of City Planning* (Montreal: Harvest House, 1972), pp. 187 and 219; and G.L. Spragge, "Canadian Planners' Goals: Deep Roots and Fuzzy Thinking," unpublished paper, 1974.

10. Frank Backus Williams, "Public Control of Private Real Estate," in John Nolen, ed., *City Planning,* (New York and London: D. Appleton and Company, 1916), pp. 53, 78, 79, 81; and Spragge, "Canadian Planners' Goals."

11. G. Frank Beer, "A Plea for City-Planning Organization," Report of The Fifth Annual Meeting (Ottawa: Commission of Conservation, Canada, 1914), p. 113.

12. See, for example, the work of F. Fraser Darling and the methodological distinctions that he makes: "The ecologist must distrust the questionnaire so beloved of the sociologists, because it fails to take sufficient notice of the ethics of a people. . . . Much the best way is observation and soaking in the culture. Ability to observe closely and interpret accurately, by way of a large grasp of the organism of a society in its habitat, is the essence of human ecology. It is an integrative science as much as an analytical one, with observation as its basis." "The Ecological Approach to the Social Sciences," *American Scientist,* Vol. 39, No. 2 (April 1951), p. 254.

13. Howard W. Odum, *Folk, Region and Society* (Chapel Hill: The University of North Carolina Press, 1964.)

14. Erich Fromm, *The Revolution of Hope* (Toronto: Bantam Books, 1968), p. 100.

15. Benton Mackaye, *From Geography to Geotechnics* (Urbana: University of Illinois, 1968), p. 120. For a general statement of Mackaye's philosophical position, see his *The New Exploration* (New York: Harcourt, Brace and Co., 1928).

16. Patrick Geddes, *Cities in Evolution* (London: Williams and Norgate Ltd., 1949).

17. Lewis Mumford, *The Culture of Cities* (New York: Harcourt, Brace and Co., 1938), pp. 480, 481.

18. Morton and Lucia White, *The Intellectual Versus the City* (Toronto: Mentor Books, 1964), p. 235.

19. Pierre Dansereau, *Contradictions and Biculture* (Montreal: Les Editions du Jour, 1964), pp. 132 and 134.

Index

A

Abrams, Charles: 59
Acadians: 16
Adams, Thomas: 20, 114
Addams, Jane: 28
Alberta: 18, 94, 96-100; Cardston, 96; New Towns Act, 71; Pincher Creek, 96; Planning Act, 98; Planning Fund, 94; St. Albert, 71; Taber, 96; Vulcan, 96; see also Oldman River Region
Alienation, immigrant: 28-29
Alonso, William: 78
Amherst, Nova Scotia: 26
Annapolis Valley: 16
Atlantic Provinces: 23; see also Maritime Provinces
Automobile: 39, 44-49

B

Bank of Montreal: 12
Baroque style: 11
Beer, Frank: 25, 107
Bell, Daniel: 107
Bender, Ian C: 65
Biggar, Saskatchewan: 18
Blumenfeld, Hans: 47, 91, 112
Borough: 81
Brandon: 26
Britain: Land Commission Act, 64; Town and Country Planning Act, 63
British Columbia: 23, 29, 96; Land Commission, 51; Lower Fraser region, 51
Burnham, Daniel: 106

C

Calgary: 96
Calhoun, John B: 90
Callaghan, Morley: 90
Cauchon, Naulon: 107
Centres: rural, 17-18; sub-regional, 78, 82, 85
Champlain, Samuel de: 11
Château Frontenac: 11
Cities: see Cities, Canadian, cities by name, and New City
Cities, Canadian: French type, 9; Ontario, 9; Maritime, 9; Western, 9
City: 76, 81; garden, 23; humanist view of, 114; industrial, 26; inner, 25-26, 30-31; regional, 7, 50, 53; see also New City

City Beautiful Movement: 106
Columbia, Maryland: 78
Commission of Conservation: 25, 58, 106, 107, 114
Communities, ethnic: 28
Community: 8, 115

D

Dansereau, Pierre: 112, 118
Darwin, Charles: 103
Depression, Great: 18
Des Barres, Colonel J.W.F.: 16
Design for Development: 53
Design, urban: 111
Development: Canadian urban, 17; gridiron pattern of, 23-25; hierarchy in urban, 17; metropolitan, 70; prairie land, 20; specialization in urban, 17
Don Mills, Ontario: 70
Downtown core: 26
Durham, Lord (on immigration): 12

E

Eastern Townships: 14
Ecology: 110
Economic Council of Canada: 104
Economics: 110
Ecosystem, human community in terms of: 8
Edmonton: 20, 29, 96; Mill Woods, 71; Regional Planning Commission, 71
Education, planning: 108, 110, 111
Emerson, Ralph W: 112, 115
Energy: 46, 49
Environment: 8, 26, 47, 49, 102, 103; motorized, 44
Environment Canada: 106
Erie Canal: 12
Ethnic communities: 28

F

Federal government: 91; and new city, 83
Fernie: 26
Flin Flon: 20
Friedman, John: 112
Fromm, Erich: 47, 112
Frontier development: 23

G

Galbraith, John Kennth: 47, 107
Galt: 26
Garden City Movement: 23
Geddes, Patrick: 112, 114
Geography: 110

121

German settlement in Nova Scotia: 16
Government: federal, 91; and new city, 83; land assembly, 67; Ministry of State for Urban Affairs, 93; provincial, 86; regional, 26, 70, 83; tri-level consultation, 6, 8, 93
Guelph: 26
Grande Prairie/Peace River: 96
Great Lakes: transportaion corridor, 52; see also St. Lawrence-Great Lakes Canal system
Greber Plan: 11
Greenbelt, Ottawa: 70
Gridiron pattern of development: 23-25
Group of Seven: 51
Grove, Frederick Philip: 51
Growth: ethic, 18; urban, 70

H

Halifax: 14, 67
Hamilton: 25, 57, 67
Haworth, Lawrence: 87, 112
Hellyer, Paul: 66, 78
Helsinki: 7
Hierarchy in urban development: 17
Holt, Sir Herbert: 106
Homestead policy: 103
Housing: 38
Hull House, Chicago: 28
Human settlement: 94
Humanism: 8; view of city, 114

I

Immigrants: 28-29, 31
Immigration: 9, 12-14, 23, 28
Indians: 31
Individualism: 102
Industrialization: 9
Inner city: 25-26
Innis, Harold: 12, 51

K

Kamloops: 26
Kanata, Ontario: 70
Kapuskasing: 112
King, William Lyon Mackenzie: 28
Kingston: 26
Kitimat, B.C.: 20

L

Land: assembly, 67-68; banks, 51, 69; British Land Commission Act, 64; cost, 8, 29, 53-59; development on prairie, 20; policy, British, 61-64; policy,

Canadian, 64-66; promotion, 18-20; public ownership of, 59-61, 68; public purchase of, 59; public reserves, 59; speculation, 18-20, 58; speculation tax, 51; strategy, 68; use; 29, values, 59; see also Real estate
Laurence, Margaret: 51
Laurier, Prime Minister: 6
Lethbridge: 96, 99; University of, 99
Lilienthal, David: 104
Lithwick, Harvey, 38, 57, 71, 92
London: 26
Lower, Arthur: 28
Lowry, Malcolm: 51
Loyalist settlement in Sydney: 16
Lunenburg: 16

M

Macdonald, John A: 51
Macdonald-Cartier Freeway: 44
Marchand, Jean: 52
Mackaye, Benton: 112
Mackenzie, William Lyon: 103
Manitoba: 6, 18, 20, 22
Marcuse, Herbert: 47
Maritime Provinces: 14-17; New England settlers in, 14; urban settlement in, 16
Mass transit: see Transportation: mass transit
McGill University: 12
McNeill, W.H.: 101
Medicine Hat: 96
Métis: 31
Metropolis: 34-36
Metropolitan phase: 34-36, 70
Ministry of State for Urban Affairs: 93
Montreal: 12, 14, 25, 41, 43, 51, 67; St. Henri, 30
Moose Jaw: 18
Mumford, Lewis: 36, 85, 112, 114
Municipal Board, Ontario: 38

N

Nader, Ralph: 58
National Council of Women: 28
National Housing Act: 66, 67
National Policy: 51
New Cities Act: 82
New City: 76-81; British, 64, 76; design, 81; integrated, 81, 90; mechanism, 82; Office of (Ontario), 83; planning process, 90-91; problems 81; provincial administration, 82; regional administration, 83; Scandinavian, 76; in United States, 76-78

123

Photograph Credits

The Publisher is grateful for the assistance of those who have provided the photographs used in this book. Every care has been taken to acknowledge below the correct sources. The Publisher would welcome information that will permit the correction of any errors or omissions.

Metropolitan Public Library: 6, 11
Notman Photographic Archives, McCord Museum, McGill University, Montreal: 9 (top)
The Northway Survey Corporation Limited, Toronto: 15
Department of Travel Industry, Victoria, B.C.: 17
Ministry of Industry and Tourism, Ontario: 23, 51, 112-113
Old Markets, New World, by Joe Rosenthal with text by Adele Wiseman.
  Copyright © 1964 by Joe Rosenthal and Adele Wiseman. Reproduced with the
  permission of the Macmillan Company of Canada Limited: 28-29
Transportation Technology Inc: 44 (top)
David Lilienthal: 101
Stratford Beacon-Herald: 109
Trois Rivières: 82
Henri Rossier: 84, 85
Helmer and Tattle, Ottawa: 112-113
Webb, Zerafa, Menkes, Housden, Architects and Engineers: 112-113

WITHDRAWN

Coleridge, Shelley,
and Transcendental Inquiry

Coleridge, Shelley, and Transcendental Inquiry

Rhetoric, Argument, Metapsychology

John A. Hodgson

University of Nebraska Press
Lincoln and London

Acknowledgments for the use
of previously published
material appear on page xvii.

Library of Congress Cataloging-in-
Publication Data
Hodgson, John A., 1945–
   Coleridge, Shelley, and transcendental inquiry: rhetoric, argument,
metapsychology / John A.
Hodgson.
      p.   cm.
   Bibliography: p.
   Includes index.
   ISBN 0-8032-2349-8 (alk. paper)
   1. Coleridge, Samuel Taylor,
1772–1834—Philosophy.
2. Shelley, Percy Bysshe, 1792–
1822—Philosophy.   3. Transcen-
dentalism in literature.   4. Discourse analysis, Literary.   5. Romanticism—England.   6. Rhetoric—Philosophy.   I. Title.
PR4487.P5H64 1989   88-27732
821'.8'09—dc19   CIP

For my family—
Sooze, Emily, Michael

Cuvier said that Metaphysics is nothing but Metaphor. . . . [I]f Cuvier was only using a metaphor himself,
and meant by metaphor broad comparison on the ground
of characters of a formal and highly abstract kind,—
then, indeed, metaphysics professes to be metaphor—
that is just its merit. . . .

—C. S. Peirce

I will not say that metaphor is the great
thing. How should I? Metaphor is a way
to handle, signify, designate;
we do not handle the great things, though we try.

All right. Still metaphor. What is it we signify?
We say lies as if they were not lies, as if
we believe. And, indeed, we do believe. No;
we know the metaphor is wrong. And yet—

—William Bronk,
"The Signification"

Contents

Abbreviations

TT   *Table Talk*. In *The Table Talk and Omniana*, ed. T.
            Ashe (London: Bell, 1909). Cited by date.

Shelley's Works Frequently Cited

DP   *A Defence of Poetry*. In Percy Bysshe Shelley, *A De-
            fence of Poetry;* Thomas Love Peacock, *The Four Ages
            of Poetry*, ed. John E. Jordan (Indianapolis: Bobbs-
            Merrill, 1965).
PU   *Prometheus Unbound*.
SL   *The Letters of Percy Bysshe Shelley*, ed. Frederick L.
            Jones, 2 vols. (Oxford: Oxford University Press,
            1964).
SP   *Shelley's Prose*, ed. David Lee Clark (Albuquerque:
            University of New Mexico Press, 1954).
SSP   *Shelley's Poetry and Prose*, ed. Donald H. Reiman and
            Sharon B. Powers (New York: Norton, 1974).
SPW   *Poetical Works*, ed. Thomas Hutchinson (London: Ox-
            ford University Press, 1905; repr. 1967). Quotations of
            Shelley's poetry are from *SPP* whenever possible, oth-
            erwise from *SPW*.

Other Works Frequently Cited

Enquiry   Edmund Burke, *A Philosophical Enquiry into the Ori-
            gin of Our Ideas of the Sublime and Beautiful*, ed. J. T.
            Boulton (Notre Dame and London: University of No-
            tre Dame Press, 1968).
Essay   John Locke, *An Essay Concerning Human Under-
            standing*, ed. Alexander Campbell Fraser, 2 vols. (Ox-
            ford: The Clarendon Press, 1894). Cited by section.
RRF   Edmund Burke, *Reflections on the Revolution in
            France*, ed. Thomas H. D. Mahoney (Indianapolis and
            New York: Bobbs-Merrill, 1955).
SE   The Standard Edition of *The Complete Psychological
            Works of Sigmund Freud*, ed. James Strachey et al., 24
            vols. (London: Hogarth Press, 1953–66).

The Interrelationship
of Rhetoric and Argument

One of the finest Paul Bunyan stories tells of the Winter of the Blue Snow, when Paul's loggers became so homesick for familiar, white snow near Christmastide that Paul journeyed far to the west to find and bring back a load of white snow for the holidays. From this load each logger saved one snowball as a memento; and years afterward, if any newcomer should doubt his story of that strange winter or of his service with Paul Bunyan, the logger would quickly silence the doubter by producing his white snowball.

The logger's white snowball is a figure of a kind; but of what kind? In one sense, it is a synecdoche, a part representing the whole—some of the very snow Paul Bunyan brought back that memorable winter. (It is a metonymy, too, almost like a relic: Paul Bunyan himself retrieved this very snow.) In another sense, though, it is a metaphor, the white snowball that stands as a substitute for the blue snow. Taxonomists of tropes can doubtless diagnose additional possibilities, but these few will serve to suggest the figurative potential of the logger's sign.

But the logger's snowball is also, very emphatically, part of an argument, produced with a purpose of persuading or proving. The rhetoric is also an argument; the argument, a rhetoric. And so, though perhaps we rarely give the matter a second thought, is it always. "Tropes," Todorov observes, "are submerged propositions. The symbol is condensed discourse"; "both discourse and symbol participate in the same logical structure."[1]

And where—for certainly we must not forget to ask this—is that blue snow? Was there ever a Winter of Blue Snow? Notwithstanding the smugness of the logger's conclusive gesture, we can have no proof that there ever was. And the impossibility of certainty reveals the rhetorical quality of his argument with wonderful starkness. That which is by definition unpresentable can necessarily be presented only by figuration. This is so whether the unpresentable be something more or less explicitly fictitious, like Paul Bunyan's blue snow, or something posited as transcendent, like God or ultimate power or the human mind or psyche.

Thus the issues this book addresses, questions about the essential interrelation of figure and discourse, are absolutely central to the field of interpretation, whether artistic, metaphysical, or psychological. At the same time, they are provoked more extremely and raised more insistently by Romantic writers than by those of any earlier period. As Friedrich Schlegel announces at the outset of his famous manifesto in the *Atheneum*, the vocation of Romantic poetry is "to establish contact between poetry and the philosophy of rhetoric."[2] The Romantics made important contributions to the rhetorical analysis of discourse. Yet their own transcendental inquiries often strive to disguise or deny their ultimate figurativeness—as so often happens when such inquiries are ostensibly not (or not merely) literary but psychological or theological or metaphysical. Such efforts tend to expose the particular rhetorical characteristics of an inquiry all the more dramatically. Hence the great Romantic writers are not merely significant practitioners of, but inviting objects for, the present kind of theoretical investigation.

Coleridge and Shelley (and the Romantics generally) agree in valuing what semiotics calls "motivated signs": their quarrel is with the arbitrary figure, and their ambition, to reduce or remove this arbitrariness in poetry. Yet such a summation does not begin to characterize Romantic rhetoric adequately. Notions of motivated signs arise early in the history of semiotics and figure largely in the theorizings of the eighteenth century.[3] As Todorov has noted, though, motivation before the Romantic period usually means no more than resemblance. And metaphor of superficial resemblance, of course, is precisely what Coleridge and his German precursors lead the Romantics in rejecting. For resemblance, Coleridge insists, can be arbitrary, accidental:

> The Fancy brings together images which have no connection natural or moral, but are yoked together by the poet by means of some accidental coincidence; as in the well-known passage in *Hudibras:*—
>
> > "The sun had long since in the lap
> > Of Thetis taken out his nap,
> > And like a lobster boyl'd, the morn
> > From black to red began to turn."
>
> (*TT,* 6/23/1834)

What Romantic rhetoric values is not simply motivation, but

determination—a genuine coherence of image and idea, a relation that is not accidental or imposed but innate, essential, and inevitable. Figures should not merely resemble, but participate in, the truths or ideas they express. In A. W. Schlegel's words (from his famous discrimination of organic from mechanical form), "Organic form . . . acquires its determination contemporaneously with the perfect development of the germ. . . . In the fine arts, as well as in the domain of nature—the supreme artist, all genuine forms are organical, that is, determined by the quality of the work."[4] Hence Coleridge's insistence on the privileged status of the synecdochic symbol, and hence Shelley's valorizing of such cause-effect metonymies as the Aeolian harp and such nonarbitrary (if not truly determined) contiguity metonymies as the "temporary dress" of costume or veil.[5] The great challenge for Romantic rhetoric is how to achieve or approach the ideal of determined figuration in the field of transcendental inquiry.

This books develops a theory of how rhetoric and argument interrelate in Romantic approaches to the transcendent. Its thesis is that Romantic transcendental inquiry evinces two fundamental, distinctive argumentative or psychological biases, each corresponding to and requiring a distinctive strategy of rhetoric. I examine Shelley and the later Coleridge (the London Coleridge, Coleridge in the last twenty or twenty-five years of his life) as paradigms of these two tendencies; and from Edmund Burke and especially the later Freud I derive a vocabulary and a psychological schema for discriminating these two fundamental modes of transcendental argument.

As their titles indicate, my two pairs of chapters bear something of a chiastic relationship to each other. Chapters one and two begin with an analysis of a theory of rhetoric and proceed thence to an investigation of the argument accompanying and (as I ultimately suggest) corresponding to that rhetoric. They begin, then, almost inevitably, with Coleridge, who more than any other Romantic demonstrates the relevance of rhetorical analysis to philosophical no less than literary inquiry. Prompted by Coleridge's famous valuation of symbol over allegory, I trace his anxious pursuit of determined figuration through the analysis of particular rhetorics into the very structure of his philosophical and theological argument. From Coleridge I also reach out illustratively to Burke and Freud, two bracketing psychological theorists, both to clarify certain implications of Coleridge's own practice and to suggest how very typical, after all, is his rhetorical strategy.

Chapters three and four, conversely, move from an initial analysis of a transcendental argument to an investigation of its supporting rhetoric, again with an ultimate suggestion that these two are mutually implicating. My starting place this time is Shelley—again, almost inevitably, for his *Defence of Poetry* is unexampled in English Romanticism as a sustained celebration of poetry's transcendental qualities. Here, though, the path we must follow becomes not merely converse, but perverse; for Shelley's argument not only reverses the emphases of Coleridge's, but also insinuates the corruptness and corrosiveness of transcendental inquiry itself. How Shelley's argument relates to Coleridge's, and why it should require a different rhetorical stance, prove to be psychological no less than rhetorical issues. The two writers' alternatives of rhetoric and of argument are ultimately alternatives of fundamental, opposed psychological attitudes—alternatives to which Burke and Freud also, and more directly, call attention, even as Coleridge and Shelley call attention to the rhetorical and argumentative strategies of these psychologists.

My Afterword is both a closure and an opening. First, I complete the psychological subplot of this study, by returning, with interest, my Freudian borrowings to their source. Here I indicate briefly how the insights gained from our study of Coleridge and Shelley can lead to a revisionist, rhetorical analysis of Freud's own argument, which we have found to be so closely related to theirs. Reaching beyond Freud and beyond Romanticism, finally, I close by ranging both forward into the present critical forum and outward into a general theory of literature. These critical issues we have been exploring in Romantic literature, I argue, are very much alive today: these very interrelationships of rhetoric and argument characterize, even as they occupy, the contemporary deconstructionist debate. Moreover, these two alternatives of Romantic rhetoric, these tensional, alternative attitudes within a Romantic text, necessarily characterize all texts; the implications of Romantic rhetoric are not merely broad, but universal.

"Rhetoric" and "argument" are both, in practice, vexed and ambiguous terms, and perhaps it will be thought that I should define and settle my usages of them at once. But their ambiguities are very much to the point here, and not to be dismissed; their most basic ambiguities are, in fact, parallel, analogous, correspondent—just as are "rhetoric" and "argument" themselves. "Rhetoric" we may regard alternatively as a theory of tropes (Nietzsche's emphasis, and a familiar usage today) or a theory of persuasion (the classical emphasis). But "argument" bears within itself much the same alternative constructions, the one again rigorous and logical, the other again desirous—argument as logical reasoning or as dispute.[6] Tropes, too, can be figures of logic no less than of rhetoric: the examples of argument from analogy and of the syllogistic status of part-for-whole synecdoche (for what is true of the whole is true of its parts) and effect-for-cause metonymy make this immediately clear. Rhetoric and argument, figure and discourse, are inextricably combined in both quests for truth and manifestations of desire. What this book particularly argues is that they combine in specific patterns of relationship, patterns which bespeak a deeper structure of text and thought.

I have applied "transcendental" indifferently to Freud's quest no less than to Coleridge's and Shelley's, to arguments and tropes of mind no less than of God, to queryings of inner no less than of outer noumena. Freud himself shows this same indifference when he speaks of the "great psychological truth" of "Kant's famous pronouncement in which he names, in a single breath, the starry heavens and the moral law within us" (*SE* 22:163–64) or when he uses the Vergilian line *"Flectere si nequeo superos, Acheronta movebo"* ("If I cannot bend the Higher Powers, I will move the Infernal Regions") as the motto for *The Interpretation of Dreams*. But the practice is also a genuinely and broadly Romantic one: Schelling's transcendental philosophy, for example, is his science of mind. In Goethe's pithy phrasing, "The god to whom a man proves devout, that is his own soul turned inside out."[7] And Homer's presentation in *Iliad* I of Achilles' self-restraint before Agamemnon as actually an intercession by Athena can serve to remind us how ancient is this ambivalence.

"Metapsychology," finally, shares with "transcendental" its double direction of reference, towards both the inner and the outer noumena. By "metapsychology" Freud means psychoanalytical theory at its most fundamental level—psychology "viewed in its most theoretical dimension," as Laplanche and Pontalis summarize.[8] Freud himself initially uses the term to suggest the inner world of the mind, a "psychology that leads behind consciousness" (*SE* 1:274), and continues to apply it to work dealing with the underlying principles and theoretical assumptions of psychoanalysis (*SE* 14:222 n.1). This same implication informs the "beyond," *jenseits*, of *Beyond the*

Pleasure Principle. But Freud also strongly implies the analogousness of metapsychology to metaphysics, as when he speaks of "transform[ing] *metaphysics* into *metapsychology*" (*SE* 6:259). Proceeding from the perception that cultures and "the events of human history" are group projections of psyches, "the very same processes [of the individual psyche's dynamic conflicts] repeated upon a wider stage" (*SE* 20: 71–72), metapsychology does not simply eliminate or displace metaphysics, but subsumes it. I speak of the metapsychology of transcendental inquiry, then, in just this double sense: my concern is both a deep structural principle informing rhetoric's relation to argument and a broad manifestation of this principle in the universe of texts.

It gives me great pleasure to acknowledge the help and support of the many friends and colleagues who have sustained me during the writing of this book. I am especially obliged to Paul Fry, Bill Keach, and Hillis Miller for their steadfast encouragement and support. I thank also Margie Ferguson and Stephen Barney, who read and commented on early chapters of the book, and Nelson Hilton, who read a late draft of the whole and greatly enriched it with his perceptive and thoughtful comments.

I am deeply and especially grateful to the National Humanities Center for fellowship support in a wonderfully congenial, fostering, and stimulating environment during the year when this book took shape and when much of it was written. To borrow an expression from Emma Woodhouse, "It was a delightful visit;—perfect, in being much too short." Without that year I could never have finished the book; without that community of fellows, it would not have become this book. I am particularly indebted to two of my fellowship colleagues, Anthony Harrison and Steven Marcus, for their careful readings of and helpful responses to several early chapters.

I am grateful to John Beer, whose edition of Coleridge's *Aids to Reflection* will soon appear as volume 9 of *The Collected Coleridge,* and Bart Winer, associate editor of *The Collected Coleridge,* for responding kindly and fully to my queries about that edition. It is on the basis of their information that I have decided to provide 1825 (first edition) as well as 1831 (second, revised edition) page numbers for all my citations of *Aids to Reflection.* Beer's definitive edition will be based on 1831 (the edition I cite in this book) but will include a running marginal check to the 1825 pagination. Thus my readers may conveniently consult Beer's edition, when it appears, by following the 1825 page citations.

Portions of chapters 1 and 4 have previously been published, respectively, in *Allegory, Myth, and Symbol,* ed. Morton W. Bloomfield, Harvard English Studies 9 (Cambridge, Mass.: Harvard University Press, 1981), pp. 273–92, copyright © 1981 by the President and Fellows of Harvard College, and in "The World's Mysterious Doom: Shelley's *The Triumph of Life*," ELH 42 (1975): 603–4. The second epigraph on page vi is excerpted from *Life Supports,* copyright © 1982 by William Bronk. It is published by North Point Press and reprinted by permission.

My thanks also to the University of Georgia for the summer fellowships that helped support my research and writing, and to the excellent staff of the University of Georgia library, whose competence and helpfulness have eased my work throughout.

Chapter 1

Rhetoric

Coleridge's Rhetoric of
Allegory and Symbol

I

More than any of his German precursors, Samuel Taylor Coleridge takes a rhetorical approach to defining the concepts of allegory and symbol. His critical strategy in comparing the two modes, to affirm the superiority of symbol to allegory, is one he shares with Goethe and many others.[1] His tactics, however, grounded in fundamental rhetorical distinctions, are very much his own. Extrapolating from the classical and Renaissance notion of allegory as extended metaphor, he further proposes a parallel association of symbol with synecdoche:

> [T]he Symbolical . . . cannot perhaps be better defined, in distinction
> from the Allegorical, than that it is always itself a *part* of that of the
> whole of which it is representative—Here comes a *Sail*—that is, a
> Ship, is a symbolical Expression—Behold our Lion, when we speak of
> some gallant Soldier, is allegorical. . . . (*LL* 2:417–18)

The rhetorical emphasis of his approach here, moreover, remains generally constant throughout the latter half of his life. Indeed, during his last two decades, as Coleridge increasingly concentrates his attention on the Bible—a book, he finds, "so strangely written, that in a series of the most concerning points, including . . . all the *peculiar* Tenets of the Religion, the plain and obvious meaning of the words . . . is no sufficient guide to their actual sense or to the Writer's own Meaning" (*AR*, pp. 81–82/74)—a theory of rhetoric, of the turning of literal meanings, becomes essential to his critical endeavor.

Whatever interest in the rhetoric of allegory and symbol Coleridge has provoked by the sheer force of his own abiding interest, however, he has also stymied by the apparent crudeness of his definitions and desultoriness of his applied criticisms. The frustration is unfortunate, for these appearances are misleading. Coleridge's initial presentation of his thesis may be simplistic, and his subsequent re-definitions of terms confusing; but his essential argument, over time, does become increasingly sophisticated and comprehensive. He is indeed guilty of certain critical lapses; but at the same time he is responsible for some of the finest rhetorical analyses of his age. Both his lapses and, far more regrettably, his accomplishments remain generally unappreciated.[2] In particular, his later analyses of metaphor and allegory—they are not those for which he is generally known—constitute a remarkably insightful investigation of the mode that the Romantics, though many of them often maligned it, did so much to redeem for Western literature.

II

As numerous critics have noted, Coleridge's advocacy of a symbolic, synecdochic mode of writing, though first declared only in 1816 in *The Statesman's Manual*, is in fact strongly implicit in his writings as much as twenty years before. In the "one life" philosophy that dominated his thinking throughout the late 1790s, synecdoche is characteristic of all participation in godhead:

> 'Tis the sublime of man,
> Our noontide Majesty, to know ourselves
> Parts and proportions of one wondrous whole!
> . . . . .
>   . . . But 'tis God
> Diffused through all, that doth make all one whole. . . .
>   ["Religious Musings," 126–31]

In a pantheistic world view, of course, man's—and any thing's—place in the cosmos is innately, definitionally synecdochic; hence Blake's urge "To see a World in a Grain of Sand," and hence Emerson's certainty that "every object has its roots in central nature, and may of course be so exhibited to us as to represent the world."[3] Coleridge's stance is notable, however, for its easy movement from ontological to rhetorical applications of this principle. In his well-known September 1802 letter to William Sotheby, for example, the comments prompted by Coleridge's dissatisfaction with William Lisle Bowles's latest volume of poetry refer to both nature and poems:

[N]ever to see or describe any interesting appearance in nature, without connecting it by dim analogies with the moral world, proves faintness of Impression. Nature has her proper interest; & he will know what it is, who believes & feels, that every Thing has a Life of it's own, & that we are all *one Life*. A Poet's *Heart & Intellect* should be *combined, intimately* combined & *unified*, with the great appearances in Nature—& not merely held in solution & loose mixture with them, in the shape of formal Similies. (*CL* 2:864)

So too Coleridge more than once in his letters shifts easily from a similar statement of this philosophic precept to an apt poetic *exemplum* (*CL* 1:334, 349–50, 397–98).

"Symbol" itself bears originally a most explicit relation to synecdoche; and Coleridge, with his great interest in etymology, his excellent Greek, and his precocious immersion in the Neoplatonic tradition (witness Lamb's famous recollection of Coleridge as a "young Mirandula" of a schoolboy at Christ's Hospital, holding casual visitors "intranced with admiration . . . to hear thee unfold, in thy deep and sweet intonations, the mysteries of Iamblichus, or Plotinus"[4]) would have known and appreciated this. A *symbolon* was a particular token of recognition—a half of a whole object, such as a die, coin, or ring, which could later be joined to the other half as proof of identity or purpose.[5] The word thus involves three attributes relevant to Coleridge's later applications: the "suggestive incompleteness" of "a single entity which yet hints at some preexisting whole . . . of which it is a part," "the necessity of some prior knowledge regarding the significance of the whole," and the revelation of meaning by way of correspondence (the *symbolon* fits into or corresponds to its other half).[6] Eventually *symbolon* came to refer more broadly to anything with a hidden but discoverable meaning; and Proclus especially uses it customarily to denote the visible object that hints at the nature of the unseen reality.[7]

On very rare occasions, Coleridge does seem to evoke this primal sense of *symbolon* in his use of "symbol." In an 1808 notebook entry, for example, he writes that the "generous mind . . . feels its Halfness—it cannot *think* without a symbol—neither can it *live* without something that is to be at once its Symbol, & its *Other half*" (*CN* 3:3325). More Neoplatonically, he once suggests in *The Statesman's Manual* that "it is the *poetry* of all human nature, to read [Nature] in a figurative sense, and to find therein correspondencies and symbols of the spiritual world."[8] Despite these isolated atavisms, however, and despite the pointedly synecdochic significance of *symbolon*, Coleridge's mature commentary on symbol and its distinctiveness from allegory owes little or nothing, at least directly, to ancient Greek or to Neoplatonic usage.[9] Conversely, when he uses the word earlier—as in his 1795 lectures, when he states that "To the philanthropic Physiognomist a Face is beautiful because its Features are the symbols and visible signs of the inward Benevolence or Wisdom—to the pious man all Nature is thus beautiful because its every Feature is the Symbol and all its Parts the written Language of infinite Goodness and all powerful Intelligence"—he uses it Neoplatonically, in the philosophic or theological sense of *allegoria,* with no particular anticipation of his later discrimination of the concepts.[10] The most straightforward explanation for this is simply that the same Neoplatonic tradition responsible for giving the term "symbol" such currency was also responsible for blurring together the concepts of symbol and allegory so thoroughly that Goethe's, Schelling's, and A. W. Schlegel's separations of the terms would strike their contemporaries with all the force of novel observation.

Coleridge's recognition of the appropriateness of synecdoche, the basic trope of immanence, to a philosophy of pantheistic monism marks the beginning of a theory of rhetoric. This beginning is rudimentary, to be sure, and undiscriminating in the same ways as is pantheism itself (for if all things are part of one whole, then all synecdoches would seem indifferently valid figures of the universal Presence). Coleridge would soon leave both the philosophy and the rhetorical theory fallow. The naturalness of the relationship, however, the perfect suitedness of the rhetorical and philosophic principles to one another, suggests a critical ideal that continues to inform his thought.

III

When Coleridge again takes up the questions of allegory and symbol in *The Statesman's Manual* in 1816, he is writing in the context of a quite different set of philosophic concerns. Most important, where before he had looked primarily for the evidences of divine immanence, now he pursues "the transcendental philosophy" and its accommodation to Christianity. "The statesman's manual," we must not forget, is the Bible; Coleridge subtitles his pamphlet "The Bible the Best Guide to Political Skill and Foresight: A Lay Sermon. . . ."

Coleridge's attitude here, then, even in dealing with literary questions, is not merely critical but polemical; correspondingly, however, he is concerned to develop critical techniques adequate not merely to lesser works of literature, but also to the supremely privileged and truthful—and challenging—Book. "Religion," he declares, in some sense "is the Poetry of all mankind,"[11] and the critical definitions of *The Statesman's Manual* serve purposes no less literary for being at the same time insistently theological. Ideally, he believes, one should "read the Bible as the best of all books, but still as a book; and make use of all the means and appliances which learning and skill, under the blessing of God, can afford towards rightly apprehending the general sense of it."[12]

The notions of symbol and allegory Coleridge now propounds (in many respects simply by paraphrasing or expanding upon the 1802 letter to Sotheby) represent an attempt to adapt his earlier rhetorical analysis to the greater demands of his new philosophy. "True natural philosophy is comprized in the study of the science and language of *symbols*," he asserts, adding that "by a symbol I mean, not a metaphor or allegory or any other figure of speech or form of fancy, but an actual and essential part of that, the whole of which it represents" (*SM*, p. 79). Soon he explains more fully:

It is among the miseries of the present age that it recognizes no medium between *Literal* and *Metaphorical*. Faith is either to be buried in the dead letter, or its name and honors usurped by a counterfeit product of the mechanical understanding, which in the blindness of self-complacency confounds SYMBOLS with ALLEGORIES. Now an Allegory is but a translation of abstract notions into a picture-language which is itself nothing but an abstraction from objects of the senses; the principal being more worthless even than its phantom proxy, both alike unsubstantial, and the former shapeless to boot. On the other hand a Symbol (ὁ ἔστιν ἀεὶ ταυτηγόρικον) [which is always tautegorical[13]] is characterized by a translucence of the Special in the Individual or of the General in the Especial or of the Universal in the General. Above all by the translucence of the Eternal through and in the Temporal. It always partakes of the Reality which it renders intelligible; and while it enunciates the whole, abides itself as a living part in that Unity, of which it is the representative. The other are but empty echoes which the fancy arbitrarily associates with apparitions of matter, less beautiful but not less shadowy than the sloping orchard or hillside pasture-field seen in the transparent lake below. Alas! for the flocks that are to be led forth to such pastures! *"It shall even be as when the hungry dreameth, and behold! he eateth; but he waketh and his soul is empty: or as when the thirsty dreameth, and behold he drinketh; but he awaketh and is faint!"* (Isaiah xxix.8) (*SM*, pp. 30–31)

We find Coleridge apparently quite settled here in discriminating allegory from symbol as metaphor from synecdoche; but now his characterizations of these two tropes, in their greater particularity, acquire also a new complexity that seems to confound where it pretends to clarify.

An allegory, as Coleridge here defines it, is typically abstract and arbitrary. A symbol, the far more admirable trope, is pointedly the opposite—both real and determined. But Coleridge's new notion of the symbol also involves a larger, even cosmic set of assumptions. First, the universe comprises a great, ultimately transcendent hierarchy: individuals, species, genera, universals, God.[14] Second, through Coleridge's sudden recourse to the notion of translucence, the symbolic synecdoche is now identifiable, *figuratively,* as the synecdoche of light; absolutely, this is to say, as the synecdoche of signification or intelligibility itself.[15] Taken together, these two larger assumptions inevitably suggest the presence in Coleridge's argument of a fundamental, if modified, Neoplatonism—with what ramifications and consequences, we shall presently try to see.

This famous *Statesman's Manual* passage, Coleridge's most sustained commentary on symbol and its difference from allegory, is also very possibly his most evasive and misleading. My misgivings about it, I hasten to add, are for the most part supported by evidence of Coleridge's own. He was continually qualifying and revising its assertions in his later writings; and all the queries I raise now anticipate reactions he would himself sooner or later evince.

We may broach the difficulties of Coleridge's position with a simple question: how real—more accurately, how free from abstractness—will a Coleridgean symbol necessarily be? As long as the symbolic trope is merely that most basic and trivial kind of synecdoche, the representation of a concrete whole by an actual part (a sail as a symbol of a ship), this issue of abstractness does not even arise. But in the *Statesman's Manual* passage Coleridge is obviously accepting as potentially symbolic the full range of synecdochic figures—not only the part-for-whole trope, but also all varieties of member-for-class: individual for species, species for genus, and the like.[16] And those very notions of species, genus, kind bring an element of abstractness into the conceptions of part and whole. As Coleridge himself elsewhere asks and replies, "Can a generic idea, as far as it is generic, have existence? No. Why not? Because it wants the entire determinateness or particularity which all existing things have; therefore, out of the mind, every generic idea is a nonentity" (*Logic*, p. 298). Some of Coleridge's own examples clearly illustrate the abstractness of such symbolism: thus, "the instinct of the ant-tribe or the bee is a symbol of the human understanding," since "the Understanding, in itself and distinct from the Reason and Conscience, differs in degree only from the Instinct in the Animal" (*AR*, p. 253n/252n).

A second crux in Coleridge's argument simply counterpoises the first on the other side of his symbol-allegory distinction: will an allegory necessarily be arbitrary? Here Coleridge's characteristically Platonic and Neoplatonic images for allegory's abstractness— shadows, echoes, reflections—dramatically counter his assertion: traditional figures of abstractness and insubstantiality these certainly are, but there is nothing arbitrary about the relation of a reflection to its original, or a shadow to the object which casts it. And if an allegory might thus relate determinedly to the concept it represents, the supposed antithesis of allegory and symbol begins to suggest instead the ambivalence or complementarity of a common signifying gesture: symbol will be to allegory as light is to reflected light, or alternatively as light is to a shadow cast from it by some object.

Light reflected from what surface? Shadow cast by what object? Coleridge does sometimes extend his meditations to these considerations, even in these or similar images. Thus in an important 1818 insertion for *The Friend* he queries, if the appearances of the world are actually mere "Nothings," illusions, yet "what is that inward Mirror, in and for which these Nothings have at least a relative existence?" (*Friend* 1:522n). Again, correspondingly using images of substance and shadow instead of mirror and reflection, he writes in a contribution to his and Southey's *Omniana*,

> I am firmly persuaded, that no doctrine was ever widely diffused, among various nations through successive ages, and under different religions (such as is the doctrine of original sin, and redemption . . .),

which is not founded either in the nature of things or in the necessities of our nature . . . I do not however mean, that such a doctrine shall be always the best possible representation of the truth, on which it is founded, for the same body casts strangely different shadows in different places and different degrees of light; but that it always does shadow out some such truth and derives its influence over our faith from our obscure perception of that truth. (*Omniana*, p. 180; cf. *Friend* 1:430)

Somewhat similarly, in marginalia distinguishing between the mode of acquiring and the mode of communicating knowledge, he characterizes the latter as "the *art* of reasoning, by acts of abstraction, which separate from the first ['Intuition, or immediate beholding'] are indeed mere Shadows, but like Shadows, of incalculable service in determining the remembered outlines of the Substance" (*Marginalia* 1:632; cf. 1:135).

To follow Coleridge through such speculations, however, would be a mistaken quest. For as these quotations no less than their numerous Neoplatonic prototypes illustrate, all such musings but proceed from or tend towards one original question—a question not of reflection or shadow at all, or even of that which reflects light or casts a shadow, but rather of the light source itself. Coleridge's cumulatively deepening puns early in *Aids to Reflection* will make this point powerfully: even granting that "He only thinks who *reflects*" and that "the light which is the eye of this soul" is "Reflection," we still need, he affirms, to ask "of what light even this light is *but* a reflection" (*AR*, pp. 4–5/4–6). As he declares in an annotation to *The Friend*, "Consciousness itself, that Consciousness of which all reasoning is the varied modification, is but the Reflex of the Conscience, when most luminous" (*Friend* 1:523n). The light source is God; it and its shining, in whatever aspect—conscience, reason, revelation—are a priori propositions. This source and essence of revelation, moreover, is ineffable, and any trope that attempts to intimate it must inevitably be metaphorical. "There is a Light higher than all, even *the Word that was in the beginning;*—the Light, of which light itself is but the *shechinah* and cloudy tabernacle";[17] of this Light, even light itself is but a metaphor, not a synecdoche. Yet repeatedly in *The Statesman's Manual* Coleridge strives to obscure this truth, asserting in defiance of and even in the very face of his own definitions that "The natural Sun is . . . a symbol of the spiritual" and that "our

Lord speaks symbolically when he says that 'the eye is the light of the body' " (*SM*, pp. 10, 79).

The finite synecdoches of part for whole, individual for species, species for genus are all genuinely symbolic in Coleridge's sense, representing a fact or truth of an order immediately higher than their own, "partak[ing] of the Reality which [they] render[] intelligible." But the translucence, the ultimately transcendent light shining down through the universal hierarchy, simply *allegorizes* this very quality of intelligibility. Thus Coleridge's expanded synecdochic definition of symbol in *The Statesman's Manual* is in part corrupt—corrupt precisely where its rhetoric is impure, in the clandestine or perverse introduction of a metaphoric figure.[18]

Once we dismiss the red herring of "translucence" in the *Statesman's Manual* passage, the reality and determinedness of a symbolic synecdoche would seem, as before, to be functions of its immediate derivation from a greater reality: a symbol is so powerful a figure because it is itself a part of the real and determined whole it represents. This prescription presents difficulties, though, once we undertake to figure transcendent concepts; for can it be possible to offer genuine symbols, substantial and immediate parts, of reason, or God, or the mysteries of faith? That Coleridge himself improperly instances light as just such a trope is hardly reassuring. And our unease can only increase when we read, in his continuation of the *Statesman's Manual* passage, his ostensibly symbolic alternative to the wages of allegorizing. This Scripture-colored exclamation, a passage consistently ignored by those who would take Coleridge's definition of symbol at face value, immediately follows the quotation of Isaiah 29:8:

> O! that we would seek for the bread which was given from heaven, that we should eat thereof and be strengthened! O that we would draw at the well at which the flocks of our forefathers had living water drawn for them, even that water which, instead of mocking the thirst of him to whom it is given, becomes a well within himself springing up to life everlasting! (*SM*, p. 31)

Here Coleridge is imaging transcendent concepts, certainly; but is his imagery—the bread given from heaven, the water of life—truly symbolic, according to his own accompanying definition? How are we to distinguish it from the very allegorizing to which Coleridge so insistently opposes it? That in fact we cannot distinguish it demonstrates the inadequacy of Coleridge's present definitions for his transcendental purposes.[19]

Nevertheless, Coleridge unshakably believes that there is a meaningful distinction to be made here, that these biblical images of bread and water are somehow too real and determined to be considered mere metaphors. As he continues in his later writings to press this point he develops what we must recognize, though he did not, as a deeply revisionary theory of rhetoric, keeping his customary synecdoche-metaphor contrast as its basis but radically changing the implications of these terms.

Let us return for a moment to the central question informing Coleridge's endeavor: is it possible to find genuinely substantial and determined tropes for transcendent concepts? The *Statesman's Manual* passage, as we have seen, as much as says "In synecdoche and symbol, yes; in metaphor and allegory, no"—and immediately gives us strong causes to mistrust both answers. Those causes, however—the abstractness and figurativeness of light, the determinedness of reflection and shadow—are themselves only features of metaphors. We still need to ask what kind of actual relationships between a transcendent concept and its representation might occasion these tropes; we need to ask whether this trope, this turning, of light conveys a metaphorical image or a synecdoche of itself. By 1825, in his *Aids to Reflection*—the title itself seriously if punningly intimates as much—Coleridge is undertaking precisely such a quest, as he asks "of what light even this light is *but* a reflection."

IV

The "Introductory Aphorisms" of *Aids to Reflection* offer a first basic rhetorical clue: reflection figures reflection; mirroring figures thought. As Coleridge soon observes, "In order to get the full sense of a word, we should first present to our minds the visual image that forms its primary meaning" (*AR*, pp. 18–19n/21n). More important to our concerns than this mirror-of-thought figure itself, however, is the contextual transition it implies, which appears clearly in Coleridge's curious appropriation of the trope: "Suppose yourself fronting a mirror. Now what the objects behind you are to their images at the same apparent distance before you, such is Reflection to Forethought" (*AR*, p. 2). Here the objects spatially behind the man observing them in the mirror figure events that are temporally behind him, incidents that belong to his history and experience. And this is a significant further clue to the answer we are seeking: the figure of reflection shows how a determined spatial relationship can represent a determined temporal one.

A similar situation obtains with respect to Coleridge's alternative determined figure for allegory: shadow figures shadowing—it figures, that is, either foreshadowing or following, both of which are determined temporal relationships. In imaginatively reviewing the creation week of Genesis 1, for example, Coleridge exclaims,

> who that hath watched their ways with an understanding heart, could, as the vision evolving, still advanced towards him, contemplate the filial and loyal Bee; the home-building, wedded, and divorceless Swallow; and above all the manifoldly intelligent Ant tribes . . . and not say to himself, Behold the shadow of approaching Humanity, the Sun rising from behind, in the kindling Morn of Creation! (*AR*, pp. 111– 12/106–7)

This kind of trope or something very like it is, of course, familiar to us as the essence of Christian typology. The figure of shadow, like that of reflection, can represent a determined temporal relationship as a determined spatial one.

These observations by themselves afford no new practical guidance to imaging the transcendent; for as Coleridge readily recognizes, "Before and After, when applied to such Subjects, are but allegories, which the Sense or Imagination supplies to the Understanding" (*AR*, p. 73/65). Thinking about such imaging in temporal terms may, however, help us recognize its essential nature by sensitizing us figuratively to the issue of priority; for "The sense of Before and After becomes both intelligible and intellectual when, and *only* when, we contemplate the succession in the relations of Cause and Effect" (*BL* 2:234). Just as spatial relationships suggest temporal ones, so do temporal relationships suggest logical ones. And what is it that makes any temporal or spatial allegory determined? One thing: a cause-effect relationship. That which is logically prior determines that which is logically consequent. We may determinedly allegorize the transcendent, which is a priori, by means of its consequences—and in no other way.

Coleridge still in *Aids to Reflection* ostensibly maintains his familiar oppositions of symbol and allegory, synecdoche and metaphor. "There is, believe me! a wide difference between *symbolical* and *alle-*

gorical" (*AR*, p. 308n/310n). The nature of symbols and symbolic expression, he reaffirms, is "always *tau*tegorical (i.e. expressing the *same* subject but with a *difference*) in contra-distinction from metaphors and similitudes, that are always *alle*gorical (i.e. expressing a *different* subject but with a resemblance" (*AR*, p. 199/197). Emphatically he insists that the similarity yoking a metaphor's tenor and vehicle is only superficial, the difference separating them fundamental: "All metaphors are grounded on an apparent likeness of things essentially different" (*AR*, p. 134/138; taken from *Friend* 2:280). Repeatedly he censures "the (I had almost said dishonest) fashion of metaphorical Glosses" in Scriptural exegesis (*AR*, p.90/83; see also pp. 149/145, 179/176, 308–9n/311n, 399/401). When he prepares to analyze the rhetoric of Paul's christological writings, however, he readily acknowledges it to be metaphoric. But by metaphor Coleridge now suddenly means not the arbitrary, fanciful similitude he has heretofore been decrying, but something far more precise and quite unfamiliar. Paul's judiciously selected figures, to Coleridge's mind, are distinctive and privileged in that they are determined: they do indeed seem to allegorize a transcendent cause by way of some of its consequences.

In Coleridge's newly restrictive sense of the term, a metaphor is a surprisingly complex figure of speech. It images

> an Act, which in its own nature, and as a producing and efficient *cause,* is transcendent; but which produces sundry *effects,* each of which is the same in kind with an effect produced by a Cause well known and of ordinary occurrence. Now when I characterize or designate this transcendent Act, in exclusive reference to these its *effects,* by a succession of names borrowed from their ordinary causes; not for the purpose of rendering the Act itself, or the matter of the Agency, conceivable, but in order to show the nature and magnitude of the Benefits received from it, and thus to excite the due admiration, gratitude, and love in the Receivers; in this case I should be rightly described as speaking *metaphorically.* (*AR*, pp. 199–200/197–98)[20]

Specifically, Coleridge finds in the Pauline Scriptures four basic metaphors for the Redemption: sacrificial expiation, reconciliation or atonement, ransom from slavery, and satisfaction of a creditor's terms by a vicarious payment of the debt. He absolutely denies that these (or any) metaphors can properly characterize the essential nature of redemption or that Paul ever intended them to be so understood, and he goes to some lengths to show that the last of them, the vicarious satisfaction of a debt, is in its literal sense irreconcilable and incongruous with Christian doctrine. The Redemption itself is necessarily unutterable, "a spiritual and transcendent Mystery, 'that passeth all understanding' " (*AR*, p. 327/329, quoting Paul in Phil. 4:7). But it does have various effects—"Sanctification from Sin, and Liberation from the inherent and penal consequences of Sin in the World to come," with accompanying "feelings of joy, confidence, and gratitude" (*AR*, p. 317/319)—which are

> the same for the Sinner relatively to God and his own Soul, as the satisfaction of a debt for a Debtor relatively to his Creditor; as the sacrificial atonement made by the Priest for the Transgressor of the Mosaic Law; as the reconciliation to an alienated Parent for a Son who had estranged himself from his Father's house and presence; and as a redemptive Ransom for a Slave or Captive. (*AR*, pp. 327/329–30)

A Pauline metaphor for the transcendent act of redemption thus is directly suggestive only of one or a few of the act's consequences, not of their unknowable cause. It figures that cause only at a further remove, by way of this intermediate resemblance of effects, and does not imply any identity with or similarity to the transcendent cause itself.

In *The Statesman's Manual* Coleridge had decried as "among the miseries of the present age that it recognizes no medium between *Literal* and *Metaphorical*," and had proposed the symbol as just such a saving medium. Metaphor or allegory, "a counterfeit product of the mechanical understanding," was "but a translation of abstract notions into a picture-language . . . the principal being more worthless even than its phantom proxy" (*SM*, p. 30). But now, in *Aids to Reflection*, Coleridge is no longer prepared to treat metaphor so lightly. First of all, he can hardly dismiss St. Paul's "abstract notions" as even relatively "worthless." But now he also recognizes that metaphors no less than symbols may at least occasionally occupy that vital, middle ground of rhetoric.

Some metaphors, to be sure, he still regards as he did in *The Statesman's Manual*, as "but empty echoes which the fancy arbitrarily associates with apparitions of matter" (*SM*, p. 30). Such metaphors he continues to denigrate. These include the metaphors and allegories he treated so condescendingly in the 1818 lectures on poetry and drama for figuring causes by causes, "employ[ing] one set of agents and images with actions and accompaniments correspondent, so as to convey . . . other images, agents, actions, fortunes and circumstances" (*LL* 2:99).

But other metaphors, such as Paul's, are, like symbols, in no way arbitrary. They are, however, liable to interpretative abuse; for the inadequate reader who senses their validity but who recognizes no medium between the literal and the metaphorical will "improperate" these figures, "taking [them] *literally*" (*AR*, p. 311/313). The error here, Coleridge argues, lies in seeking in causes for a similitude attributed only to effects. As he elaborates in *Aids to Reflection*,

> the article of Redemption may be considered in a twofold relation—in relation to the *Antecedent*, *i.e.* the Redeemer's Act, as the efficient cause and condition of Redemption; and in relation to the *Consequent*, *i.e.* the effects in and for the Redeemed. Now it is the latter relation, in which the Subject is treated of . . . by St. Paul. . . . It is the *Consequences* of the Act of Redemption, that the zealous Apostle would bring home. . . . (*AR*, p. 312/314)

The former relation, the similitude of causes or agents, leads to such figures as those "dullest and most defective parts of Spenser . . . in which we are compelled to think of his agents as allegories" (*LL* 2:103). St. Paul's figuration, in contrast, must be read for what it is, not an arbitrary metaphor for an ineffable cause but a genuine "similitude of *effect*" (*AR*, p. 317/319).

What Coleridge is now in *Aids to Reflection* terming metaphor, then, would seem to be either a subclass of the trope or a new way of looking at it. We might accurately, if clumsily, describe it as a particular way of combining two cause-effect metonymies: a familiar act or agent, a known cause, serves as a trope for its known effect, while this effect already conversely images a different, transcendent cause of which it is alternatively a consequence.[21] In order to preserve the discriminations on which Coleridge insists, I shall call this new figure a determined metaphor, meaning thereby to distinguish it from the mechanical fancy's "empty echoes," which are indeed, as Coleridge asserts, arbitrary.[22]

The new theory of metaphor Coleridge propounds in *Aids to Reflection* is of biographical no less than critical significance, for it underlies and even constitutes an important turn in the development of his religious beliefs. In this respect, as Coleridge himself recognizes, the pattern of his spiritual growth parallels St. Augustine's: both men earlier found the Bible's language often incongruous and crude, but both learned to appreciate it by reading it—and especially the writings of St. Paul—figuratively. In *Biographia Literaria,* Coleridge says of his earlier religious beliefs that he could not reconcile in his moral feelings his "doubts concerning the incarnation and the redemption by the cross . . . with the sacred distinction between things and persons, the vicarious payment of a debt and the vicarious expiation of guilt," and proceeds to liken his "final re-conversion to the whole truth of Christ" to Augustine's (*BL* 1:205). The problem of the redemption is the last obstacle to his faith, even as it is the catalyst of his hermeneutics; and in fact Coleridge still has not resolved it to his satisfaction when he writes this *Biographia* passage in late 1815. A marginal comment in a volume of Donne's *LXXX Sermons,* apparently written in 1816, shows him still frustrated by the crux—"this strange *metabasis eis allo genos* [translation to another kind], this Debtor and Creditor Scheme of expounding the mystery of Redemption!" (*Marginalia* 2:263).[23]

By the spring of 1819, however, when he recorded its essentials in a two-paragraph note to Field's *On the Church* (*Marginalia* 2:657–58), Coleridge had fully developed his theory of Pauline metaphor. After this time, his insistence on the "wide difference between *symbolical* and *allegorical*" proves to be highly qualified, and not only in *Aids to Reflection.* Thus in his 1818 lectures Coleridge had declared straightforwardly that a fable was a species of allegory, distinguishable from other allegories in that its allegoric agents and images were conventional: for example, "A Bear, a Fox, a Tyger, a Lion, Diana, an Oak, a Willow, are *every man's* Metaphors for clumsiness, cunning, ferocious or magnanimous Courage, Chastity, unbendingness, and flexibility" (*LL* 2:100). In an 1821 notebook entry, though, Coleridge significantly revises this position, stating instead that in an allegory

> where the Metaphors [are] adopted conventionally by all classes of a society, so that the objects, to which the assimilation is implied, are Symbols or partake of the Nature of Symbols, and are assumed as already known & understood by the Auditor,—this Allegory, so qualified, is *A Fable;* & this alone merits the name of an Esopic Fable.— The Ass, the Fox, the Lion, the Oak, the Wolf, the Lamb are all either συμβολα, or ωσ συμβολα. . . .[24]

In his 1825 lecture "On the Prometheus of Aeschylus," delivered to the Royal Society of Literature, moreover, Coleridge terms the play simultaneously a ταυτηγορικον, *tautegorichon* (in Coleridge's usage, always the exclusive status of symbol) and an allegory, and concludes that in parts of it "symbol fades away into allegory, but . . . never ceases wholly to be a symbol or tautegory."[25] And in an 1830 notebook entry alluding to 1 Corinthians 13:12 ("For now we see through a glass darkly; but then face to face"), to cite a final example, Coleridge asserts that "to see dimly as in a mirror—i.e. by reflection" is also to see "symbolicaly [*sic*]" (*Marginalia* 1:237n).

V

As Coleridge extends and revises his rhetorical theory of the symbol in *Aids to Reflection,* he crafts his argument with a certain cautious evasiveness not unlike that of *The Statesman's Manual.* At the center of this evasiveness, as of the argument itself, is his new emphasis on and understanding of the trope of analogy.

Clearly Coleridge intends analogy here to share the burden of meaning and value earlier borne by symbol alone. His association of the two terms is most explicit:

> The language is analogous, wherever a thing, power, or principle in a higher dignity is expressed by the same thing, power, or principle in a lower but more known form. . . . [T]hese analogies are the material, or (to speak chemically) the *base*, of Symbols and symbolical expressions; the nature of which [is] always *tau*tegorical (i.e., expressing the *same* subject but with a *difference*. . . . (*AR*, pp. 199/196–97; see also pp. 315/318, 330/332)

Analogy in this sense is thus but another name for that kind of synecdoche wherein "a *lower* form or species [symbolizes] . . . a higher in the same *kind*" (*AR*, p. 254n/253n).

Coleridge's appropriation of analogy for his present transcendental purposes prompts two questions, one of which we have had occasion to ask before. First, is it even possible to image synecdochically the transcendent by the perceptible? (This is, of course, the question that Coleridge begged by his sophistic use of light and translucence in the *Statesman's Manual* passage.) Can a transcendent concept, that is, also be in part—and be known to be—a phenomenal fact? Metaphysically, as Coleridge would have learned from Kant, the answer must be no.[26] Theologically, however, Coleridge finds two occasions for answering yes: the Incarnation and the Eucharist. Hence his privileging of the Johannine "living water" and "bread of life" as symbolic, something we have already seen in *The Statesman's Manual* (and here it is worth remembering that baptism and Holy Communion [the Eucharist] are the only two sacraments that the Church of England recognizes). Any other instance of such a trope, however, would have to be illicit. Coleridge himself, moreover, several times says as much: "All the mysteries of faith . . . are intelligible *per se*, not discursively and *per analogiam*. For the truths are unique, and may have shadows and types, but not analogies."[27]

Second, is analogy indeed, as Coleridge here assumes, a way of representing one thing by another *in the same kind?* In fact, quite the contrary is true. As Coleridge himself had earlier realized, "Analogy always implies a difference in kind and not merely in degree" (*CN* 1:2319). His example demonstrates his meaning very clearly: "It is the sameness of the end, with the difference of the means, which constitutes analogy. No one would say the lungs of a man were analogous to the lungs of a monkey, but any one might say that the gills of a fish and the spiracula of insects are analogous to lungs."[28] Countering the lucidity of his example, however, Coleridge's immediately prefatory theoretical statement cannot but give us pause: "It is the sameness of the end, with the difference of the means, which constitutes analogy." As a description of analogy this is somewhat unusual, not to say skewed; but how very aptly it describes determined metaphor![29] We need, then, to explore the relationship of these two tropes.

For a more generally acceptable definition of analogy we might look to Kant's *Critique of Judgment,* which Coleridge knew well. Analogy, Kant declares, "is the identity of the relation between reasons and consequences (causes and effects), so far as it is to be found, notwithstanding the specific differences of the things or those properties in them which contain the reason for like consequences (i.e., considered apart from this relation)."[30] Kant here helps us to appreciate that the root trope of analogy is again the cause-effect metonymy. Where a determined metaphor turns on the similarity of two effects, however, and an arbitrary metaphor on the similarity of two causes, an analogy turns on the similarity of two relations between causes and effects. Thus analogy, distinct from determined metaphor yet rhetorically cognate with it, affords another means of determinedly imaging the transcendent.[31]

As Kant goes on to suggest, it is quite possible, even traditional, to use analogy to image transcendent concepts. But that Coleridge actually is, as he claims, talking about analogy in *Aids to Reflection* is not at all apparent. Ostensibly he is trying, along the lines of his earlier distinction of symbol from allegory, to demonstrate the presence in the Bible of two alternative modes of representing the spiritual mysteries of Christianity, taking as his examples of analogy and metaphor the Gospel of John (preeminently John 3:6, "That which is born of the flesh, is flesh; that which is born of the Spirit, is Spirit") and the writings of Paul, respectively. His presentation of John 3:6 as an analogy, however, seems notably sophistic. "The latter half of the verse contains the fact *asserted;* the former half the *analogous* fact, by which it is rendered intelligible" (*AR,* pp. 198–99/196). But as an analogy this is not tautegorical; it is merely tautological, and therefore trivial—like saying that lungs are analogous to lungs. We can analyze Christ's statement to Nicodemus more meaningfully than this by recognizing in it two distinct causes productive of two similar or identical effects: flesh generates, spirit generates. We can, in other words, take birth as a common effect rather than as a common ratio. And despite his vehement denials, this is clearly what Coleridge is doing:

> [T]he interpretation of the common term is to be ascertained from its known sense, in the more familiar connexion—Birth, namely, in relation to our natural life and to the Organized Body, by which we belong to the present World. Whatever the word signifies in this connexion, the same *essentially* (in *kind* though not in dignity and value) must be its signification in the other. (*AR,* p. 330/332).

But this is, after all, simply to read John 3:6 as a determined metaphor. Once again, as before in *The Statesman's Manual,* Coleridge's great rhetorical opposition, now conceived as that of analogy versus metaphor, ultimately resolves into a common figure.

VI

Coleridge's too hasty valuation of symbol over allegory in *The Statesman's Manual* may perhaps best be understood as symptomatic of his more fundamental ambition to honor imagination over fancy. The relationships of the two pairs of terms are especially apparent when he identifies the imagination as "that reconciling and mediatory power, which . . . gives birth to a system of symbols . . . consubstantial with the truths, of which they are the *conductors,*" and correspondingly sees allegories as "empty echoes which the fancy arbitrarily associates with apparitions of matter" (*SM*, pp.29, 30). Such an excuse seems irrelevant to the parallel and similarly flawed distinction of analogy from metaphor in *Aids to Reflection*, though, for obviously Coleridge does not regard Paul's tropes as empty or arbitrary. Indeed, he cites Paul frequently throughout his writings as paradigmatic of the Bible's excellence; and when, soon after writing *The Statesman's Manual*, he again contrasts the hollow fancifulness of the "mechanic philosophy" (the tradition of Locke and Newton) with the vital imaginativeness of the Scriptures, he turns to Paul for his exemplary text (*BL* 1:277–78, *CL* 4:768; cf. *SM*, pp. 28–29).

But while in *The Statesman's Manual* Coleridge is concerned to distinguish between "the *product[s]* of an unenlivened generalizing Understanding" and "the living *educts* of the Imagination" (*SM*, pp. 28–29), in *Aids to Reflection* his rhetorical analysis works to discriminate between two different kinds of biblical, imaginative figuration; and apparently this changed need dictates his changed rhetorical approach. Although the Johannine and Pauline tropes are not, after all, different in kind, they may be considered to differ in degree. Paul's metaphors tend to be determined by relatively few effects; Coleridge, in fact, typically speaks of a Pauline metaphor as figuring Christ's redemption by way of a single effect only. John's metaphor of birth, on the other hand, has the special virtue of yielding simultaneously a great many determined effects, some of Paul's among them: "In the Redeemed it is a re-*generation*, a *birth*, a spiritual seed impregnated and evolved, the germinal principle of a higher and enduring Life, of a *spiritual* Life . . . [It is] an assimilation to the Principle of Life, even to him who is *the* Life. . . . [It] is at the same time a redemption from the spiritual death" (*AR*, pp. 315–16/318). We find, then, the following distinction: where Paul's tropes are determined metaphors, John's central trope is an overdetermined metaphor. Though Coleridge does not make the distinction explicit in *Aids to Reflection*, he did in fact figuratively anticipate it years before, in the *Omniana*. We have already noted a passage that can aptly illustrate the simultaneous cognation and variety of Paul's determined metaphors: "The same body casts strangely different shadows in different places and different degrees of light; but . . . it always does shadow out some such truth." But presently Coleridge follows this image up with another:

Let a body be suspended in the air, and strongly illuminated. What figure is here? A triangle. But what here? A trapezium . . . and so on. The same question put to twenty men, in twenty different positions and distances, would receive twenty different answers: and each would be a true answer. But what is that one figure, which being so placed, all these facts of appearance must result, according to the law of perspective . . . ? Aye! this is a different question . . . this is a new subject.[32]
(*Omniana*, pp. 180, 181)

The new subject, we can now recognize, is that of a highly overdetermined metaphor.

VII

The famous Romantic opposition of symbol and allegory, whatever its value in analyzing the rhetoric of ordinary thought, nevertheless in transcendental rhetoric is but an irrelevancy. Coleridge, who made this opposition a commonplace, has thus far misled us badly. But his error points unerringly to a matter of great critical significance. Beneath the false issue of synecdochic versus metaphoric tropes there lies hidden a genuine, significant crux, that of determined versus arbitrary figuration, the unavoidable issue for any rhetoric that would strive to be transcendental. That Coleridge should have found his way to this issue redounds greatly to his credit as a critic. That he should nevertheless have remained blind and vulnerable to its deconstructive implications for his own work, as the next chapter argues he did, is perhaps simply the price his criticism had to pay his faith.

Chapter 2

Argument and
the Rhetoric of Argument

Coleridge, Burke, and the
Catenary Curve of
Determined Metaphor

I

In *Aids to Reflection* Coleridge carries his thesis of transcendental figuration to its highest refinement. His theoretical valuation of determined over arbitrary figures, his practical analyses of the rhetoric of Johannine and Pauline texts, both culminating in his presentation of determined metaphor as a distinct and uniquely powerful trope, mark a significant advance in Romantic critical sophistication.

These are great virtues; but they are not, by the standards of Coleridge's objectives, sufficient. It is time now to insist without further ado that Coleridge's rhetorical theory is also fundamentally flawed and invalid.

Since Coleridge is particularly concerned with the determinedness, the logical rigor, of tropes—hence his denigration of metaphor as contrasted with symbol—we may well begin to test his theory by looking at the logical status of determined metaphor. Our examination need not be protracted; for any simple, non-transcendental example will immediately show that, logically speaking, a determined metaphor is no less arbitrary than an ordinary one, and for much the same reason—if not transition into a new kind, then transition into a new cause. For instance—and the example is Coleridge's own, as we have already seen—we can speak of the sun as the lamp of heaven, because its "effec[t] on us is th[e] same as tha[t] of a lamp" (*Marginalia* 1:200). The shining sun causes an effect (light) on us; the shining lamp causes the same effect. If we link these two potential cause-effect metonymies (sun → light, lamp → light) into a single figure, we may accordingly take the lamp as a determined metaphor for the sun—we might then speak metaphorically of the sun as the lamp of heaven; but the relation of sun and lamp remains as arbitrary as that of any other metaphor. Indeed, the trope very clearly *is* a simple metaphor, nothing more; from a logical point of view, the Coleridgean distinction of determined from ordinary metaphor is entirely specious. "Determined metaphor" is an oxymoron.

Do all Coleridge's increasingly subtle and involved analyses of metaphor, then, come to no more than this? *Parturient montes, nascetur ridiculus mus;* the phenomenon is not, after all, so uncharacteristic of Coleridge's work. Still, we should not dismiss too lightly his particular concern with tropes of causality, for it corresponds precisely to the central, motivating anxiety of his philosophical and religious thought. Coleridge was fully aware that the issue of causality is the crux of all transcendental inquiry. As he noted even in 1798, "Hume's system of Causation—or rather of non-causation" is "the pillar, & confessedly, the *sole* pillar, of modern Atheism" (*CL* 1:385–86). Now Hume had argued that, as Shelley succinctly paraphrases, "We know no more of cause and effect than a constant conjunction of events" (*DP,* p. 43), and that what we commonly take to be a causal relationship is, in Coleridge's words, "a blind product of delusion and habit" (*BL* 1:121; cf. *Logic,* p. 192); the notion of causality, then, is due not to an innate, a priori necessity at all, but simply to a tacit *a posteriori* attribution.[1] Such an argument, Coleridge saw, poses a devastating threat to religious faith: "If no connection can be affirmed unless both *antecedent* and *consequent* are *alike* facts of experience, and no analogical conclusions are valid between subjects of diverse kind . . . , a spiritual antecedent cannot be presumed from a material phenomenon" (*Logic,* p. 190). We can readily see here that in this philosophical debate the privileged status of transcendental determined metaphors is also at stake.

Coleridge defends faith against Hume's skeptical challenge by recurring derivatively to Kant's argument that some synthetic (i.e., experiential) judgments, including those of causality, are in fact nonetheless a priori; and clearly it is in this Kantian context of "synthesis *a priori*" and "transcendental logic" that Coleridge's special valuation of transcendental determined metaphor seeks its justification. But Hume's skepticism is not to be so easily repressed. It returns with new vigor, for example, in Nietzsche's suggestion that the cause-effect metonymy originates not with an a priori truth but with a rhetorical construction. In his "criticism of the concept 'cause'" Nietzsche argues,

We believed that an effect was explained when we could point to a
state in which it was inherent. As a matter of fact, we invent all causes
according to the scheme of the effect: the latter is known to us. . . .
There is no such thing as a cause or an effect. From the standpoint of
language we do not know how to rid ourselves of them. But that does
not matter.

His diagnosis is that "the so-called instinct of causality is nothing
more than the *fear of the unfamiliar*, and the attempt at finding something in it which is already *known.—*It is not a search for causes, but
for the familiar."[2] As Jonathan Culler observes of this,

> Causation involves a narrative structure in which we posit first the
> presence of a cause and then the production of an effect. . . . But, says
> Nietzsche, this sequence is not given; it is constructed by a rhetorical
> operation. What happens may be, for example, that we feel a pain and
> then look around for some factor we can treat as the cause. The "real"
> casual sequence may be: first pain, then mosquito. It is the effect that
> causes us to produce a cause; a tropological operation then reorders
> the sequence pain-mosquito as mosquito-pain. This latter sequence is
> the product of discursive forces, but we treat it as a given, as the true
> order.[3]

This same kind of rhetorical operation, Freud suggests in *The Future
of an Illusion*, lies behind all superstition and religion.

In thus inquiring beyond Hume into the theological and psychological implications and extrapolations of determined metaphor,
Freud not only indicates the metapsychological potential of the trope
but also clarifies—and exemplifies—the threat such inquiry poses to
Coleridge's fideism. Coleridge's entire theory of determined metaphor arises from an impulse to affirm the logical validity of Pauline
no less than Johannine rhetoric; yet, like any transcendental affirmation, it is itself vulnerable to logical challenge, though this is a vulnerability it anxiously obscures. Determined metaphor is an oxymoron of a very particular kind: as "determined," it is an appeal to
logic; as "metaphor," a defense against logic.

And herein lies the crisis of Coleridge's metaphysics: he can neither do without logic, nor with it. Not without, because then there
would be no standard for judgment, no occasion or instrument for
preferring one theory over another. It is logic that discriminates the

sophisms or "paralogisms" of a weak philosopher like Hartley (_BL_ 1:123) from the rigorous coherence of a Kant, logic which constitutes the very vehicle of reason. But not with, because the transcendent is beyond it: "We do not win heaven by logic" (_TT_, 4/4/1832).

Hence Coleridge's simultaneous celebration of logic's better and alternative, "that vital passion which is the practical cement of logic" (_BL_ 1:9n), "that fortunate _inconsequence_ of our nature, which permits the heart to rectify the errors of the understanding" (_BL_ 1:217; my emphasis).

We cannot hope to grasp the strategies and objectives of Coleridge's metaphysical argument, then, without exploring this issue at its heart, the logical status of his project. And one immediately relevant way of doing this, we can now see, is to inquire whether Coleridge's is a symbolic or a metaphorical discourse.

II

We have already followed at some length Coleridge's concern with the logical status of symbol and metaphor, but it may be helpful to summarize here. The symbol, as a part-for-whole synecdoche, is (like the effect-for-cause metonymy) logically determined; for that which is true of the whole is true of the part. What is true of the symbol, moreover, must of course be consistent with (though not necessarily universally true of) the whole. Thus, that which is true of the part is at least partly true of the whole; or, hierarchically speaking, that which is true of the lower form or species is at least partly true of all higher forms or species of that same kind. Metaphor, on the other hand, has an entirely different logical status. Where synecdoches relate different degrees of a single kind, in contrast "all metaphors are grounded on an apparent likeness of things essentially different" (_AR_, p. 138/134; _Friend_ 2:280), things of different kinds. Thus a metaphor is, as Coleridge knows, a sophism, logically speaking—what Aristotle calls a _metabasis eis allo genos_, a "Transition into a new kind" (_AR_, pp. 215/213, 311–12/314).

When we ask whether Coleridge's project is itself ultimately symbolic or metaphorical, then, we are asking how it relates to the ultimate truths it asserts—that is, whether it is of the same kind as these truths, or of a different kind. Central among these truths are Coleridge's fundamental distinction of Reason from Understanding and his fundamental association of man's Reason with God.

Coleridge is explicitly and repeatedly insistent on the absolute distinctiveness of Reason and Understanding. As he says in *Biographia Literaria*, he is convinced "of the importance, nay, of the necessity of the distinction, as both an indispensable condition and a vital part of all sound speculation in metaphysics, ethical or theological" (1:174–75). "To establish this distinction was one main object of *The Friend*," he continues (see especially *Friend* 1:153–61); it is one also of *Aids to Reflection*, where he argues at length "On the Difference in Kind of Reason and the Understanding" (pp. 208–28/206–27, 407–08 [1831 only]), and of *The Statesman's Manual*, where he devotes to the distinction an appendix almost as long again as the sermon itself (pp. 59–93). As he later summarizes at the end of a long marginalium to this last, "Therefore the [theoric] and [practical] Reason differs in kind from the [theoric] and [practical] Understanding—and Reason and Understanding are diverse Faculties. *Q.E.D.*" (*SM*, p. 61n).

Reason itself is ultimately identifiable with God, "the Supreme Reason." "God, the Soul, eternal Truth, &c. are the objects of Reason; but they are themselves *reason*. We name God the Supreme Reason; and Milton says, 'Whence the Soul *Reason* receives, and Reason is her Being'" (*Friend* 1:156). Between human Reason and "the Supreme Reason" the difference, as Coleridge's terminology implies, is thus one of degree only, not of kind. In an 1814 letter he even sketches the degrees within the kind:

> Mind . . . may be regarded as a distinct genus, in the scale ascending above brutes, and including the whole of intellectual existences; advancing from *thought*, (that mysterious thing!) in its lowest form, through all the gradations of sentient and rational beings, till it arrives at a Bacon, a Newton, and then, when unincumbered by matter, extending its illimitable sway through Seraph and Archangel, till we are lost in the *Great Infinite!* (*CL* 3:483)

But this means that his Reason relates man synecdochically to God, as an actual part of that Whole which he represents. And Coleridge affirms this in his 1818 "Essays on Method," it is worth noting, in language pointedly evocative of his *Statesman's Manual* characterization of the symbol: God is "a Being whose ideas are creative, and consequently more real, more substantial than the things that, at the height of their *creaturely* state, are but their dim reflexes"; and man is the "representative of the Creator, as far as he partakes of that reason in which the essences of all things coexist in all their distinctions yet as one and indivisible" (*Friend* 1:516). Reason is "substantial knowledge" because it is synecdochic knowledge, "that intuition of things which arises when we possess ourselves, as one with the whole" (*Friend* 1:520).

Coleridge's strategy, then, is clearly to present his project as a symbolic argument—a work of the reason, not merely of the understanding; a work synecdochically partaking of the great truths it represents and enunciates, not merely figuring them metaphorically.

Coleridge's absolute distinction of Reason from Understanding raises problems for his larger strategy in that the very logic by which he makes the distinction is itself the expression of the Understanding—logic is but "the forms of the understanding and the rules grounded on same," limited to "the acts and conclusions of the understanding or the sense" (*Logic*, pp. 204, 77; cf. *Friend* 1:156)—and is thus, his own argument would insist, only metaphorically relevant to any acts and conclusions of reason. Coleridge tries to sidestep this difficulty by asserting that "there is a higher logic—that of ideas," which "proves, but at the same time supersedes" the logic of the understanding (*TT*, 4/30/1830, 12/21/1833; cf. *SM*, pp. 104–5, *Friend* 1:518–19). This assertion is part of a larger insistence that, though "the Understanding and Experience may exist without Reason," yet "Reason cannot exist without Understanding; nor does it or can it manifest itself but in and through the understanding" (*Friend* 1:156).[4] But these problematic blurrings of the distinction between Understanding and Reason are of only secondary importance: while they leave Coleridge open to the ripostes of the empirical philosophers he is challenging, they do not affect the larger movement of his argument.

The primary postulate of Coleridge's metaphysics, however, his assertion of the synecdochic relationship between human Reason and God, raises far more serious difficulties. Only by building upon this synecdoche can Coleridge claim to be advancing a symbolic theological argument; but in fact, as we have repeatedly seen, his claim is spurious, for his ostensible symbols are actually masquerading metaphors. Coleridge consistently rejects or evades this knowledge in his public pronouncements; occasionally, however, he does advert to it in his private addenda. In an important 1818 annotation of his concluding "Essay on Method," for example, he explicitly if obscurely admits that his argument ultimately must abandon Reason as it approaches transcendence, that man's Reason is not part of but is absolutely separated from God. Reason alone, he now acknowledges, can at most affirm a "Supreme Reality, "an *absolute* Being. But here it stops"; for Reason alone cannot discriminate this Supreme Reality from the world itself, and so cannot move beyond pantheism—a purely synecdochic theology, indeed, but only an immanent one. To go beyond pantheism to the conviction of a Supreme Reason, man must leave Reason behind: "[F]rom whichever point the Reason may start, from the things that are seen to the One Invisible, or from the Idea of the Absolute One to the things that are seen, it will find a chasm, which the Moral Being only, which the Spirit and Religion of Man can alone fill up" (*Friend* 1:522–23n).Reason's path is stopped by a chasm; Reason is not a part of, continuous with, what lies beyond, but separate from it.

In an 1827 annotation of the *Statesman's Manual* appendix on Reason and Understanding, Coleridge speaks to much the same effect of man's correlativeness to God:

> The principle of personal individuality being the transcendent—(that is, the highest *species* of *genus* X, in which X rises, *moritur, at dum moritur resurgit* ["dies, but in dying rises again"], into the higher *genus* Y,)—the personal principle, I say, being the transcendent of all particulars, requires for its correspondent opposite the transcendent of all universals: and this is God. (*SM*, p. 73n)

Transcendence is not a difference in degree but a transition into a different *genus*, a different kind: it is a *metabasis eis allo genos*. The pursuit of transcendence, then, is not symbolic, but metaphorical.

III
Determined Metaphor and
Edmund Burke's Conception of a Sublime God

The rhetorical twists and psychological ambivalences that everywhere shadow Coleridge's transcendental inquiry are not his merely, but faith's. If we too readily regard them as idiosyncrasies, the "logical swim-bladders, transcendental life-preservers" of Carlyle's devastating portrait,[5] this is surely because we have been swayed by Coleridge's own never-ending insistence on the absolute difference between the "mechanic philosophy" of the empiricists ("the philosophy of death") and his own "living and spiritual philosophy" (*SM*, p. 89). But the genuine and significant differences between Coleridge and the empiricists—"The pith of my system," he once summarized, "is to make the senses out of the mind—not the mind out of the senses, as Locke did" (*TT,* 7/25/1832)—should not blind us to the fact that the theological starting points of their systems are quite similar. For Locke no less than Coleridge sets out from the "I am," man's certainty "that he is *something that actually exists*"; like Coleridge, Locke finds that "from the consideration of ourselves, and what we infallibly find in our own constitutions, our reason leads us to the knowledge of this certain and evident truth,—*That there is an eternal, most powerful, and most knowing Being*" (*Essay* IV.x.2,6). The empiricists no less than Coleridge imagine and figure God anthropomorphically, by moving from effect (man) to cause (God) in a determined metaphor.

Although we have now seen something·of faith's impact on Coleridge's argument and its rhetoric, we have not considered his rhetoric's implications for his faith. But these same implications, which so often take deep cover in "the holy jungle of transcendental metaphysics,"[6] stand out with somewhat greater clarity in the more open (if still shadowy), immanent terrain of the empiricists. A particularly apposite example, by a thinker Coleridge respected (as he did not Locke), is Edmund Burke's *A Philosophical Enquiry into the Origin of Our Ideas of the Sublime and Beautiful* (1757).

Burke's analysis of the sublime is at once empiricist and psychological: he inquires after the origins of the sublime exclusively among the sensations and passions. Yet he also acknowledges the idea of God as an ultimate source of the sublime, and one which, moreover, "frequently occurred to me, not as an objection to, but as a strong confirmation of my notions in this matter" (*Enquiry,* p. 68). How, then, does he accommodate the transcendent idea of God within his analysis of the immanent sources of the sublime?

Burke derives all experiences of the sublime from a single occasion, terror, but he distinguishes three modes of the emotion: "Whatever is fitted in any sort to excite the ideas of pain, and danger, that is to say, whatever is in any sort terrible, or is conversant about terrible objects, or operates in a manner analogous to terror, is a source of the *sublime*" (p. 39). In an alternative version of this tripartite schema, he states that "Besides these things which *directly* suggest the idea of danger, and those which produce a similar effect from a mechanical cause, I know of nothing sublime which is not some modification of power. And this branch rises as naturally as the other two branches, from terror, the common stock of every thing that is sublime" (p. 64).

Power, not in itself terrible, is clearly that which "is conversant about terrible objects"; for "pain is always inflicted by a power in some way superior, because we never submit to pain willingly. So that strength, violence, pain and terror, are ideas that rush in upon the mind together" (p. 65). Terror implies power, then, though power need not imply terror—though it will not then be sublime, for "power derives all its sublimity from the terror with which it is generally accompanied" (p. 65). Burke cites the ox, powerful but not terrible, as an illustrative counterexample: "An ox is a creature of vast strength; but he is an innocent creature, extremely serviceable, and not at all dangerous; for which reason the idea of an ox is by no means grand." The bull, in contrast, "is strong too; but his strength is of another kind; often very destructive, seldom (at least amongst us) of any use in our business; the idea of a bull is therefore great, and it has frequently a place in sublime descriptions" (p. 65).

When Burke tries to locate the idea of a transcendent God within this scheme, however, his categories begin to break down. He judges that the idea of God is fundamentally the idea of ultimate power, "the highest of all" (p. 70), and it is accordingly into his section on "Power," not that on "Terror," that he introduces his brief discussion of God. But no sooner does Burke take this position than he begins to compromise it. "I know some people are of opinion, that no awe, no degree of terror, accompanies the idea of power," he begins—and he himself has already both admitted the general possibility and cited the ox as just such an example. But that these people further "have hazarded to affirm, that we can contemplate the idea of God himself without any such emotion" (p. 67) constitutes a critical threat to his theory, which Burke cannot allow to go unchallenged. "I can contemplate the idea of God without terror," the threatening enthymeme runs, "therefore I can experience the sublime without terror."

Not only does Burke implicitly accept the suppressed premise, "to contemplate the idea of God is to experience the sublime"; he even— to the overthrow of his entire argument—accepts the whole syllogism.

> I say then, that whilst we consider the Godhead merely as he is an object of the understanding, which forms a complex idea of power, wisdom, justice, goodness, all stretched to a degree far exceeding the bounds of our comprehension, whilst we consider the divinity in this

> refined and abstracted light, the imagination and passions are little or
> nothing affected. (p. 68)

God so considered, in other words, is *not* terrible. Burke's defense
against this admission is simply to deny that such "refined and ab-
stracted" contemplation is either common or practicable:

> But because we are bound by the condition of our nature to ascend to
> these pure and intellectual ideas, through the medium of sensible im-
> ages, and to judge of these divine qualities by their evident acts and ex-
> ertions, *it becomes extremely hard to disentangle our idea of the cause
> from the effect by which we are led to know it.* Thus when we contem-
> plate the Deity, his attributes and their operation coming united on the
> mind, form a sort of sensible image, and as such are capable of affect-
> ing the imagination. (p. 68; my emphasis)

God's awesomeness, then, is a construct of the impressionable but illogical imagination, which confusedly figures cause by effect, divine
attributes by sensible acts—the very operation whose logic Coleridge had in *Aids to Reflection* so assiduously tried to demonstrate
and defend.

Burke's explanation (like Coleridge's) is particularly remarkable in
that this same tangled confusion of cause and effect that he is discussing immediately becomes a feature of his own argument:

> Now, though in a just idea of the Deity, perhaps none of his attributes
> are predominant, yet to our imagination, his power is by far the most
> striking. . . . [N]o conviction of the justice with which it is exercised,
> nor the mercy with which it is tempered, can wholly remove the terror
> that naturally arises from a force which nothing can withstand. (p. 68)

Terror, then, arises from power; but more than this, Burke now begins to insist, terror *inevitably* arises from power: "this dread *must
necessarily follow* the idea of such a power, when it is once excited in
the mind" (p. 70; my emphasis). But this is as much as to say that
power implies terror—something Burke has just finished denying.

Burke's theory clearly indicates that he can keep God sublime only
by keeping him not merely powerful but terrible. But our idea of God
then becomes, not "a just idea of the Deity," but our passionally,
imaginatively distorted notion of Him, and so a notion that, in contradiction to Burke's classification of it, does indeed directly suggest

the idea of danger. Power is not, as Burke wants to say it is, the indirect suggestion of danger; rather danger is the indirect suggestion of power. Thus Burke's argument in fact tends to the theological conclusion he cites with intent to deny, that *primos in orbe deos fecit timor* (Fear made the first gods in the world). "The maker of the maxim saw how inseparable these ideas were, without considering that the notion of some dread power must always be precedent to our dread of it" (p. 70), he rejoins; but Burke himself has already insisted that not from power, but from the dread of power, does the religious sense arise.

Burke's ostensibly all-inclusive categorization of the sublime, then, suffers a logical breakdown when it tries to encompass the sublimity of God. Its failure of logic, however, is at the same time a precise rhetorical operation, the troping of cause by effect; and it is only through this contrary figuration that our conception of God becomes "capable of affecting the imagination," only thus that God seems sublime. Burke's logic fails the requirements of the understanding, we see, precisely so that his antagonistic rhetorical strategy can serve the requirements of the imagination.

The logical dilemma into which Burke's "psychological observations" and theological speculations led him was apparent to Kant, who effectively responds to and corrects the errors of Burke's understanding in his own "Analytic of the Sublime."[7] To appreciate his imagination's demands, though, we must consider to what ends Burke's rhetoric opposes his logic. Why, then, should "our just idea of the Deity" be emotionally and imaginatively inadequate?

If our only God is in effect our misunderstood terror-God, as Burke argues, then our just idea of Him, an idea Burke posits, has a problematic status. The idea arose, Burke suggests, when Christianity "humanized the idea of the divinity, and brought it somewhat nearer to us." Before this happened, Burke notes, "there was very little said of the love of God"; and the culmination of this spiritual development, gained through "infinite attention" and "long habits of piety and contemplation," is "an entire love and devotion to the Deity" (p. 70). Such an accommodation, as we have seen, nonetheless poses an immediate threat to the sublime in Burke's eyes, for it is inimical to the sense of terror.[8] But this terror, though not a necessary implication of power, has just become Burke's figure for power; and the deeper thrust of Burke's rhetorical counter-argument is that our just idea of God, and especially our love of Him, is inimical to our sense of His power. "Knowledge and acquaintance make the most striking causes affect but little. It is thus with the vulgar, and all men are as the vulgar in what they do not understand" (p. 61). So Burke anticipates his theological dilemma with paradoxical ("knowledge" of "what they do not understand") aptness.

"The love of God" thus lays reverence open to fatal compromise. For love is condescending: "We love what submits to us" (p. 113). To call such a God "humanized," then, is—at least for Burke—after all to speak figuratively; and not just metaphorically, but euphemistically so. Elsewhere Burke is much more forthright about the status of power considered apart from terror: it is the status of dogs as opposed to wolves, of domesticated animals as opposed to beasts of prey, of the "social useful" as opposed to the "pernicious" and "unmanageable" (pp. 65–67), of the draft or plough horse as opposed to the horse of Job 39, *"whose neck is cloathed with thunder, the glory of whose nostrils is terrible, who swalloweth the ground with fierceness and rage"* (pp. 65, 66). Such humanizing is in reality taming; to contemplate God without terror is, for Burke, to tame and domesticate Him.

Perhaps even this metaphor is something of a screen for a darker one. Many of Burke's examples, it is worth noting, are allusively sexual. Often their sexual potency is traditional, or, in his mythical instances, implicit in their Jobean context: the lion, the tiger, the panther, the rhinoceros, the unicorn, the leviathan. The dog's sexual status and significance is as much as explicit: dogs are "the most social, affectionate, and amiable animals," but "though we caress dogs, we borrow from them an appellation of the most despicable kind, when we employ terms of reproach; and this appellation is the common mark of the last vileness and contempt in every language" (p. 67). And Burke's first and foremost pair of examples makes his implication especially clear: the ox and the bull are both figures of great strength, but "the idea of an ox is by no means grand," while "the idea of a bull is . . . great, and it has frequently a place in sublime descriptions" (p. 65). To humanize is to tame, but to tame is to make dogs of wolves and oxen of bulls—is to possess or castrate. "Love approaches much nearer to contempt than is commonly imagined" (p. 67); or proverbially (and the maxim preserves Burke's sexual implications), familiarity breeds contempt.

The sexual implications of Burke's theory of the sublime and the beautiful are by no means incidental, but, like the theological implications, break easily out of the limiting categorizations within which he proposes to contain them. Burke argues that the sexual passions "have their origin in gratifications and *pleasures,*" not in pain and danger, and so pertain not to the sublime but to the beautiful. Yet he immediately characterizes the sexual experience as "rapturous and violent" (p. 40), and by these very words effectively assimilates it to the sublime, which threatens "rapine and destruction" (p. 65). Quickly an implicit sexual model of brute, masculine tyranny and ingratiating female subservience begins to inform Burke's respective notions of the sublime and the beautiful:

> [W]e submit to what we admire, but we love what submits to us; in one case we are forced, in the other we are flattered into compliance. (p. 113)
> [P]leasure must be stolen, and not forced upon us; pleasure follows the will; and therefore we are generally affected with it by many things of a force greatly inferior to our own. But pain is always inflicted by a power in some way superior, because we never submit to pain willingly. (p. 65)
> Beauty in distress is much the most affecting beauty. (p. 110)

According to this sexual model, the sublime and the beautiful are complementary or reciprocal sides of a single, antagonistic relationship. The dominant member of this relationship, because he (figuratively this member is always male in Burke's inquiry) threatens pain, rapine, and destruction, will seem sublime, if perhaps ugly (p. 119), to the subjugated member, while she or it (this member is almost always either female or neutered), because she is weak (p. 116), compliant, and pleasing (pleasure-yielding), will seem beautiful to him, yet perhaps contemptible. Burke's association of sexual passion with the beautiful proves to be one-sidedly masculine: "its object is the beauty of women" (p. 51). It is only from this masculine viewpoint that love can be characterized by "complacency" (p. 149), and desire enjoy "that smooth and voluptuous satisfaction which the assured prospect of pleasure bestows" (p. 38).

Thomas Weiskel has written suggestively of the recapitulated Oedipus complex and the still deeper reaction formation underlying the sublime moment, and noted that "inevitably, for . . . Burke, the myth of the superego takes a theological form."[9] We find ourselves now approaching much the same conclusion, though from a very different set of evidence and models. We shall pursue some of the Freudian implications of this myth at a later time; for now, let us note simply that the "just idea" of God, against which Burke's rhetorical counterargument protects him, is the very inversion of this myth. Though a God whom we love, a God of power without terror, be posited to possess "a power in some way," figuratively physical, "superior" (p. 65), nevertheless in some other way, figuratively sexual, we have already shown ourselves to be His superior. If not our creation, yet surely He is thus our chattel; and our actions—our love and devotion—show that, somehow, we know it. Burke's "just idea" of God is inadequate not merely because its idea is not sublime, but because its God is not transcendent of us, but subordinate to us.

IV
Determined Metaphor and
the Rhetorical Structure of the Uncanny

Though we have considered Burke's difficulties with the idea of God, we have not yet exhausted his scheme for the sublime. Burke resists locating the theological sublime within the direct mode of terror, yet fails to fix it, as he would wish, within the indirect mode of things conversant about terror. But what of his third and final mode, that of things "operat[ing] in a manner analogous to terror"? If Burke has, after all, no room in his theory for the Christian God per Se, does he at least have room for the divine analogy?

It soon becomes apparent that Burke is using "analogous" rather loosely—much, as Coleridge would say, like calling a monkey's lungs analogous to a man's. What Burke actually has in mind for this third mode of the sublime, in fact, is unmistakably a determined metaphor. Since terror, the source of the sublime, "produc[es] an unnatural tension and certain violent emotions of the nerves; it easily follows . . . that whatever is fitted to produce such a tension, must be productive of a passion similar to terror, and consequently must be a source of the sublime, though it should have no idea of danger connected with it" (p. 134). Burke is far readier than Coleridge, moreover, to reverse one of the cause-effect metonymies of a determined metaphor to serve the requirements of his thesis. Witness his clinching anecdote about "the celebrated physiognomist Campanella":

> [T]his man, it seems, had not only made very accurate observations on human faces, but was very expert in mimicking such, as were any way remarkable. When he had a mind to penetrate into the inclination of

those he had to deal with, he composed his face, his gesture, and his whole body, as nearly as he could into the exact similitude of the person he intended to examine; and then carefully observed what turn of mind he seemed to acquire by this change. So that . . . he was able to enter into the dispositions and thoughts of people, as effectually as if he had been changed into the very men. (p. 133)

In this anecdote Campanella does not merely seek, like a Method actor, to discover what mood he need cultivate to recreate such an expression, but conversely mimics the expression to discover what mood it might produce. Thus here again, as in his other modes of the sublime, Burke's theory involves him in a confusion of cause and effect, and a clandestine literalizing of a determined metaphor.

We can already see Burke's Campanella anecdote pulling him toward the transcendent even as it does toward the sublime: in Campanella's "mind to penetrate" the minds of others, it is eerily "as if he had been changed into the very men.""Coleridge himself supposes such spiritual powers only in certain unusual dreams of sensitive individuals—not the ordinary "under-consciousness" of sleep in which "We dream *about* things," but states in which seemingly "we *dream the things themselves;* exact, minute, and vivid beyond all power of ordinary memory is the portraiture, so marvellously perfect is our brief metempsychosis into the very *being,* as it were, of the person who seems to address us." Such dreams, Coleridge continues, sometimes impress theologically naive men as "supernatural visitations"; sometimes, even, they seem to be "sublimed into foresight and presentiment," "possess[ing] a character of divination" (*SM,* pp. 80–81). These implications and intimations are equally apparent in Edgar Allan Poe's elaborate adaptation of the Campanella anecdote in "The Purloined Letter." Here Poe's detective, Auguste Dupin, tells of the eight-year-old schoolboy who was remarkably successful at the game of "even and odd," the object of which is to win marbles, one by one, by successfully guessing whether one's opponent is holding an even or odd number of them. This boy's "principle of guessing . . . lay in mere observation and admeasurement of the astuteness of his opponents." As he explains it,

"When I wish to find out how wise, or how stupid, or how good, or how wicked is any one, or what are his thoughts at the moment, I fashion the expression of my face, as accurately as possible, in accordance with the expression of his, and then wait to see what thoughts or sentiments arise in my mind or heart, as if to match or correspond with the expression."[10]

Thus Dupin's schoolboy shares Campanella's assumptions—and successes—in applying the determined metaphor of physiognomical and psychological identification with another.[11] Poe extends Burke and other earlier theorists of sympathy, though, by identifying the boy's opposite as his opponent, and stressing what is only latent in the earlier accounts, the competitiveness of the schoolboy's exercise of his skill. More clearly even than Campanella and Burke, Dupin and Poe emphasize the shrewdness of the empathic insight: the schoolboy continually triumphs at "even and odd" because he consistently outthinks his opponent.

The implications of this shift in emphasis become clearer if we oppose our viewpoint to Dupin's or Campanella's for the moment and instead consider the schoolboy's successes from the antagonistic perspective of his opponents, or Dupin's from the perspective of the workaday Prefect of Police. What those others may at first dismiss as luck will gradually provoke stronger and less confident emotions—admiration, astonishment, amazement—all of which, Burke tells us, are the effects and signs of the sublime (*Enquiry,* pp. 57–58, 113, 136). More precisely, here these emotions are responses to—and to defeat by—the uncanny. From Dupin's viewpoint, of course, he and the schoolboy are simply always cannier than their opposites, for canniness can recognize its own inferior degrees (cf. what Coleridge calls *"understand[ing] a writer's ignorance,"* as opposed to being *"ignorant of his understanding"* [*BL* 1:232]). From the opposing viewpoint, however, Dupin and the schoolboy are not merely cannier, but truly uncanny, *unheimlich.* "Incredulity," as Coleridge sagely observes, "is but Credulity seen from behind" (*SM,* p. 81).

Freud's conception and analysis of the uncanny as "something repressed which *recurs*" clearly accommodate the implications we are now considering:

> [I]f this is indeed the secret nature of the uncanny, we can understand why linguistic usage has extended *das Heimliche* into its opposite, *das Unheimliche;* for this uncanny is in reality nothing new or alien, but something which is familiar and old-established in the mind and which has become alienated from it only through the process of repression. This reference to the factor of repression enables us, furthermore, to understand Schelling's definition of the uncanny as some-

thing which ought to have remained hidden but has come to light.
("The 'Uncanny,'" *SE* 17:241)

In Poe's story, what is hidden but nevertheless comes to light is simply the parity of the hidden marbles, even or odd, which itself is but a sign of the opponent's hidden thoughts. The schoolboy's consistent, improbable discovery of what his opponent hides will increasingly seem to that opponent to be either telepathic or omniscient, and in either case uncanny.

Dupin's anecdote helps us further to appreciate that the uncanny is essentially not an isolable or absolute condition but a relative and reciprocal one, the superior antagonist but also the complement of the canny. This relation of canny to uncanny, moreover, is precisely that of the beautiful to the sublime—of love to fear, for example, and again of our just to our imaginative ideas of God—in Burke. The uncanny is uncanny because it is not merely preternatural, but preterlogical—because it successfully reasons, in despite of logic, through a literalization of determined metaphor.

Freud, too, insofar as he insists that *unheimlich* is not simply the opposite but also "in some way or other a sub-species of *heimlich*" (*SE* 17:226), initially encourages us to see *heimlich* and *unheimlich* as unequal complements of each other. Yet Poe goes further than Freud here in clarifying this insight as it pertains to relations between men; for Freud's comments on this matter, like Burke's on the relations between his two ideas of God, bespeak either blindness or obscurantism.[12] Just as Burke utilizes a rhetorical counterargument to disguise (perhaps even from himself) the illogic of his argument about the theological sublime, so Freud, through a similar blurring of cause and effect, works in "The 'Uncanny'" to obscure the relation of another's uncanniness to one's own inferior canniness. This vagueness is particularly striking in the most sustained of his essay's very few analyses of uncanniness in another (as opposed to uncanniness in coincidental events or in fictions):

> One of the most uncanny and wide-spread forms of superstition is the dread of the evil eye. . . . There never seems to have been any doubt about the source of this dread. Whoever possesses something that is at once valuable and fragile is afraid of other people's envy, in so far as he projects on to them the envy he would have felt in their place. A feeling like this betrays itself by a look even though it is not put into words;

and when a man is prominent owing to noticeable, and particularly owing to unattractive, attributes, other people are ready to believe that his envy is rising to a more than usual degree of intensity and that this intensity will convert it into effective action. What is feared is thus a secret [*geheime*] intention of doing harm, and certain signs are taken to mean that that intention has the necessary power at its command. (*SE* 17:240)

Whose is the betraying look here? This would seem at first to be identifiable with the feared evil eye, the gaze of the uncanny other— uncanny in that he sees what one would wish to keep hidden from him, the valued possession. But what the look in question here actually betrays, according to Freud's odd tangle of referents, is not envy but a projection of envy, a fear of the envy of the other; and this is the gaze of the original possessor, not of the other. Moreover, the fear born of the projection of envy may, it seems, itself be mistaken for envy; and thus cause and effect of the evil eye come to be reversed, and the evil eye becomes increasingly hard to distinguish from the eye that perceives it.[13] As "The Tell-Tale Heart" shows Poe well knew, not he who bears the putative evil eye, but he who so imputes it to the other, is the truly dangerous man. Yet the fear or envy that makes him dangerous (the narrator of "The Tell-Tale Heart" kills the evil-eyed old man) also makes him vulnerable (the narrator, like each of Dupin's schoolboy's opponents, "loses his marbles," goes mad[14]). Thus the uncanny member of one relationship may become the relatively less canny of another, for all uncanniness is relative: the narrator's police interrogators function like uncanny psychoanalysts, and once again that which ought to have been kept concealed—this time, the old man's dismembered corpse—comes to light.

V

As we have been finding over and over in the works of Coleridge, Burke, and Poe, the logical and the rhetorical implications of determined metaphor and of arguments structured by it work at cross-purposes. Logic teaches us to see the metaphor as arbitrary; rhetoric would have us feel it as persuasive. Coleridge affords a brilliant, succinct instance of this struggle when he reminds us explicitly in his *Logic* of the logical "inadequacy of every metaphor (*simile non est idem*, or as we say, no likeness goes on all fours)"—to which rhetoric's responsive and not merely rhetorical question might well be: no likeness, including this one? Logic insists that the metaphor is a figure, is rhetorical and illogical; rhetoric, on the defensive, will try to disguise (that is, figure) the trope as logical—or, on the offensive (as with Nietzsche), will argue in "return" that causation, the postulate of propositional logic, is itself but a rhetorical construct, a figure. There are sides to be taken in this contest, and consequently setbacks to be endured—but not, perhaps, victories to be won.

We seem to have seen Coleridge unhesitatingly take a side. In his later years, at least, he is first of all, and outspokenly, a Christian—a believer, an apologist, something of a dogmatist—and only subordinately a metaphysician and logician. Always a stimulating interpreter of the Bible, he is never a disinterested one. Thus he defends the determinedness of Johannine "analogy" and Pauline metaphor not, we must conclude, because they are logical, but because as sacred texts they are privileged: if logic cannot justify these tropes, then faith must.

Where faith could be set aside, however—where the rhetoric in question was not, to his mind, privileged—Coleridge was perfectly able to see and ready to contest the logical sophism inherent in determined metaphor. This becomes particularly evident in his critique of a fellow Christian philosopher, the mystic Jakob Boehme. Of Boehme's grand theory of nature's origin Coleridge acutely notes,

> Imagine a Poet intensely watching a Tree in a Storm of Wind, unconsciously imitating its motions with his body, and then transferring to the Tree those sensations and emotions that accompanied his own gestures: and then you may understand Behmen, and his mode of describing the acts of Nature by ante-dating the passions, of which yet those acts may be, perhaps, the nascent state and fluxional quantities. (*Marginalia* 1:612)

Boehme's interpretative method, then, like Campanella's and Burke's and Dupin's—and John's and Paul's—turns simply on a rhetorical reversal of cause and effect, a determined metaphor. Here, however, Coleridge clearly recognizes the sophistry of such an argument. He sees its sophism, moreover—"the confusion of the creaturely spirit . . . for deific energies in Deity itself"—as the fundamental and pervasive flaw of Boehme's entire pantheistic argument: Boehme "preposterizes [makes an after-event come first] the Consequent of the Fall into the absolute First . . ." (*Marginalia* 1:602). But this very "preposterousness," this "hysteron proteron of the Fancy" (*Mar-*

ginalia 1:647), is the essence of all determined metaphor. Thus the very method that Coleridge not only accepts but celebrates as a rhetorically heightened logic in Paul and John, he also rejects as a rhetorically disguised illogic in Boehme.

This inconsistency of Coleridge's interpretations seems indeed to show his faith at odds with his logic. Yet Coleridge himself would not have abided such a judgment; he insistently regarded deductive logic as a servant of faith, and was concerned to expose Boehme's illogic in order to reveal Boehme's unorthodoxy, his essential pantheism (*Marginalia* 1:556, 602). And how, after all, could faith wish to diverge from logic in the interpretation of determined metaphor? For to presume that one can thoroughly identify oneself with some other, as Dupin's schoolboy does—to presume, in effect, that one can be "uncanny" with respect to that other—suddenly constitutes egregious arrogance and heresy when that other is God. This was evident even to the empiricists Coleridge so strenuously criticizes for their theological reductiveness: as Locke notes, "This is to make our comprehension infinite, or God finite, when what He can do is limited to what we can conceive of it. If you do not understand the operations of your own finite mind, . . . do not deem it strange that you cannot comprehend the operations of that eternal infinite Mind" (*Essay* IV.x.19). Wherever Coleridge does draw back from such presumptuousness toward God, then, he is arguably being more pious than he is in his ostensibly devout theological assertions.

Where does Coleridge so draw back? During the last twenty-five years of his life, it is surprisingly accurate to answer simply, in his poetry. In his metaphysical and theological prose writings Coleridge typically, even compulsively, exceeds the limits of logic in his desire to affirm the tenets of his faith. He could joke about his own youthful mistranslation of *sermoni propiora* as "Properer for a Sermon" (*CL* 2:864; cf. *Marginalia* 2:353–54n), but almost all of his published metaphysical prose works are in effect lay sermons, rhetorical refusals to be frustrated by the "chasm" yawning, beyond the brink of logic, between "the things that are seen" and "the Idea of the Absolute One" (*Friend* 1:523n). In his poetry, however, Coleridge displays a much greater recognition of and respect for this chasm, and a logically honest hesitation before it.

The images expressing this barrier to transcendental inquiry will necessarily be tropes of uncertainty: Coleridge's are most frequently figurations of infinite regress, disorientation, and blankness. In his philosophical speculations, Coleridge introduces such figures only to dismiss them with ridicule. So in *Biographia Literaria,* for example, he exposes and laughs at the epistemological inadequacies of materialism:

> The formation of a copy is not solved by the mere pre-existence of an original; the copyist of Raphael's Transfiguration must repeat more or less perfectly the process of Raphael. It would be easy to explain a thought from the image on the retina, and that from the geometry of light, if this very light did not present the same difficulty. We might as rationally chant the Brahmin creed of the tortoise that supported the bear, that supported the elephant, that supported the world, to the tune of "This is the house that Jack built." (*BL* 1:137–38; see also *Logic,* p.169)

On what, though, does the tortoise stand? Coleridge insists on the logical absurdity of such innately regressive postulates.[15] Metaphysics, he argues, must have some first principle, some absolute ground:

> A chain without a staple, from which all the links derived their stability, or a series without a first, has been not inaptly allegorized, as a string of blind men, each holding the skirt of the man before him, reaching far out of sight, but all moving without the least deviation in one strait [sic] line. It would be naturally taken for granted, that there was a guide at the head of the file: what if it were answered, No! Sir, the men are without number, and infinite blindness supplies the place of sight? (*BL* 1:266; repeated with minor changes in *Logic,* p. 86).[16]

In his later poetry, however, Coleridge responds to such uncertainty quite differently, not insisting that it must be surmounted but recognizing that it cannot be.

"Coeli Enarrant," for example, alludes almost perversely to Psalm 19. There David affirms,

> The heavens declare the glory of God; and the firmament sheweth his handywork.
> Day unto day uttereth speech, and night unto night showeth knowledge.
> . . .
> The law of the Lord is perfect, converting the soul: the testimony of the Lord is sure, making wise the simple.

The statutes of the Lord are right, rejoicing the heart: the commandment of the Lord is pure, enlightening the eyes.

The fear of the Lord is clean, enduring for ever: the judgments of the Lord are true and righteous altogether.

. . .

Moreover by them is thy servant warned: and in keeping of them there is great reward.

[1–2, 7–9, 11]

In contrast to David's confident reading of the great book of the world, however, Coleridge can responsively read and exclaim nothing that is not there, and only the nothing that is:

The Stars that wont to start, as on a chase,
And twinkling insult on Heaven's darkened Face,
Like a conven'd Conspiracy of Spies
Wink at each other with confiding eyes,
Turn from the portent, all is blank on high,
No constellations alphabet the Sky—
The Heavens one large black Letter only shews,
And as a Child beneath its master's Blows
Shrills out at once its Task and its Affright,
The groaning world now learns to read aright,
And with its Voice of Voices cries out, O!

[CN 2:3107; cf. CPW 1:486]

Whatever heaven's secrets, they are not ours; its texts, to us, are indifferently ciphers or blanks.

In the early manuscript version of "Coeli Enarrant" Coleridge figures his "visual powers" blending with the world as "mirrors each reflecting each" (CN 2:3107). This image reappears in an 1811 letter, modified into an emblem of "Love, true human Love—i.e. two human hearts, like two correspondent concave mirrors, having a common focus, while each reflects and magnifies the other, and in the other itself, . . . an endless reduplication, by sweet Thoughts & Sympathies" (CL 3:303), and then recurs in Coleridge's early draft of what was to become "Work without Hope," where he speaks prefatorially of "hav[ing] often amused myself with the thought of a self-conscious Looking-glass, and the various metaphorical applications of such a fancy[17]—and this morning it struck across the Eolian Harp of my Brain that there was something pleasing and emblematic (of what I did not distinctly make out) in two such Looking-glasses fronting, each seeing the other in itself, and itself in the other" (*CL* 5:414). In the poem itself, cast as "a complaint of Jacob to Rachel as in the tenth year of his Service he saw in her or *fancied* that he saw Symptoms of Alienation," Coleridge (signing himself "JACOB HODIERNUS") laments that, as the world's walls daily pressed nearer,

> My faith (say I: I and my Faith are one)
> Hung, as a Mirror there! and face to face
> (For nothing else there was, between or near)
> One Sister Mirror hid the dreary Wall.
> But *That* is broke! And with that bright Compeer
> I lost my Object and my inmost All—
> Faith *in* the Faith of THE ALONE MOST DEAR.
>
> [*CL* 5:416]

Face to faith, eye to I—in this house of mirrors no perceived or reflected image, if there be an image, can be known as objective rather than subjective; the real cannot be distinguished from the virtual. Not only Coleridge's identification of his mirror-self with his faith, moreover, but also the exegetical tradition concerning Rachel (the *via contemplativa*) prompt not a narrowly personal but a metaphysical reading of these dark lines. Certainly Coleridge himself so applies the image soon afterward when he figures a world without a prior absolute as "a Universe of mere Relations without focuses, to which they refer—i.e. when the Looking-glasses are themselves only Reflections" (*Marginalia* 2:1019). Metaphysically, in his prose, he still rejects this as an "intolerable Position[ ]" (ibid.); but rhetorically, in his poetry, he increasingly identifies with it.[18]

In "Limbo," to cite a final example, Coleridge takes the meaningless signification of moonlight on a sundial as an image of "Human Time," then revises and compounds his figure into one of moonlight falling upon a blind old man who, by chance turning his face upward, "Gazes the orb with moon-like countenance" (*CPW* 1:430). The old man appears to cast "a steady look sublime" despite his blindness, and "His whole face seemeth to rejoice in light!" But all this is no more than seeming and lunacy, two mirrors and two blindnesses facing each other: "He seems to gaze at that which seems to gaze on him!"

Just as Coleridge privately casts "Work without Hope" as the utterance of a persona, Jacob, so he subsequently characterizes these

erance of a persona, Jacob, so he subsequently characterizes these lines of "Limbo" as a "pretended fragment" of the mad dramatist Nathaniel Lee, spoken while he was in Bedlam (*CL* 6:758). Given Coleridge's attitude toward Lee, however, this dramatic displacement cannot vitiate the blankness of the poem's vision, but only multiplies its explicit insistence on relative subjectivities and its implicit one on ignorance of absolutes. We should recall Coleridge's anecdote: " '*I* asserted that the world was mad,' exclaimed poor Lee, 'and the world said, that I was mad, and confound them, they outvoted me' " (*BL* 1:262).[19]

VI

We have seen that Coleridge's philosophy tries to present itself as a symbolic, synecdochic activity, while his later poetry by contrast acknowledges its own allegorical, metaphorical character. This is but to say in another way that Coleridge's later poetry tends to respect the logical limitations of its rhetoric, while his philosophy tends rather to push beyond logic on the strength of its rhetoric alone. In both these fields, we have been examining the logic (or illogic) of Coleridge's argument. But we have also found that this argument implies and correlates with a larger rhetorical structure, so that, as above, we can meaningfully characterize Coleridge's philosophy in rhetorical terms, as ostensibly symbolic but essentially metaphorical. I would now like to look further at these rhetorical structures of Coleridge's argument and at the rhetorical implications of his attempt to make rhetoric a vehicle for his metaphysical arguments.

When Coleridge says that the nature of symbols and symbolical expressions, such as John's, is "always *tau*tegorical (i.e. expressing the *same* subject but with a *difference*) in contra-distinction from metaphors and similitudes [such as Paul's], that are always *allegori*cal, (i.e. expressing a *different* subject but with a resemblance" (*AR*, p. 199/197), he is insisting that the difference between these two tropes is one not merely of degree but of kind. Their relation to each other, then, could itself only be metaphorical: whatever their degree of resemblance, they are different subjects. But as we have already seen, this is precisely the argument that Coleridge also makes about the distinctiveness of Reason from Understanding. Both arguments, moreover, are identically flawed. The difference between Johannine analogy and Pauline metaphor, as we saw in the preceding chapter, is after all one not of kind but of degree. Both, in fact, are types of meta-

ter. Thus the two tropes actually relate to each other synecdochically, while their relation, John's as well as Paul's, to the transcendent is only metaphorical. Similarly, it would now seem that Reason and Understanding differ only in degree from each other, while both differ in kind from the Supreme Reason (see above, section II). The same subversive pattern informs both Coleridge's theory of rhetoric and his metaphysical argument. It is perhaps only to be expected, then, that we should also find it in the famous *Biographia Literaria* passage on Imagination and Fancy; for we have already noted (Chapter 1, section VI) Coleridge's insistent association of fancy with metaphor and of imagination with synecdoche, while his extensions of these parallels to include understanding and reason, respectively, are similarly prominent and consistent in his work (cf. *SM*, pp. 28–30). Yet the rhetorical implications of the imagination/fancy account are more than usually interesting, for here Coleridge seems particularly sensitive to the threat they pose.

> The IMAGINATION then I consider either as primary, or secondary. The primary IMAGINATION I hold to be the living Power and prime Agent of all human Perception, and as a repetition in the finite mind of the eternal act of creation in the infinite I AM. The secondary I consider as an echo of the former, co-existing with the conscious will, yet still as identical with the primary in the *kind* of its agency, and differing only in *degree*, and in the *mode* of its operation. It dissolves, diffuses, dissipates, in order to recreate; or where this process is rendered impossible, yet still at all events it struggles to idealize and to unify. It is essentially *vital*, even as all objects (*as* objects) are essentially fixed and dead.
>
> FANCY, on the contrary, has no other counters to play with, but fixities and definites. The Fancy is indeed no other than a mode of Memory emancipated from the order of time and space; and blended with, and modified by the empirical phenomenon of the will, which we express by the word CHOICE. But equally with the ordinary memory it must receive all its materials ready made from the law of association. (*BL* 1:304–05)

As he would with analogy and metaphor in *Aids to Reflection* and with Reason and Understanding throughout his work, Coleridge suggests in *Biographia Literaria* that imagination and fancy differ fundamentally, differ in kind. The imagination itself, however, may be of two types, primary and secondary. The primary imagination is consciousness itself, "the living Power and prime Agent of all human Perception," while the secondary imagination is the "shaping and modifying power" (*BL* 1:293). As their shared name suggests, these two types are synecdochically related: the secondary imagination is "identical with the primary in the *kind* of its agency, and differ[s] only in *degree*, and in the *mode* of its operation."

Disturbing the tendency of these discriminations, however, are some curious intimations of a very different argument. The primary imagination, to begin with, is "a *repetition* [my emphasis] in the finite mind of the eternal act of creation in the infinite I AM." More strikingly still, the secondary imagination is "an *echo*" (my emphasis) of the primary—an abstraction, a reflection, a shadow, like all the arbitrary works of the fancy. Thus the secondary imagination relates not synedochically but metaphorically to its objects—and these are not only transcendent objects, but all objects of perception.

This secondary imagination, moreover, "dissolves, diffuses, dissipates, in order to recreate"; and while these decreating activities would seem to be the very antitheses of perception, they strongly evoke Coleridge's characterization of fancy as "emancipated from the order of time and space."[20] If fancy is, as Coleridge says, memory (which depends on perception) so emancipated, the secondary imagination may be similarly identified as perception so emancipated. And while we may regard perception as the paradigmatically symbolic condition, "partak[ing] of the Reality which it renders intelligible," whereas memory is paradigmatically metaphorical, a "phantom proxy," yet their "emancipat[ion] from the order of time and space" in which their objects exist makes both of them something new and strange, sets both at a metaphorical remove from us.

Thus the secondary imagination no less than the fancy is, after all, essentially a metaphorizing operation. Coleridge himself figuratively admits as much, despite the generally contrary assertions of his argument: the secondary imagination is an echo, and an echo of a repetition at that. We are very close here to the complexity of the *Statesman's Manual* discussion of allegory and symbol, where Coleridge disparages the "empty echoes" and mirrored reflections of allegory and contrastingly extols the satisfying fullness and reality of symbols, only to identify the stuff of this symbolic fullness and reality with two exemplary metaphors, the bread of life and the water of life. Like his celebration of symbol in *The Statesman's Manual*, Coleridge's celebration of the secondary imagination in *Biographia Lit-*

eraria is a celebration, despite itself, of metaphorization, of allegoresis.

VII

Early in the introduction of his *Logic*, Coleridge posits a remarkable theory of the intellect's development, which may well serve as a summary paradigm of rhetoric's relation to argument in his work. "Not only memory," he suggests,

> but even perception, beyond a very limited extent, is impossible otherwise than by the sense of likeness. And here again, we see the beneficent effects of that promiscuous presentation of objects, of which we have before spoken [Nature's "gay and motley chaos of facts, and forms, and thousandfold experiences"], and which, like a puzzle invented for the purpose of evoking the faculties, at once sustains and relieves the attention by the charms of novelty and continual change, and at the same time by a gentle compulsion solicits the mind to make for itself from the *like* effects of different objects on its own sensibility the links which it *then* seems to *find*, unconscious that both the form, and the light by which it is beheld, are of its own eradiation and but *reflected* from external nature. We may confidently affirm that this catenary curve of likeness is the line in which all the senses evolve themselves and commence their communion with the world, and their *purveyorship* for the understanding. (*Logic*, p. 11; the interpolated quotation is from p. 8)

A catenary (from *catena*, chain) curve is a precise mathematical term for the curve formed by a chain hanging from two fixed points. Alternatively and more obscurely, however, "catenary" can mean "related to a catena or series"; and though a catena can be simply a chain or string, it also has a specific theological meaning: "a string or series of extracts from the writings of the fathers, forming a commentary on some portion of scripture; also a chronological series of extracts to prove the existence of a continuous tradition on some point of doctrine" (*OED*).

Coleridge's image thus affords a brilliant, ambivalent figure—an allegory, of course, not a symbol—for his own puzzling and evocative work. Is the catenary curve of his speculations logical or only exegetical; is the "catenary curve of likeness" in the present passage a mathematical or a theological figure of speech?

Coleridge would claim that his catenaries are genuinely logical

constructions. The image of argument as a logical chain of many deductive links—Spinoza's "iron Chain of Logic" (*CL* 4:548), Kant's
"adamantine chain of . . . logic" (*BL* 1:153), "the Chain and Mechanism of Cause and Effect" (*AR*, p. 71n/63n)—is in fact a frequent one
in his work. The chain, of course, depends on its staple; the argument, on its first principle. Thus Coleridge finds that Spinoza's un-
breakable chain "falls of itself by dissolving the rock of Ice, to which
it is stapled," which the pantheistic Spinoza had "mistake[n] for a
rock of adamant" (*CL* 4:548), and scorns any infinitely regressive argument as "a chain without a staple" (*BL* 1:266; *Logic*, p. 86). But he
insists that God and the self-consciousness—God, from the standpoint of being; the self-consciousness, from the standpoint of
knowing—constitute such a staple for his own chain of argument—
"the fixt point, to which for *us* all is morticed and annexed" (*BL*
1:284).[21] Just so, in the *Logic* passage, his use of the phrase "catenary
curve" demands a figuratively mathematical interpretation. Given
the staple and the chain, this curve is deducible and inevitable; thus it
aptly images the course of logical, deductive argument.

On the other hand, with God as the first staple for his chain, Coleridge would certainly argue that his catenaries are theological figures, too. The two types of figures are thus compatible and indif-
ferent. But are they? Does a continuous tradition, like interpretation
linked to like, demonstrate a truth, or only a tradition of continuity?
Does the chain, because it reaches far out of sight, guarantee the staple? The argument suddenly becomes only inductive, and logic yields
to ignorance or faith—as Coleridge well knows: "link follows link
by necessary consequence; . . . Religion passes out of the ken of Reason only where the eye of Reason has reached its own Horizon; and
. . . Faith is then but its continuation" (*BL* 2:247). That it assumes
the guise of deductive argument ("follows . . . by necessary consequence"), a catenary calling itself a catenary curve, does not make it
such, and is but a device of its rhetoric—a metaphor. The catenary
that would present itself as a catenary curve thus becomes a figure for
the course of rhetorical argument.

Coleridge's own catenaries, curved though they usually are, are
not logical, but rhetorical; not mathematical, but theological. But if
his rhetoric subsumes and compromises yet it never suppresses his
logic. Impoliticly, honestly, as if with pangs of conscience, his argument repeatedly calls attention to its own figurativeness, even where
it strives most desperately for logical grounding: thus, in preparing

to discuss the senses as premises in all logical reasoning, Coleridge pauses to caution, "And yet a knot of uncommon difficulty meets us here at the very outset, of such difficulty indeed that, if the reader will excuse an apparent contradiction, resulting from the necessary inadequacy of every metaphor . . . , it must be first cut in order that it may afterwards be untied" (*Logic*, p. 132).

Here the knot, the cutting, and the untying are all alternatively logical and metaphorical (and all, at a further remove, allusive—to the Gordian knot).[22] It would seem that metaphor ties knots in logic that will yield to only metaphorical denouements, while logic, if not murdering to dissect, yet severs where it would wish only to unravel.[23]

And underlying and informing the rhetorical pattern of Coleridge's argument is the identical pattern of his theory of psychology and sensation itself. For Coleridge's catenary curve of likeness is again the curve of determined metaphor, linking different objects by way of their like effects: Nature, the supreme rhetorician, "solicits the mind to make for itself from the *like* effects of different objects on its own sensibility the links which it *then* seems to *find*."

Chapter 3

Argument

Shelley's Defense against Poetry and the Freudian Schema of the Psyche

I

Just as Coleridge regards religion as the poetry of mankind, so Shelley may be said to regard poetry as the religion of mankind. Shelley himself was well aware of the mirror-relationship (potentially, then, the metaphorical relationship) of his poetics to Coleridge's theology. As he noted in a draft of "A Philosophical View of Reform," "Religion may be called Poetry; though distorted from the beautiful simplicity of its truth—Coleridge has said that every poet was religious, the converse, that every religious man must be a poet was more true."[1] Many of Shelley's most striking and provocative aphorisms on poetry, moreover, simply particularize his general reversal of Coleridge's trope—his assertions, for example, that "Christianity, in its abstract purity, became the exoteric expression of the esoteric doctrines of the poetry and wisdom of antiquity"; "Poetry redeems from decay the visitations of the divinity in Man"; "Imagination is as the immortal God which should assume flesh for the redemption of mortal passion."[2] We should not be surprised, then, to discover Shelley's poetics and poetry reflecting the patterns of Coleridge's metaphysical rhetoric and argument. The figurative resemblance of Shelley's thought to Coleridge's warns us not to take too absolutely the ostensible differences of their credos.

But is this last sentence not an implicit privileging of rhetoric over argument? Can we reverse it—can we say instead that "The obvious differences of their credos warn us not to take too absolutely the figurative resemblance of their thought"—with equal, or greater, or any, validity? Shelley, reversing Coleridge as he does, affords an inviting opportunity for the experiment.

Coleridge's particular attention to the workings of rhetoric provides a convenient starting place for a consideration of rhetoric's relation to argument. While denying that his metaphysical argument is metaphorical, he yet gives us the rhetorical training to see that it is. In contrast Shelley, the logically more rigorous thinker, openly avows that his hypotheses are fundamentally metaphorical. But he has very little to say about metaphor itself; and how his own metaphors actually work is often an unusually difficult question. Just as Coleridge helps us appreciate how tropes relate to propositions, then, Shelley may well be able to help us appreciate how propositions conversely relate to tropes.

The general pattern of the preceding two chapters on Coleridge is a progressive consideration of, first, his rhetoric, then his (metaphysical) argument, and finally what I have termed the deeper rhetoric, the rhetorical implications, of his argument. With Shelley I propose to invert this pattern, progressing from his (poetical) argument to his rhetoric to, finally, the deeper argument of his rhetoric. I shall begin, then, with Shelley's fullest statement of his poetic theory, *A Defence of Poetry.*

II

"A poet participates in the eternal, the infinite, and the one. . . ." "A great poem is a fountain for ever overflowing with the waters of wisdom and delight," a "divine effluence." "Poetry thus makes immortal all that is best and most beautiful in the world. . . ." "A poem is the image of life expressed in its eternal truth" (*DP*, pp. 32, 63, 73, 35).

We are increasingly prepared nowadays to view Shelley as a sober and tough-minded skeptic; yet it is very possibly in such ringing, hierophantic affirmations as these that we most surely recognize his distinctive voice. Always, for Shelley, poetry aspires to the status of transcendental utterance. Granting that "the deep truth is imageless" (*PU* II.iv.116), he nevertheless celebrates poets for "draw[ing] into a certain propinquity with the beautiful and the true, that partial apprehension of the agencies of the invisible world which is called religion" (*DP*, p. 31).

How, though, does the poet—or critic—recognize this apprehension for what it is? There would seem to be one crucial sign: relation. The language of poets, thus, "is vitally metaphorical; that is, it marks the before unapprehended relations of things and perpetuates their apprehension" (p. 30). Yet such an answer, of course, merely begs the question. For what do the poet's metaphors relate? The relations of things to what? But here, we find, Shelley gives a dual answer, alternatively ontological and epistemological. On the one hand, what the poet marks is the relations of things to things, the world's "indestructible order" (p. 31), the "similitudes or relations . . . finely said by Lord Bacon to be 'the same footsteps of nature impressed upon the various subjects of the world' " (p. 30). In this sense the poet works to reveal universal essences, "unveil[ing] the permanent analogy of things by images which participate in the life of truth" (p. 35). In another sense, though, the poet's accomplishment is primarily epistemological, even as the relations he marks are phenomenological: "to be a poet is to apprehend the true and the beautiful, in a word, the good which exists in the relation, subsisting, first between existence and perception, and secondly between perception and expression" (p. 30). Thus Shelley clearly sees poetry as a field of both being and knowing, inasmuch as "thoughts have relation both between each other and towards that which they represent" (p. 33); and throughout the *Defence* he plays off these two perspectives against each other.

Ontology

We may well begin testing Shelley's ontological assumptions in the *Defence* by recurring to his admiring citation of Bacon's figure, "the same footsteps of nature impressed upon the various subjects of the world." Shelley tracks poetry by its footsteps several times in the *Defence,* alluding, for example, to poetry's voice as "heard, like the footsteps of Astraea" (p. 50), and marking the poetic "interpenetration of a diviner nature through our own" by its "footsteps . . . like those of a wind over a sea" (p. 72). But these last two figures make explicit what was already strongly implicit in the first, the *absence* of the very cause that the figure strives to locate and identify. For Astraea's footsteps signal that she is "departing from the world" (p. 50), while "the coming calm erases" the footprints of the wind over the sea (p. 72). Nature's or poetry's footprint, however longingly read as a sign of near-presence, can be but a sign of absence, "The path of its departure" ("Mutability," 14; cf. "Alastor," 270–71, 368).

The poet's defensive claim, as Shelley presents it, is to catch glimpses. If the visitations of divinity be evanescent, yet poetry "arrests the vanishing apparitions" (p. 73). Yet who or what is thus seen and revealed? "Poetry lifts the veil from the hidden beauty of the world" (p. 40), "it strips the veil of familiarity from the world, and lays bare the naked and sleeping beauty, which is the spirit of its forms" (p. 74); but is this sleeping beauty truly to be identified with our peripatetic quarry? We readers can in fact know it only as an "impersonation[ ]" (p. 40), the revealing, after all, of yet another hiding: "Veil after veil may be undrawn, and the inmost naked beauty of the meaning never exposed" (p. 63). What we perceive in poetry, then, must abide the epistemological question of how truly we perceive there.

Epistemology

We have already noted Shelley's statement that poetry develops through two sequential relations, "first between existence and perception, and secondly between perception and expression." In both stages of this transmission, it would seem, the poet is a uniquely suitable agent for truth. He "beholds intensely the present as it is, and discovers those laws according to which present things ought to be ordered" (p. 31), while his expressive medium, language, superior to all others in that it alone "has relation to thoughts alone" (p. 32), "is as a mirror which reflects . . . the light" it communicates (p. 32). Beneath the surfaces of these optimistic affirmations, however, Shelley sometimes indicates a darker, bottomless realm of skeptical suspension. What, first, of the relation between existence and perception? We can conclude only that "All things exist as they are perceived; at least in relation to the percipient" (p. 74). The relation thus is at once so tautological and so absolutely subjective as to be meaningless. "What wonder," then, as Shelley comments on the same observation in another essay, "if we grow dizzy to look down the dark abyss of how little we know" (*SP*, p. 174). The relation between perception and expression, moreover, would seem to be equally (though oppositely) subjective and unintelligible: for it is necessary, Shelley cautions, to "distinguish words from thoughts" (p. 55), and important to recognize that "language is *arbitrarily* produced by the imagination" (p. 32; my emphasis). As he insists again elsewhere, "Words are the instruments of mind, . . . but they are not mind, nor are they portions of mind" (*SP*, p. 185). Thus poetry, the purely arbitrary expression of purely subjective perception, can after all affirm no truth beyond itself. "How vain is it to think that words can penetrate the mystery of our being!" (*SP*, p. 172).

To the reader accustomed to hearing in Shelley's phrases a rhapsodic Ion rather than an ironic Socrates, this initial presentation of the *Defence* will doubtless seem excessively and reductively skeptical, especially as it refuses to privilege as transcendent the inspirations of the poet. But does Shelley himself ever so privilege them? The accommodating Aeolian lyre, which is the *Defence*'s first sustained figure for imaginative power, for example, can bespeak the wind, but knows nothing of the wind's origins or motives; the "corresponding antitype" (p. 27) of its music is not the wind, but the trembling of the lyre's own strings. The wind itself can be likened only to the "series of external and internal impressions" (p. 26) that constitutes our thoughts, and conveys no sublimer message than that of its own existence. The "indestructible order" that the poet imagines is no preexistent or transcendent scheme, then, but precisely—and only—the order of the imagination itself. The light that the mirror of language reflects (p. 32) is no radiance from beyond, but simply the creation of imagination itself—and out of itself, "its own light" (p. 25), as self-referential as it is self-creative. As Shelley says of its manifestation in ancient Rome,

> The true poetry of Rome lived in its institutions; for whatever of beautiful, true, and majestic, they contained, could have sprung only from the faculty which creates the order in which they consist. . . . The imagination beholding the beauty of this order, created it out of itself according to its own idea. . . . (p. 52)

"A poem is the image of life expressed in its eternal truth" (p. 35), but this ambiguously referential ("its") verity is not any truth of life but the truth of the *image*, "containing within itself the principle of its own integrity" (p. 25).

Such speculations are truly but grim food for thought. For if the imagination is so isolated and self-contained a power, then its expression, poetry, is but a whistling in the metaphysical dark. So be it. "A Poet is a nightingale, who sits in darkness and sings to cheer its own solitude with sweet sounds; his auditors are as men entranced by the melody of an unseen musician, who feel that they are moved and softened, yet know not whence or why" (p. 38). It is time for us to acknowledge the unsparing bleakness of such a picture.

III

Early in the *Defence* Shelley speaks of "the vanity of translation" as "the burthen of the curse of Babel" (pp. 33–34). His allusion here, coming as it does close upon his acknowledgment of the arbitrariness of language, would seem more largely relevant to the essay as a whole. For the men of Shinar too aspired to "those eternal regions" (p. 70) that are the poet's lure and bourne, and the frustrated Tower of Babel remains a monument to and type of the impossibility of that ascent—which is to say (and both Dante and Milton would already have suggested this to Shelley), a monument to and type of the fall itself. The attempt to create Babel—that is, Bab-El, "gate of God," a portal to the transcendent—ends miserably in Babel—that is, babble, the derisive, punitive gift of tongues. The burden of this curse is uncomfortably like the burden—the poetic refrain or theme—of Shelley's very *Defence*.

But poetry, Shelley seems eager to add, makes no part of the world's corruption. "It is not inasmuch as they were Poets, but inasmuch as they were not Poets," that men have been corrupt (p. 49); evil springs "from the extinction of the poetical principle" (p. 55), not from its operation. These conclusions follow naturally from Shelley's famous, central affirmation that "The great instrument of moral good is the imagination; and poetry administers to the effect by acting upon the cause" (p. 40). Yet even here, perhaps, Shelley impels us to consider more curiously. For if, as he also affirms, corruption "*begins* at the imagination and the intellect as at the core" (p. 50; my emphasis), then poetry more than anything else in life may be susceptible, even uniquely vulnerable, to the very sickness it strives to cure.

A hint of this dark characteristic of poetry appears early in the *Defence* in a passage usually taken to be entirely celebratory. "The story of particular facts is as a mirror which obscures and distorts that which should be beautiful: Poetry is a mirror which makes beautiful that which is distorted" (p. 36). Distorted by what? Not, despite the assumption of some critics, by story, which Shelley defines here as an antithesis rather than a component of poetry.[3] The distortion seems to proceed rather from imagination itself, which inevitably deforms in its reflections the thoughts or perceptions upon which it acts (p. 25).[4]

We are now poised, I think, to engage the very center of Shelley's defense, his insistence on the accidentality, the superficiality, of poetic error. "The distorted notions of invisible things which Dante and his rival Milton have idealized," he claims, "are merely the mask and the mantle in which these great poets walk through eternity enveloped and disguised" (p. 59). Poetry's imperfection lies in the "thin disguise of circumstance" (p. 45)—distracting, perhaps, but extrinsic. For

> a poet considers the vices of his contemporaries as the temporary dress
> in which his creations must be arrayed, and which cover without concealing the eternal proportions of their beauty. An epic or dramatic
> personage is understood to wear them around his soul, as he may the
> antient armour or the modern uniform around his body; whilst it is
> easy to conceive a dress more graceful than either. The beauty of the
> internal nature cannot be so far concealed by its accidental vesture,
> but that the spirit of its form shall communicate itself to the very disguise, and indicate the shape it hides from the manner in which it is
> worn. A majestic form and graceful motions will express themselves
> through the most barbarous and tasteless costume. (p. 39)

But is the costume, after all, separable from or extraneous to the essence? Despite all Shelley's talk of "the inmost naked beauty," he
hedges significantly on this point. It is noteworthy, in the passage just
quoted, that he speaks of conceiving "a dress more graceful," not an
underlying nakedness. And though he hastens to suggest that a poetry of absolute unveiling, however rare, can yet exist, he immediately calls even this suggestion into question: "Few poets of the
highest class have chosen to exhibit the beauty of their conceptions in
its naked truth and splendour; and it is doubtful whether the alloy of
costume, habit, & c., be not necessary to temper this planetary music
for mortal ears" (p. 39).

As we have seen, there are two veilings at issue here, an ontological and an epistemological. Like poetry itself, the personages of poetry are dressed in the circumstances of their existence, but dressed
also in words. Shelley quietly admits in his *Defence* that poetry is
necessarily a veiling in language, but he seeks to deny that it must
also be a veiling in circumstance: "A Poet therefore would do ill to
embody his own conceptions of right or wrong, which are usually
those of his place and time, in his poetical creations, which participate in neither" (p. 41). This position explicitly evokes and repeats
that of the Preface to *The Cenci,* where Shelley acknowledges it his
business "to clothe [the story] to the apprehensions of my countrymen in such language and action as would bring it home to their
hearts," but seeks "to avoid the error of making [the characters] actuated by my own conceptions of right or wrong, false or true, thus

under a thin veil converting names and actions of the sixteenth century into cold impersonations of my own mind" (*SPP*, pp. 239–40). Yet characters will necessarily be "actuated" by *something*—if not by their author's conceptions, then by some other's, or their own. And while the Cencis' motivating conception, sixteenth-century Italian Catholicism, is to Shelley's mind "not, as in Protestant countries, a cloak to be worn on particular days," yet even as something instead "interwoven with the whole fabric of life" it works to reveal life itself as but another layer of clothing (*SPP*, pp. 240–41). And precisely this is, for Shelley, ultimately the lesson of Beatrice Cenci herself: "The crimes and miseries in which she was an actor and a sufferer are as the mask and the mantle in which circumstances clothed her for her impersonation on the scene of the world" (*SPP*, p. 242). The mask and the mantle are not merely the costumes of "the distorted notions of invisible things" in which such poets as Dante and Milton envelop their creations, then, but the very garb and matter of being. Not merely all characters but all persons are impersonations; for men no less than for poetry, to be is to be disguised.

In all ways, then, poetry is not only inextricably but inherently self-implicated in a cover-up. Its veiling, moreover, is always a distorting: in terms of Shelley's other primary images, the mirror is flawed, the lyre defective or untuned. This is most interestingly apparent, perhaps, in the paradigmatic case of tragic drama, "poetry in its most perfect and universal form" (*DP*, p. 45). For however insistently Shelley would characterize the poetic power as harmonious and harmonizing, he is yet driven to acknowledge "an inexplicable defect of harmony in the constitution of human nature," whereby

> the pain of the inferior is frequently connected with the pleasures of the superior portions of our being. Sorrow, terror, anguish, despair itself, are often the chosen expressions of an approximation to the highest good. Our sympathy in tragic fiction depends on this principle; tragedy delights by affording a shadow of the pleasure which exists in pain. (p. 66)

Similarly, if we pursue the implications of Shelley's suggestion that "The drama, so long as it continues to express poetry, is as a prismatic and many-sided mirror" (p. 46), we can again recognize poetry's refractory distortedness or coloring as the innate *hamartia* of the imagination. This last quotation, it is worth noting, darkly and powerfully evokes a crucial passage in *Prometheus Unbound* wherein the

Spirit of the Earth is describing the revival of the world and mankind upon the coming of the new, Promethean age:

> Hate and Fear and Pain, light-vanquished shadows, fleeing,
>
> Leave Man, who was a many-sided mirror
> Which could distort to many a shape of error
> This true fair world of things—a Sea reflecting Love;
> Which over all his kind, as the Sun's Heaven
> Gliding o'er Ocean, smooth, serene and even,
> Darting from starry depths radiance and light, doth move. . . .
>
> [IV.381–87]

Shelley's allusion to this passage from *Prometheus Unbound* suggests that undistorted mirroring is incompatible with the surface-distorting winds of the very emotions that the *Defence* finds essential to tragedy and inherent in life.

To be is indeed to be disguised; for custom is costume, and life, by its very nature, is habit-forming. Shelley clearly intends the puns on "costume" and "habit," as he indicates when he associates "the temporary dress" of "costume, habit, & c." (p. 39) with "the veil of familiarity" (p. 74; cf. p. 40) as the vesture of naked truth. But we may well be taken aback to find this inevitable garb implicitly identified as inevitable viciousness, and "the alloy of costume, habit, & c." euphemistically substituted, by way of the intermediary "barbarous and tasteless costume," for "the *vices* of [one's] contemporaries" (my emphasis). It is one thing to suggest, as I began by doing, that beneath Shelley's idealistic affirmation lies a depth of skepticism, which throws all affirmation into abeyance; several critics have observed as much in recent years, and Shelley himself acknowledges it more than once.[5] It is quite another, though, to find that such affirmation in the face of skepticism is not merely tentative but dangerous, not merely a placebo but a poison. Yet such, I think, is the deeper drift of Shelley's argument. Not only will transcendental assurances, as Shelley's deeper skepticism teaches, be baffled; they will also—which skepticism by itself does not and cannot teach—be corrupted.

IV

As the skeptic's certain bafflement constitutes Shelley's constant undersong throughout the first half of his *Defence of Poetry,* so does the poet's certain corruption, already intimated in his talk of poetry's distortings, throughout the second half. To a degree, Shelley fore-stalls our recognition of this closing theme by celebrating "the energy and magnificence" of Milton's Satan, whose career prototypically presents just such a progress through bafflement and corruption, while dismissing Satan's evils as the venialities of a slave (p. 60). Per-haps it is then but slightly disturbing to find Shelley identifying his own epistemology with Satan's (*Paradise Lost* I.254–55): "All things exist as they are perceived; at least in relation to the percipient. 'The mind is its own place, and of itself can make a Heaven of Hell, a Hell of Heaven' " (p. 74). But such allowances make it all the more discon-certing shortly afterwards to hear Shelley, as he momentarily plays devil's advocate against the poets he would defend, again quoting the devil's own speech (cf. *Paradise Lost* IV.829): "Let us for a moment stoop to the arbitration of popular breath, and . . . let us without trial, testimony, or form, determine that certain motives of those who are 'there sitting where we dare not soar' are reprehensible" (pp. 75–76).

There are terrible ironies already implicit in Satan's own position: now fallen, he scornfully—but uselessly—boasts to unfallen angels of his earlier, unfallen eminence. These ironies are compounded by Shelley's substitution here of *we* for Milton's *ye*, for Satan's position is now both identified with the boorish multitude's and divorced from the poet's.[6] But more devastating still is Shelley's proleptic un-dercutting of Satan's position in an earlier allusion to the same speech: what were the value of life, "if Poetry did not ascend to bring light and fire from those eternal regions where the owl-winged fac-ulty of calculation dare not ever soar?" (p. 70). Taken together, these passages powerfully suggest that poetry's position, no less than Sa-tan's, is seriously compromised. If to be Satan is to be poetic, nev-ertheless it is also to be fallen irredeemably from poetry.

Satan is by no means Shelley's only self-refuting poetic model, or even his most damning. The ambivalence of his role in the *Defence* can prompt, for example, a new look at even so seemingly secure a figure as Dante—"the Lucifer," as Shelley calls him, "of that starry flock which in the thirteenth century shone forth from republican Italy, as from a heaven, into the darkness of the benighted world" (pp. 62–63). The ominousness of the epithet, Shelley's apologists to the contrary notwithstanding, is unmistakable. We must remember, too, that a starlit world remains a benighted one. And for Shelley to preface this sentence by calling Dante "the first awakener of entranced Europe" (p. 62) only thickens the ambiguity; for does he awaken Europe *from* a trance, or *into* one? Our memory of an earlier figure in the *Defence,* the benighted nightingale-poet whose "auditors are as men entranced by the melody" (p. 38), prevents too facile or optimistic an answer. And while Shelley also celebrates Dante's "apotheosis of Beatrice in Paradise, and the gradations of his own love and her loveliness" as "the most glorious imagination of modern poetry" (p. 58), it is from neither Paradise nor Beatrice nor Dante's purified love, but their antitheses, that Shelley appropriates a Dantean text to the ostensibly greater glory of poetry:

> The freedom of women produced the poetry of sexual love. Love became a religion, the idols of whose worship were ever present. . . . The familiar appearance and proceedings of life became wonderful and heavenly; and a paradise was created as out of the wrecks of Eden. And as this creation itself is poetry, so its creators were poets; and language was the instrument of their art: "Galeotto fù il libro, e chi lo scrisse." (p. 57)

The book was a Galeotto, a pander, as was he who wrote it. Whether deliberate subversion or devastating misprision, Shelley's perverse use of Francesca's infernal, incestuous confession (*Inferno* V) presents poets as not legislators but panders, and poetry as creation firmly in the service of corruption.

This unexpected, antithetical judgment finds equally chilling confirmation, moreover, in the course of Shelley's call to his contemporaries for a new cultivation of poetry:

> There is no want of knowledge respecting what is wisest and best in morals, government, and political economy, or at least, what is wiser and better than what men now practice and endure. But we let "*I dare not* wait upon *I would,* like the poor cat i' the adage." We want the creative faculty to imagine that which we know; we want the generous impulse to act that which we imagine; we want the poetry of life. . . . (pp. 68–69)

Once again, the quoted words of a persuasive tempter or temptress—here, Lady Macbeth (I.vii.44–45)—allusively expose the imagination's impulses, in direct and dramatic opposition to Shelley's pretended message, as not generous but selfish, not vital but deadly. To let "I dare not" wait upon "I would" is, in its original context, to *hesitate* to kill Duncan; Macbeth, despite his wife's scornful taunts, is not less (a "poor cat") but more of a man so long as he refrains from the deed: "I dare do all that may become a man, / Who dares do more is none." Shelley would advocate "the creative faculty," "the generous impulse"; but these are to be identified, after all, with "the milk of human kindness" (that is, humankindness), not with the "spirits" of the imagination—intoxicating, selfish, poisonous—which Lady Macbeth proffers in its place.[7]

Beneath Shelley's sustainedly enthusiastic defense of poetry, then, beneath or beside even the quieter but more fundamental skepticism that defends against the excesses of this vatic enthusiasm, there runs a sustainedly pervasive attack, an ultimate counterplot, against all these defensive assumptions.[8] Even while Shelley's skepticism is undercutting his transcendental affirmations, it is itself being sapped by a deeper pioneer. If *The Four Ages of Poetry* displays Peacock as the devil's advocate, *A Defence of Poetry* complementarily presents Shelley as the devil's fifth column.

V

But why should this be so? Even granting that poetry's transcendent claims as Shelley advances them must be unfounded, by what doom must they also be corrosive?

Shelley's skepticism and his pessimism work in different ways. His skepticism, more prominent than but no different from Coleridge's, marks the necessary hesitation of logic at the brink of the unknowable; as in Coleridge, the tension between Shelley's transcendent affirmation and his skeptical reserve is a tension between rhetoric and logic. The deeper, nihilistic pessimism implicit in Shelley's essay, however, has no real parallel in Coleridge. Nor, clearly, has it any logical force; for if logic cannot confirm our pleasing notions of the transcendent, neither can it confirm our dismaying ones.

We can readily see that whereas Shelley's skeptical counterargument in the *Defence* is logical, his implicit, pessimistic thesis (poetry is corruptive), like his explicit, optimistic one (poetry is redemptive), is merely rhetorical, figurative. Just how its rhetoric works is a subject I shall defer to the next chapter. At present I would simply note that Shelley's pessimistic thesis here remains a figurative one; and to our question of why corruption should be the poet's doom his *Defence* offers only a figurative response. There would seem to be two interrelated scenarios for this fall. First, one may be not merely baffled, but deceived, by the disguises he everywhere perceives. Alternatively, one may in the first place be watching the wrong performance, or, like a magician's misdirected audience, be attending to the wrong part of it.

Deception

To be, to be disguised, is not merely to be veiled; disguise does not merely obscure an identity, but misrepresents it. However much Shelley would suggest that poetry's distortions are not *too* distorting, that the internal nature will after all express itself through its accidental vesture, his own admissions of oxymoron—of "the delight which is in the grief of love" (p. 57), "the pleasure which exists in pain" (p. 66)—confuse and vitiate his claims. Just as behind a veil there may hang another veil, moreover—"Veil after veil may be undrawn, and the inmost naked beauty of the meaning never exposed"—may not a disguise lie beneath a disguise? In such circumstances Shelley's poet renders himself, by virtue of his very assumption of superior perspicuity, particularly liable to misprision.

Hence, for example, the ultimate blindness of Shelley's own final attempt to defend the poet from the charge of moral blindness. More than most men, he argues, the poet is sensitive to pain and pleasure and eager to avoid the one and pursue the other. He exposes himself to calumny, Shelley adds, "when he neglects to observe the circumstances under which these objects of universal pursuit and flight have disguised themselves in one another's garments" (p. 77). The appearances of the world, this is to say, may be very effective and misleading disguises indeed, and even the poet may well be deceived by them—a telling enough concession, given the premises of Shelley's defense. Yet behind this seeming display of weakness Shelley is on a second level affirming a stronger defense; for his words here evoke his prior observation that "Sorrow, terror, anguish, despair itself, are often the chosen expressions of an approximation to the highest good" (p. 66). Thus the poet, himself undeceived, may simply be presenting such superficial deceptions with heuristic intent, not failing to perceive but only neglecting to proclaim and thus destroy the disguise. Educing pain or pleasure in his works through the figurative disguise of its opposite, he becomes liable to (unjustified) "calumnies against poetry and poets" (p. 76) just insofar as his readers or auditors fail to attend more than superficially to his words. At a deeper level still, however, Shelley's defense suggests despite itself that even the poet's disguised insights will themselves be vulnerable to a deeper decep-

tion. For those "circumstances" under which pain and pleasure mas-
querade in each other's garments are themselves, Shelley has already
reminded us, another layer of disguise, the very "disguise of circumstance" itself (p. 45). The circumstances of disguises are themselves
disguises. Disguise always lies behind disguise, forever ready to
mock the poet's claim of recognition.

Misdirection

"Neither the eye nor the mind can see itself," Shelley asserts in the
course of his meditation upon drama, "unless reflected upon that
which it resembles" (p. 46). The awkwardness of his phrasing—why
not say simply "unless imitated in that which it resembles" or even
"unless by reflection"?—calls attention to his claim. Can the eye then
see itself only as reflected in another eye? Does a mirror resemble an
eye? How does the eye or the mind recognize something else as re-
sembling it, unless it knows what it looks like in the first place? The
drama, Shelley says, resembles a mirror; but what kind of self-
recognition does it afford? In it at best "the spectator beholds himself, under a thin disguise of circumstance, stript of all but that ideal
perfection and energy which every one feels to be the internal type of
all that he loves, admires, and would become" (p. 45). What he admittedly beholds, then—stripped and then disguised and, beneath it
all, idealized—is not his self, but a type of his hope and ambition for
self. Far from "teach[ing] . . . self-knowledge" (p. 46) as Shelley
claims, such imaging, so long as it is thought to be a mirroring, will
make self-knowledge impossible. Here, perhaps, lies the root of at
least the poet's (if not all mankind's) error: a mistaken notion of what
he resembles, or of what reflects him.

Perhaps, moreover, the poet mistakes even the sources of his
power. "[T]he mind in creation is as a fading coal, which some invisible influence, like an inconstant wind, awakens to transitory brightness" (p. 71); but thus to celebrate the wind that figures the poet's inspiration is correspondingly to scant the inimitable fire that figures
his power and origin. Do the poet's inspirations, then, distract him
from a greater, ultimate enlightenment? The implication, as we have
already seen, is disturbingly present just before this in the allusively
satanic insinuation that to be poetic is also to be fallen irredeemably
from poetry. And Shelley strengthens this implication in his next
paragraph with the assertion that poetry records "as it were the interpenetration of a diviner nature through our own; but its footsteps are

like those of a wind over a sea, which the coming calm erases, and whose traces remain only, as on the wrinkled sand which paves it" (p. 72). This conjoined reference to "the interpenetration of a diviner nature through our own" and imagery of a wind-stirred sea soothed by a succeeding calm unmistakably evoke a passage from Act IV of *Prometheus Unbound* which we have already had cause to remember (above, section III), Earth's joyous description of the world's renewal. "It [Love] interpenetrates my granite mass," Earth sings, so that "Man, who was a many-sided mirror / Which could distort to many a shape of error / This true fair world of things" is transformed by Love's arrival into "a Sea reflecting Love," "smooth, serene and even" (IV.382–86). But this Promethean context exposes the poet's original error. The coming calm that Shelley regrets as an erasure of a divine signature is actually something quite the opposite, a renewing or smoothing of the faulty mirror in which heaven may only then be truly reflected. Correspondingly, in attending to the evanescent footsteps of the wind and to their traces on the sea-bottom, the Earth's song suggests, the poet is in fact celebrating precisely those events and signs that are antagonistic to the sea's reflection of heaven. The wind of inspiration destroys the sea's mirroring of heaven's enlightenment. Poetry is antagonistic to its own greatest aims.

To Shelley's way of thinking, *Paradise Lost* "contains within itself a philosophical refutation of that system, of which, by a strange and natural antithesis, it has been a chief popular support" (p. 60). The judgment is equally applicable, I have been arguing, to his own *Defence of Poetry*. Far from defending poetry, Shelley's essay covertly, subversively undermines all of poetry's defenses. Yet—and the perverseness of this increasingly seems to be not Shelley's but poetry's— by virtue of this very subversiveness it proclaims all the more forcefully its own kinship with Milton's epic, and implicitly with all great poetry.[9]

VI

This antithetical, even parodic subversiveness of argument in Shelley's *Defence* is that feature which, more than any other, sharply distinguishes his transcendental inquiries from Coleridge's. Their differences of relative skepticism and faith are matters of proportion only. Coleridge, the fideist, nevertheless shows symptoms of genuine skep-

ticism in his later poetry, as we have seen, and even in the lay sermons
of his prose admits the inevitability and propriety of such doubt:

> [W]hether the Knowing of the Mind has its correlative in the Being of
> Nature, doubts may be felt. Never to have felt them, would indeed be-
> tray an unconscious belief, which traced to its extreme roots will be
> seen grounded in a latent disbelief. How should it not be so? if to con-
> quer these doubts . . . be the purpose, the means, and the end of our
> probation. . . . (*Friend* 1:512; cf. *AR*, pp. 101/96, 152/148)

Likewise Shelley, the skeptic, nevertheless repeatedly "express[es]
various degrees of assent to [affirmative] propositions regarding ultimate reality,"[10] so that he has often been read as a kind of Neoplato-
nist. But where Coleridge perceives only a struggle of true faith with
the various incompetencies of doubt and error, Bab-El versus babble,
Shelley additionally intimates a third position, Babylon, a damna-
tion opposing all attempted affirmations of redemption. To use the
Christian terminology they both so often adopted, Shelley, in a way
Coleridge never does, takes Hell seriously.

Why, though, does subversiveness make a part of Shelley's field of
argument but not of Coleridge's? Perhaps we may more readily begin
to explore the nature and implications of this question by examining
it in the sublime *topos* that poses it most explicitly, that of the transcendental quester halted at the abyssal brink of the unknowable.
This figurative situation, already present in Coleridge's sense of the
"chasm" separating the phenomenal from the noumenal (*Friend*
1:523n), is equally familiar to Shelley: "We are on that verge where
words abandon us, and what wonder if we grow dizzy to look down
the dark abyss of how little we know" (*SP*, p. 174). Poised now on
that verge, we may pause to isolate and identify the tendencies we
seek to understand.

Burke, surprisingly and significantly, has almost nothing to say
about this archetypal *topos* of the sublime—merely, "I am apt to
imagine . . . that height is less grand than depth; and that we are
more struck at looking down from a precipice, than at looking up at
an object of equal height, but of that I am not very positive" (*Enquiry*, p. 72). His strange silence here, I would suggest, has much to
do with the rare potential for ambivalent reaction that a precipice affords. For Burke can imagine only one possible course of action by
the individual at the brink, a sane holding on and keeping back. As he
says in summarizing his major argument,

The passions which belong to self-preservation, turn on pain and danger; they are simply painful when their causes immediately affect us; they are delightful when we have an idea of pain and danger, without being actually in such circumstances; this delight I have not called pleasure, because it turns on pain, and because it is different enough from any idea of positive pleasure. Whatever excites this delight, I call *sublime. (Enquiry,* p. 51)

But the individual poised upon a precipice, unlike the one looking up from below, is not certainly but only volitionally free from the circumstances of pain and danger. He could, if he wished, react otherwise. While Burke in his *Enquiry* does not acknowledge an alternative, others certainly do. Thus William Drummond, the skeptical empiricist who so greatly influenced Shelley, argued on the question of moral versus physical causality,

> *A man at the top of St.Paul's,* says Doctor Price, *will not jump down; but a man at the bottom cannot jump up.* This illustration avails nothing. We are just as certain, that a man cannot resist the strongest motive, as we are, that he cannot overcome a physical impossibility. If the love of life had been the prevailing motive in the mind of Empedocles, he could no more have leaped of his own accord into the center of Aetna, than he could have flown over its summit.[11]

This obvious incompleteness in Burke's scheme of the sublime correlates directly with the self-contradictoriness we have already seen in his notions of God. The cliff, like our emotional idea of God, is fearsome; yet our very terror, oxymoronically a sobering passion, works to make us behave reasonably—that is, with our own self-preservation in mind—in the presence of such danger. So long as reason thus masters passion, Empedocles will never jump. Burke predicates his entire thesis, moreover, upon the pious or rational assumption that ultimately reason does indeed master passion: hence his assertion that he himself is providing "a consideraton of the *rationale* of our passions" as a partial means to his end, "the elevation of the mind" (*Enquiry,* p. 53; my emphasis).

Burke does not mean, of course, that man always behaves rationally. On the contrary, he demurs, "I should imagine, that the influence of reason in producing our passions is nothing near so extensive as it is commonly believed" (p. 45). He does acknowledge in passing, then, the unreasonable possibilities of madness (pp. 41, 74) and "self-murder" (p. 135). And repeatedly he founds the sublime upon the precedence of passion over reason—arising "antecedent to any reasoning, by an instinct that works us to its own purposes, without our concurrence" (p. 46). At the sublime moment, "the mind is so entirely filled with its object, that it cannot entertain any other, nor by consequence reason on that object which employs it. Hence arises the great power of the sublime, that far from being produced by them, it anticipates our reasonings, and hurries us on by an irresistible force" (p. 57). Beneath these concessions to passion, however, lies an assumption that these very departures from reason occur in the service of a higher reason, the wisdom of God:

> The more accurately we search into the human mind, the stronger traces we every where find of his wisdom who made it. If a discourse on the use of the parts of the body may be considered as an hymn to the Creator; the use of the passions, which are the organs of the mind, cannot be barren of praise to him, nor unproductive to ourselves of that noble and uncommon union of science and admiration, which a contemplation of the works of infinite wisdom alone can afford to a rational mind. . . . (p. 52)

The passionate imagination, then, "anticipates our reasonings" in a dual sense, not only anteceding and preempting them but conducting our minds to reason's proper destination more quickly than reason alone could take us there.

Yet even as Burke is insisting most forcefully on this ultimate supremacy of reason, he betrays with a quick glance his suppressed awareness of the alternative he is determined to deny.

> Whenever the wisdom of our Creator intended that we should be affected with any thing, he did not confide the execution of his design to the languid and precarious operation of our reason; but he endued it with powers and properties that prevent the understanding, and even the will, which seizing upon the senses and imagination, captivate the soul before the understanding is ready either to join with them *or to oppose them.* (p. 107; my emphasis)

Burke's closing words here allow a new, discordant element into his argument. Can the sublime force ever impel imaginings or actions that the understanding, even upon consideration, would oppose? Here again, as with the correlative case of the imagination's opposition to Burke's "just idea of God," we find the imagination seizing power not as the reason's harbinger or regent but as its antagonist. As Burke notes in an architectural context shortly afterwards, there are allurements of beauty that "will make the imagination *revolt* against the reason" (p. 109; my emphasis). Despite his uneasiness at the idea, there would seem, by his admission, to be such unreasonable allurements of sublimity, too.

Years later, when his attendance on the "great drama" of the French Revolution playing on the stage of events had so ominously broadened his experience of the fearful and terrible, Burke finally, reluctantly admits the missing element into his scheme of the sublime. He still insists—especially for the English—that "[nature's] unerring and powerful instincts . . . fortify the fallible and feeble contrivances of our reason" (*RRF*, p.39); thus the shocking spectacles of the French Revolution are so affecting, he says, because "in those natural feelings we learn great lessons; because in events like these *our passions instruct our reason.* . . . We are alarmed into reflection; our minds . . . are purified by terror and pity, our weak, unthinking pride is humbled under the dispensations of a mysterious wisdom" (*RRF*, p. 91; my emphasis). But his very admission of the reason's "fallible and feeble" condition evinces his new awareness of how precarious is her perch. As events in France had proved, most if not all men potentially harbor the "spirit of fanaticism" (*RRF*, p. 177); in all, the passions of revolution may "break prison to burst like a *Levanter*, to sweep the earth with their hurricane and to break up the fountains of the great deep to overwhelm us" (*RRF*, pp. 66–67). Though the more stolid English, with their "sullen resistance to innovation" and "cold sluggishness of [their] national character," remain generally unaffected by the French madness—as "thousands of great cattle, reposed beneath the shadow of the British oak, chew the cud and are silent" (*RRF*, p. 97)—yet the contagion nonetheless most certainly threatens; for the English, too, the great no less than the poor, range "the wild and unbounded regions of imagination" (*RRF*, p. 116).

And now Burke must finally admit, though he will never approve, that the attractions of the sublime extend not only toward reason and self-preservation. Fittingly, Empedocles is his paradigm:

> Men have no right to what is not reasonable and to what is not for
> their benefit; for though a pleasant writer said, *Liceat perire poetis,*
> when one of them, in cold blood, is said to have leaped into the flames
> of a volcanic revolution, *Ardentem frigidus Aetnam insiluit,* I consider

such a frolic rather as an unjustifiable poetiç license than as one of the franchises of Parnassus. . . . (*RRF,* p. 71)

"To perish may be permitted to poets": the poetic license may be licentious. The self-indulgent poet, like the revolutionary fomenter, becomes for Burke a type of the imagination's self-destructive turn against reason.

Shelley, by the evidence of his *Defence,* has some experience with the imagination's antagonism to "the understanding, and even the will." He knows, and from his gothic juvenalia through "Alastor" to "Adonais" declares, that one can be "lured . . . to the brink" ("Adonais," 423). At the end of his life, he finds that he has approached it himself: "I stand, as it were, upon a precipice, which I have ascended with great, and cannot descend without *greater,* peril, and I am content if the heaven above me is calm for the passing moment" (*SL* 2:436)[12] And his awareness that sometimes a man "longs—although he fears—to die" and "pants to reach what yet he seems to fly, / Dull life's extremest goal" (*SPW,* p. 841), correlates with the belatedly supplied piece of the psychological scheme informing Burke's aesthetic. That scheme, we are now ready to see, comprises a matrix of the possible responses of the self to the (divine, natural, or human) other.

Two parameters demarcate the psychology implicit in Burke's *Enquiry* and *Reflections:* first, one's relative power over (or powerlessness before) the other, and second, one's sympathy for (or antipathy toward) the other. Setting aside the static, equilibristic cases of parity of power and indifference of regard, we find here a four-part scheme involving two intersecting dualities of dynamic relationship— though at first Burke willingly recognizes only three of the four psychological situations his theory entails.

Burke does, to begin with, consider that the other will be either more or less powerful than oneself. When the other is less powerful, so that one is not terrified but terrifying, one's relational experience may according to Burke range from contempt to pleasure, love, and the beautiful: one may (and may wish to) idolize or dissect (*Enquiry,* p. 108), love or disdain, mate or castrate—according, apparently, to the predominantly sympathetic or destructive tendencies of one's nature. If the other is more powerful, however, Burke argues, one is necessarily in a position of danger, and so naturally in a state of terror. One may then experience pain or, alternatively, delight and the sublime; but this depends entirely on the event, for one is motivated by a passion for self-preservation throughout.

This last premise, however, experience no less than art repeatedly denies: sometimes an Empedocles will jump, sometimes the flames of volcanic revolution will entice. The imagination can, as even Burke darkly suspects, sometimes revolt against the reason. One's response to the superior as to the inferior other, then, can be urged by either of two very different drives. If delight, as Burke insists, is "the sensation which accompanies the removal of pain or danger" (*Enquiry*, p. 37), nevertheless there is also, as the iconography of swoons and self-sacrifice suggests, a quite contrary emotion, a fierce delight of horror, a desire to yield to the threat that confronts us.

We find in this completed Romantic scheme, then, not only similar dualisms of response to superior and inferior powers, but also fundamentally identical passions informing these dualities—on the one hand a conservative desire that the weaker power (whether that be oneself or the other) be spared from pain or destruction, on the other hand an aggressive desire that the weaker be dominated or destroyed. We might easily label the four categories of this psychological matrix according to these four possible desires, as follows:

| | | Desire | |
		Conservative	Destructive
Relative Power of the Other	More Powerful	Self-Preservation	Self-Destruction
	Less Powerful	Preservation of the Other	Destruction of the Other

With "preservation of the other" are to be associated what Burke classifies as the passions that belong to society, originating in gratification and pleasures: love, lust, sympathy, imitation, ambition. The antipathetic desires for "destruction of the other" include the "murder to dissect" impulse of the anatomist (*Enquiry*, p. 108) and the "contempt . . . attendant on a strength that is subservient and innoxious" (p. 66), a contempt that prompts such subjugating acts as castration, rape, domestication, and enslavement.

VII

Burke's psychological scheme clarifies a categorical difference between Coleridge's transcendental argument and Shelley's: Coleridge's is ultimately conservative and self-preserving, Shelley's ultimately self-destructive. These categorizations in themselves still, of course, do not explain why the two poets' arguments should so diverge. But certainly the issue is at least potentially a psychological one; and one kind of sophisticated psychological answer is, I think, already implicit in Burke's apparently simple scheme.

The particular virtue of Burke's psychological matrix comes from its careful distinction of situations wherein the other is relatively more or relatively less powerful than the self. Thus organized, his matrix affords a strikingly compatible precedent and context for certain central elements of Freudian theory—specifically, of Freud's later metapsychology.[13] There is most obviously, to begin with, the close consistency of Burke's conservative versus destructive desires here with Freud's life instincts versus death instincts, respectively. The conservative urges Burke notes—of self-preservation, love, and reproduction—are precisely those Freud in his final theory includes within the life instincts, as are the destructive urges—of self-destruction, hatred, and aggression—within the death instincts. In their categorization of human desires, at least, there exists between the early Burke and the late Freud a strong congruence and sympathy.

If we consider the other parameter of our Burkean matrix, however, we find, if much that is again highly evocative of the late Freud, yet also much that is strangely dissonant from him. We may readily perceive the nature and source of this tension between the two theories simply by translating the four categories of Burke's matrix into their obvious Freudian counterparts, thus:

ego-love	masochism
object-love	sadism

What have we really changed here? Very simply, we have redefined the occasioner of desire. In Burke, we distinguished between a more powerful and a less powerful other; in the present Freudian redaction, however, we are distinguishing instead between the self and the other. The Romantic notion of the potential instinctive responses to a more powerful other seems directly translatable into the late Freud's notion of potential instinctive responses to the self.[14]

We are accustomed nowadays (and quite rightly) to regard Freud as a precursor of structuralism, while we find in Burke all the trappings of painstaking discrimination and categorization that characterize the more stultifying taxonomic tendencies of the eighteenth century. Yet now we are tending at a deeper level to blur these discriminations. For there is something fundamentally relational and structuralist about Burke's analysis, in that he sees the occasioner of desire not as an entity but as itself a relationship, a power-relationship. And conversely there is something initially substantive about Freud's, with its discrete compartmentalizations of self and other. The relational quality of Freud's later psychology becomes apparent and important to him only gradually (we may recall, for example, his initial insensitivity to or deemphasis of the purely relative status of the uncanny [see above, chapter 2, section IV]). Yet this quality is already, we find, a fundamental feature of the Romantic psychology that anticipates his.

Our comparison of Burke's and Freud's schemes does suggest one apparent incompatibility between them. Freud is quite specific about the purely assimilative tendency of the life instinct or Eros and the contrastingly dissimilative tendency of the death instinct or instinct of destruction. Associating them with the two fundamental principles of Empedocles, he declares that the former "endeavours to combine what exists into ever greater unities, while the second endeavours to dissolve those combinations and to destroy the structures to which they have given rise" ("Analysis Terminable and Interminable," *SE* 23:246; cf. *An Outline of Psycho-Analysis, SE* 23:148). But while Burke and Shelley also find these characteristics in one's potential responses to a less powerful other, yet they find just the opposite tendencies when the other is more powerful. In such a situation, to their minds, the self-preservative, life instinct serves as a kind of defense against agglomeration or fusion, with its consequent loss of identity or life, while the perverse, self-destructive urge expresses a contrary attraction, a desire for just such a merging with the other: "No more let Life divide what Death can join together" ("Adonais," 477).

The divergence at this point of Freud's scheme from Burke's seems clear-cut. Yet we cannot, after all, fairly cite this as an incompatibility of theories, for Freud himself is aware of and deeply interested in the presence of just such a divergence within his own theory. Despite the apparent straightforwardness of his neo-Empedoclean classifications, he recognizes important cases wherein an attraction is also an impulse to self-sacrifice. What Freud calls the "Nirvana principle," the pleasure principle "entirely in the service of the death instincts" ("The Economic Problem of Masochism," *SE* 19:160), is certainly such a case. By Nirvana Freud denotes a state of "the extinction of the tensions of instinctual needs" (*An Outline of Psycho-Analysis, SE* 23:198). But that this fatal tendency is also an attraction toward a merging seems inescapably implied by the word "Nirvana" itself, with its additional suggestion of selfless—self-sacrificing—fusion into the collective soul. Such implications soon become explicit, moreover, in Freud's evolving notion of the ego-ideal and of the objects, the Others, which can step into its place: the idealized beloved, the hypnotist, the primal father or group leader (*Group Psychology and the Analysis of the Ego, SE* 18:112–16, 125–27). In all these relationships, "the ego becomes more and more unassuming and modest, and the object more and more sublime and precious, until at last it gets possession of the entire self-love of the ego, whose self-sacrifice thus follows as a natural consequence" (*SE* 18:113); in all, the principle of attraction serves not the life but the death instinct.

What we are in fact beginning to find here is that latent within the simplistic Freudian matrix we initially sketched there lies, not simply a repetition of Burke's matrix, but also various extensions—or, more accurately, internalizations—of that matrix. Not only does Freud ultimately agree with Burke's scheme of potential psychological relationships with a less or more powerful Other, but he further suggests that the scheme remains valid with reference not only to an external Other, but even to an internal one—that is, to another agency (the superego, the id) of the psyche.

But if Freud, after all, accepts and includes the psychological scheme present in Burke, what then are we to make of his explicit divergence from that scheme—his reversal of its association of assimilation with self-destruction and of dissimilation with self-preservation? Here we confront one of the crucial, fundamental ambiguities or contradictions of Freud's theory—a crux indeed.

We have already seen that Freud's identification of Eros with assimilation causes him certain problems; for assimilation sometimes seems to be instead the task of the antithetical death instinct. Acknowledging such evidence, and responding more immediately to the apparent interchangeableness of love and hate, Freud finds that he can save his theory of the two fundamentally distinct classes of instincts only by assuming the existence in the mind of a displaceable, neutral energy that can be added to either an erotic or a destructive impulse. He further infers that this displaceable and neutral energy "is desexualized Eros," "is employed in the service of the pleasure principle," and "would still retain the main purpose of Eros—that of uniting and binding—in so far as it helps towards establishing the unity, or tendency to unity, which is particularly characteristic of the ego" (*The Ego and the Id, SE* 19:44–45).

Clearly Freud has still not solved his problem here: how, for example, can he maintain simultaneously that this displaceable energy is neutral and that it nevertheless retains its drive to unite and bind? Yet in this formulation he does bring us very close to recognizing what is the truly fundamental issue in question. Freud himself later— at the very end of his career—speaks of this as the question of "the still unassessed relations between the pleasure principle and the two primal forces, Eros and the death instinct" (*An Outline of Psycho-Analysis, SE* 23:198). Derrida poses it with blunt purity: "What is the difference between a principle and a drive?"[15]

We already have at hand, I think, the materials with which to begin framing an answer to Freud's question—which is, we must remember, a question not of identities but of relationships. Freud himself may seem to be offering a unifying perspective on both drives and principles insofar as he variously discusses both in terms of binding; but his usage proves to be ambivalent and inconsistent, allowing him, for example, to characterize sexuality at one time as an unbinding, at another as a binding force.[16] Let us avoid such equivocations here, and resolve such ambiguities, by speaking simply of *binding* versus *bounding*. A binding process comprises tendencies to merge, with either a stronger (which engulfs one) or a weaker (which one engulfs); a bounding process, on the other hand, comprises tendencies to maintain separation—either to preserve one's own separateness (and so one's identity) or to impose separateness on another. And in these terms, at last, we can discover consistent characterizations for Freud's two fundamental principles. The pleasure principle—whether serving the death instinct, as in "Nirvana,"[17] or the life instinct, as in object-love—corresponds to the binding process; the reality principle—whether serving the death instinct, as in sadism, or the life instinct, as in self-preservation—corresponds to the bounding process. We may thus elaborate and explicate our psychological schema in a way that demonstrates Burke's and Freud's fundamental consistency with each other:

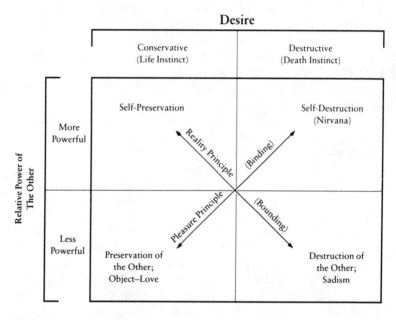

How do the principles relate to the drives? In a word, chiastically.[18]

VIII

These inquiries into Freudian metapsychology do not merely give us a fresh sense of Freud's fundamental Romanticism, but importantly clarify the psychological issues at stake, and the propositions at hand, in all transcendental inquiry. We are ready now to argue, for example, that a poetry attempting to move beyond immanent, demonstrable propositions to urge transcendent ones must choose between divergent psychological pathways. Thus Shelley's *Defence* maintains its adherence to the pleasure principle, even though this principle, as it carries him toward the transcendent, changes its allegiance from the life to the death instincts. Coleridge's poetry and theology, in contrast, their differences from each other notwithstanding, maintain their allegiance to the life drive, even though to do so they must, as they approach the transcendent, find support not from the pleasure principle but from the reality principle. Shelley's ultimate transcendental gesture is toward self-destruction; Coleridge's, toward self-preservation.

Beyond these psychological translations of earlier insights, moreover, our metapsychological model can give us a much surer sense of what kinds of rhetorical strategies to expect from each major branch of transcendental inquiry.

The stimulus to Freud's speculations on the death instinct, and hence to the formulation of his late metapsychology, was the strong and perplexing evidence of the compulsion to repeat. Freud found himself obliged to regard many instances of the repetition compulsion as existing "beyond the pleasure principle." At times he seems willing to associate the repetition compulsion with the death instinct (*SE* 18:14, 44); but his increasing recognition that the pleasure principle itself can serve the death instinct forces him to reconsider, and in chapter 6 of *Beyond the Pleasure Principle* he recasts his notion of the life instinct (via Plato's Aristophanic myth of the origin of the sexes) to enable it, too, to accommodate "the characteristic of a compulsion to repeat" (18:56). In this final formulation it is thus often the *life* instinct that the repetition compulsion serves. The compulsion to repeat is sometimes—perhaps really it is always—not an expression of but a *defense* against the death instinct.[19] That which had led Freud to suspect the existence of the death instinct proves to be something not necessarily deathly at all, but potentially vital.

Repetition of an unpleasurable experience will serve the life instincts insofar as it attempts to master an actual or potential threat to life; and any Other more powerful than oneself constitutes such a threat.[20] There is thus a natural correlation between the repetition compulsion and the uncanny, so much so that "whatever reminds us of this inner 'compulsion to repeat' is perceived as uncanny" (*SE* 17:238). As Freud notes in his 1909 "Analysis of a Phobia in a Five-

Year-Old Boy," "a thing which has not been understood inevitably reappears; like an unlaid ghost, it cannot rest until the mystery has been solved and the spell broken" (*SE* 10:122).[21] More accurately, such a thing, such a threat, cannot be allowed to rest; so long as it is a mystery to the self, it is a mastery over the self. The repetition compulsion here marks the desire for self-preservation. A similar situation obtains in psychoanalytical treatment whenever "an alliance [is] made between the treatment and the compulsion to repeat, an alliance which is directed in the first instance against the pleasure principle but of which the ultimate purpose is the establishment of the dominion of the reality principle" ("Remarks on the Theory and Practice of Dream-Interpretation," *SE* 19:118).

We do not need Lacan's suggestion that symptoms are metaphors[22] to recognize here, in the repetition compulsion's support of the reality principle in the service of the life instinct, a prescription for multiple metaphoricity. Coleridge has already taught us to recognize reflections, echoes, shadows, and all such instances of repetition as paradigms of metaphor. Freud's psychological model encourages us to anticipate further, though, that when the self confronting the transcendent maintains its allegiance to the life drive with the support of the reality principle, as Coleridge does, the result will be not merely repetition but compulsive, repeated repetition—or again, not merely metaphorization but multiple metaphorization, whether metaphor succeeding metaphor or metaphor metaleptically compounding metaphor.

And so in fact it is with Coleridge. We have already seen how images of extended repetition and reflection—facing mirrors, infinite regresses—inform his later poetry. But the repetitive activity that is his subject there becomes the very essence of his later prose. Anyone who reads at all widely in Coleridge's writings will be struck by the seemingly compulsive repetitiveness of his meditations on a few central notions—preeminently reason and understanding, subject and object, and the thesis-antithesis-synthesis triad (sometimes with prothesis and mesothesis thrown in for good measure). It is just this compulsive repetitiveness that makes Carlyle's portrait of the Sage of Highgate's pontifications on "om-m-mject" and "sum-m-mject" so very telling.[23] Voyaging endlessly and irresolutely through what Carlyle styled "the high seas of theosophic philosophy," he becomes at last a striking antitype of his own daemonic, autobiographically proleptic Ancient Mariner, continually compelled to repeat his narrative; and if such behavior seems to mark him as Life-in-Death's, whose creature he now is, yet it defends him from the alternative fate of being Death's.[24]

The other psychological pathway of transcendental aspiration, wherein the pleasure principle remains dominant but enters the service of the death instinct, will necessarily command—or obey—a somewhat different rhetorical strategy. Repetitions, metaphors, will still be possible here, but not potentially endless repetitions; instead there must come some kind of a death to the continuum, whether by contradiction or dwindling, by negation or entropy. We are ready to see now something of how this rhetorical suicide declares itself in the poetry of Shelley.

Chapter 4

Rhetoric and
the Argument of Rhetoric

The Mistakes and Atonement
of Shelley's Gloomy Passion

I

Rhetorical suicide? The very phrase is an ambivalence showing rhetoric to be very much alive. Are we speaking now of a figurative suicide, or a suicide of figuration?

It is in fact surprisingly difficult to imagine what the death, much less the suicide, of rhetoric might be. Silence? Perhaps; but surely this is overkill, an obliteration not merely of rhetoric but of all language and communication—as is the alternative of noise, the colorless all-color of unassimilable communicative excess. And cannot even silence (the pregnant pause, the musical rest) be a trope? Literalness, transparency, clarity? So Harold Bloom suggests, when he argues that "from the standpoint of poetry, *literal meaning is a kind of death. Defenses can be said to trope against death, rather in the same sense that tropes can be said to defend against literal meaning. . . .*"[1] But such a condition as this literalness does not, after all, seem possible. Bloom himself knows that "Tropes . . . are *necessary* errors about language" (p. 94; my emphasis), and so repeats Barthes' recognition that there can be no "zero degree" of writing, for "clarity is a purely rhetorical attribute, not a quality of language in general."[2] As Todorov summarizes, "The contrary of the figure, transparency—the invisibility of language—exists only as a limit . . . , a limit which it is necessary to conceive but which we must not attempt to grasp in the pure state."[3] However much we may wish to believe that rhetoric, like a dome of many-colored glass, stains the white radiance of pure expression, we ultimately find instead that to fragment the dome is inevitably to put out the light, and further that the colors also inhere in and even constitute the light itself.

Our first concern with Shelley's poetry now, though, is not how he there argues the question of rhetoric, but how he raises it. The poems are, of course, rife with what we might uncertainly regard, at least in our more skeptical moods, as rhetorical questions: "O Stream! / Whose source is inaccessibly profound, / Whither do thy mysterious waters tend? / Thou imagest my life"; "What was that curse?"; "O Wind, / If Winter comes, can Spring be far behind?"; "Who art thou?"; "Then, what is Life?" Not a few of these, I would suggest, are indeed also questionings of rhetoric. But nowhere in Shelley, I think, is rhetoric more questioning, questioned, and questionable than in "Mont Blanc." Vexed though its verses are, and partly because they are, I would like to adduce especially the first two sections of this poem as a paradigm of Shelleyan rhetoric.

II

Admittedly "Mont Blanc" is a difficult poem—not only abstruse, but full of syntactical and grammatical cruxes and ambiguities that make, it is often argued, no very meaningful contribution to the work. Surely, though, Shelley's interpreters have made this poem seem even more difficult than it really is, burdening it with extraneous metaphysical assumptions that it neither invites nor admits. If my own reading of the poem seems novel, my defense shall be simply that this reading is both internally coherent, which I have not found other readings of "Mont Blanc" to be, and consistent with Shelley's speculations elsewhere in his poetry and prose.

Crucial to an understanding of "Mont Blanc" is the poem's opening section, a complex, extended metaphor complete in eleven lines. Here Shelley establishes the fundamental set of correspondences that informs the entire poem, and here he has always been casually misread. To read him well, we must first be prepared to see that the poem absolutely, explicitly (thus the "Thus" opening the second section) insists upon the mutual consistency of the metaphor of section I and the scene of section II. As Judith Chernaik properly observes, the poem's second section "illustrate[s] point for point the metaphor of Section I."[4] "The everlasting universe of things / Flows through the mind" as a river flows through its valley—specifically, as the Arve flows through its ravine: all of "Mont Blanc" proceeds from this basic figure.

Once we grant Shelley this extended metaphor, we are committed to accepting the specific identifications it entails. In particular, we cannot blink away Shelley's explicit reading of the Ravine he addresses:

> when I gaze on thee
> I seem as in a trance sublime and strange
> To muse on my own separate phantasy,
> My own, my human mind. . . .
>
> [34–37]

The ravine, Shelley's image for the mind, he now takes specifically as imaging his own mind. What seems the natural and likely meaning of "mind" in section 1 is here quite clearly confirmed: the ravine images the individual human mind. It cannot be taken, then, as it so often improperly is, to refer instead to "the One Mind" or "the Universal Mind,"[5] for such a reading would be not merely superfluous but inconsistent with Shelley's scheme. Yet this "universal mind" reading of the Ravine of Arve does not arise unprovoked. For Shelley's opening metaphor presents not only a mighty river flowing through a valley, but also a modest tributary stream, "a feeble brook" (7), there "where from secret springs / The source of human thought its tribute brings / Of waters . . ." (4–6). Would not this tributary seem to figure the individual mind?[6] And so the Ravine of Arve must figure some greater, encompassing mind. This interpretation, once launched, seems quite plausible—at least until it bumps up against lines 34–37. But actually there are problems with such a reading from the very beginning—the inconsistency, to begin with, of seeing mind on one level (the One Mind) as a valley but on another level (the individual mind) as a stream. Yet what better sense can we make of Shelley's imagery here?

It will help us now, I would suggest, to remember that, according to Shelley's philosophical beliefs, his opening statement that "The everlasting universe of things / Flows through the mind" is something of a tautology. As he several times asserts in his prose, "Nothing exists but as it is perceived" (*SP*, p. 174; cf. p. 173; *DP*, p.74); accordingly, "A catalogue of all the thoughts of the mind and of all their possible modifications is a cyclopaedic history of the Universe" (*SP*, p. 182). Following from this skeptical principle, "The difference is merely nominal between those two classes of thought which are vulgarly distinguished by the names of ideas and of external objects" (*SP*, p. 174); and further, "By the word *things* is to be understood any object of thought—that is, any thought upon which any other thought is employed with an apprehension of distinction" (*SP*, p. 174). Thus what flows through the mind is the everlasting universe of thoughts.[7] Most of these, in the terms of Shelley's imagery, flow down from the "secret throne" (17) of the Arve's primary, glacier-hidden source; some of them, however, come from that secondary, tributary "source of human thought." Both sources contribute water to the Arve, thoughts to the mind; as far as the river of the mind is concerned, the difference between these two kinds of water or thought is, indeed, merely nominal. And this, too, is quite consistent with Shelley's imagery: he is taking care to distinguish not discrete kinds of water, but different sources. He makes precisely the same distinction, we should note, in the *Defence* when he describes man as "an instrument over which a series of *external and internal* impressions are driven, like the alternations of an ever-changing wind over an Aeolian lyre" (p. 26; my emphasis).[8]

This distinction of sources, rather than of resultant classes of thoughts or "influencings" (38), also characterizes Shelley's skeptical forebears. Thus Locke, though he denies the existence of innate ideas per se, does recognize two sources of ideas, which he even calls "the *fountains* of knowledge": sensation (perception of external things, conveyed by the senses), which is the "great source of most of the ideas we have," and reflection, or "internal sense," "that notice which the mind takes of its own operations, and the manner of them" (*Essay* II.i.2–4; my emphasis). The mind's operations, moreover, proceed "from powers intrinsical and proper to itself" (II.i.24). Since its original operations, in Locke's view, must be upon sensations, reflection is itself at once innate yet secondary, for it depends upon extrinsic perceptions for its initial impetus or occasion. Similarly, Locke argues that the mind has innate powers to combine, relate, and abstract already received ideas to create new, "complex ideas":

> [A]s the mind is wholly passive in the reception of all its simple ideas, so it exerts several acts of its own, whereby out of its simple ideas, as the materials and foundations of the rest, the others are framed. . . . [W]hen it has once got these simple ideas, it is not confined barely to observation, and what offers itself from without; it can, by its own power, put together those ideas it has, and make new complex ones, which it never received so united. (*Essay* II.xii.1–2)

Here again, the mind's active power is both innate and secondary. Thus Shelley is being absolutely true to Locke's theory in attributing the continuous flow of ideas through the mind to two sources, a primary source in the external world as perceived by the senses and a tributary, secondary source, contributing to the primary flow "with a sound but half its own" (6), in the mind itself, "The source of *human* thought."

A similar epistemological model is also available in Shelley's more immediate philosophical mentor, David Hume. Thus Hume argues, much as does Locke, that "all the materials of thinking are derived either from our outward or inward sentiment; the mixture and composition of these belongs alone to the mind and will";[9] and again,

> Thus the distinct boundaries and offices of *reason* and of *taste* are easily ascertained. . . . The one discovers objects, as they really stand in nature, without addition or diminution: the other has a productive faculty, and gilding or staining all natural objects with the colours, borrowed from internal sentiment, raises, in a manner, a new creation.[10]

Not only in its suggestion of what constitutes the universe, then, but also in its discrimination and characterization of that thought-universe's primary and secondary sources, the first section of "Mont Blanc," far from evoking an idealistic "one mind," gives a remarkably careful exposition of contemporary skeptical and empirical epistemology.

"The understanding, like the eye," Locke notes, "whilst it makes us see and perceive all other things, takes no notice of itself; and it requires art and pains to set it at a distance and make it its own object" (*Essay* "Introduction"). But when that epistemological object also perceives or reflects, careful exposition will inevitably be "dizzying" and "tumultuous" (*SP*, p. 186). Such giddiness waits menacingly everywhere in the sober Locke: for example, "When the mind turns its view inward upon itself, and contemplates its own actions, *thinking* is the first that occurs" (*Essay* II.xix.1). Shelley at least recognizes and plays with his dilemma even as he provokes it. Imagining, as he is, the Ravine of Arve as a figure of his own mind, he persists in exploring this figure for, and accommodating it to, his very act of imagining; and as he thus extends and compounds his contemplations, he decisively leaves behind the static landscape allegories of an earlier age.

Shelley's figurative locus for this figuring is "the still cave of the witch Poesy" (44), a cavern in the Ravine. As he pushes his speculations and his metaphor into this cave, he is now not merely imagining his mind, but imagining his mind imagining. And this figured imagining, we are perhaps not surprised to find, is itself self-reflexive,

Seeking among the shadows that pass by,
Ghosts of all things that are, some shade of thee,
Some phantom, some faint image. . . .[11]

[45–47]

"All things that are" refers to the opening "universe of things" (1), as Shelley now reaffirms by repeating the phrase in line 40. This flowing universe of things—that is, of ideas—comprises the "influencings" that the mind "renders and receives" (38), the "legion of wild thoughts" (41). What pass through the cave are "shadows" and "ghosts"; Shelley is now figuratively alluding, I take it, to *reflections* of the water upon the sides of the cave, even as argumentatively he is reminding us that the mind has no knowledge or experience of things, but only of *perceptions* of things.[12] And in these shadows and ghosts Shelley imagines himself as seeking "some shade of *thee*," of the Ravine—that is, of his own mind. He is trying to discover some image for the mind within the flux of sensation. But is this not what he had been doing in the first place by taking the Ravine of Arve as an image of his mind? Only now, as he pursues his quest, he is, we might say, imagining imagining imagining; and so his objective continues to recede, in a potentially infinite regress.

Thus we find the opening sections of "Mont Blanc" developing toward an elaborate, thoughtful *mise en abîme*. But what is the effect of this rhetorical strategy? In truth such figuration seems ambivalent, at once conservative and entropic, suggesting as it does both a stable continuum but also an ineluctable dwindling and fading away. Customarily the *mise en abîme* structure has conveyed a bewildering disorientation ("Dizzy Ravine!") to critics. "[A]s to an infinite retrogression," Coleridge muses, "it is identical with the Reason determining to abandon its own essence, & commit an act of suicide" (*CN* 3:4047). But Jacques Derrida experientially demurs: "I distrust the confidence that [the *mise en abîme*], at bottom, inspires, and I find it too representational to go far enough, not to *avoid* the very thing into which it pretends to plunge us."[13] And Shelley in fact neither yields to the seductiveness of this abyss structure nor relies on it for his most unsettling effects. For the very perception of the infinite regress implies a certain stability, even a hypnotised fixity, in the observer: "I seem as in a trance." But Shelley, rather than simply beholding the world's "fast influencings" from the fixity of trance, simultaneously "bound[s]" from the bounds of that trance (cf. 90–91), leaping into that experience of vertiginous flux. On the one hand, that is, he posits a disorienting hypothesis; on the other, he experiences that disorientation. So the rive-er and riveter Arve: aver; rave.[14]

Thus "Mont Blanc" presents an "unremitting interchange" between metaphysical speculation and a consequent corruption of speculative ability notably similar to the interchange between skepticism and imaginative corruption we have already found informing *A Defence of Poetry*. Our concern now is with the rhetorical characteristics of this interplay, particularly as it accommodates an impulse to corruption. What, then, are the rhetorical symptoms of this maddening?

There is at least a certain tension accumulating in the numerous puns, near puns, and verbal ambivalences Shelley so characteristically scatters through the poem: "vale"/"veil" (13, 63, 123; 26, 54) "lie" (19, 54: recline or rest—but also, potentially, deceive), "repeal" (80: annul—but possibly instead to echo), "recall" (48: revoke, or remember? Cf. *PU* I.59), "bound" (90: leap, but with overtones of boundary; with 90–91 cf. "Alastor" 207).[15] But more sustained disturbances seem to well up whenever, for example, the poem touches with the barest allusiveness on the "faith so mild" (77) of greatest concern to Shelley, Christianity. That winged "legion of wild thoughts" (41), for example, evoking the multitudinousness and unrestraint of Shelley's musings, also ominously but unmistakably recalls the wild thoughts afflicting the raving, lunatic Gadarene of Mark 5:1–20, thoughts whose name is "Legion."[16] Those daemonic thoughts, moreover, are not only madly wild, but also apparently devoted to death: the man, while they possess him, "had his dwelling among the tombs," while the swine into which they flee when Jesus appears immediately stampede into the sea and drown. And so Shelley's scriptural allusion here darkly haunts this second section of "Mont Blanc," burdening its sublime speculations with the suggestion that what flits through "the still cave of the witch Poesy" might be the thoughts of a madman.

An oddly related uncertainty also informs an earlier passage of part II, "the strange sleep / Which when the voices of the desart fail / Wraps all in its own deep eternity" (27–29). The very relevance of these lines to their context is highly ambiguous. Do they, like all around them, refer to the Ravine of Arve? But in the midst of Shelley's apostrophizing catalogue of the ravine's attributes—"Thy giant brood of pines" (20), "thine earthly rainbows" (25), "Thy caverns" (30)—his carefully unattributive "*the* strange sleep" (it could so easily have been another *thy*) seems pointedly exceptional. Nor is it easy to see how these voices might be said or imagined to fail here, in the very path of "unresting sound" (33). Yet the voices of the desert, after all, are surely in one sense the "mysterious tongue" (76) of these "desart" (67) mountains, preeminently Mont Blanc, whose voice is a great silence. The failure of such a voice would be its veiling by sound—here, the sound of falling, raving waters, like the adjacently mentioned and apposite "waterfall, whose veil / Robes some unsculptured image" (26–27). That which hides the unimaginable image, that which drowns the silent voice of the power, is none other than the Arve, "the everlasting universe of things"—the "commotion" (30), "ceaseless motion" (32), and "fast influencings" of thought itself.

In another sense, however, "the voices of the desart" are allusively prophetic and prophesied, preparatory and revelatory, for their great original is the Paraclete's, *vox clamantis in deserto,* the voice of one crying in the wilderness—a voice crying, we might well note in this context of Mont Blanc and the Ravine of Arve, that "every valley shall be exalted [filled up], and every mountain and hill shall be made low" (Isaiah 40:4). The failure of this voice would be the failure of religion itself.

But should we, in this poem, take the voices of the desert as belonging to the wilderness, or only as spoken in or for it? Do the voices fail to proclaim the truth, or fail only to communicate it? Such questions rearrange themselves to form the poem's closing query. They also inform the famous crux of lines 76–79, whose vexatious phrasing may, after all, serve a purpose:

> The wilderness has a mysterious tongue
> Which teaches awful doubt, or faith so mild,
> So solemn, so serene, that man may be
> But for such faith with nature reconciled.

"Doubt, or faith": back and forth across this conjunctive "or" the great argument of Romantic transcendental inquiry ranges and struggles: babble or Bab-El. Doubt or faith—"but." Certainly the manuscript evidence, as Wasserman and Chernaik note, suggests that Shelley's "but" in line 79 is adverbial, meaning "only" or "merely."[17] Nevertheless, generations of readers have immediately and naturally taken the word as a conjunction, however puzzling.

Shelley's obfuscating final departure from the clarity of his earlier drafts ("With such a faith," "In such wise faith") sets up a certain tension between semantics and syntax. This network of mutually interfering significations, moreover, is precisely that which we have been discovering elsewhere in the poem, as before in *A Defence of Poetry*.

Not simply a paradoxical conjunction, Shelley's "but" in line 79 ambivalently oscillates or wavers between adverb and conjunction, again introducing a genuinely deconstructive awareness and imbalance into the poem, and a hint of potential corruption: babble or Bab-El, yes, but then, withal, Bab-El or Babylon, too.

III

As its closing open question once more affirms, "Mont Blanc" never settles on a final answer or position, but remains carefully unpolemical. If it does not yield to entropy, raving, and corruption, however, it more than glances toward them. It signals these attractions, as we have seen, by way of two rhetorical devices in particular, allusion and the regress structure. Since the same two figures, we remember, play similar roles in the *Defence of Poetry*, we should look more closely at how they function in Shelley's work.

In "Mont Blanc," to be sure, the figures of allusion and regress retain a certain vagueness—appropriate, perhaps, for the poem's careful impartiality. The biblical allusions we have noted, for example, are by no means insistent: however pointed they may be, the fact remains that no one seems to have called attention to them before.[18] The regress structure is more obvious, at least in its first stages, but we still cannot easily say whether this regress be finite or infinite, a figurative Chinese boxes structure or a true *mise en abîme*. Elsewhere in Shelley, however, allusions are often more explicit, regresses more clearly infinite or finite; and in particular Shelley seems to use these figures in specific and consistent ways just there where his argument seems most defeatist, entropic, or nihilistic.

Shelley's poetry is of course full of examples of eternal cycles, infinite regresses or progresses. Mutability, "the revolving world" (*PU* II.iv.118), is one of his most insistent themes, and the Spenserian interplay of all transience against great Constancy itself is rarely absent from his writing. Whatever he takes to be the nature of the One, whatever its relation to the many, he continually proposes not only that "The One remains, the many change and pass" but that they change and pass in cycles, like the cycles of life, celestial motions, weather, tide, seasons. Thus not merely a man's thoughts or life, not merely the successive generations of men, but even the sequential ages of language and poetry, of social and political structures, proceed through time in recurrent patterns or alternations no less than do the phases of the moon, the alternations of night and day, the generations of plant and animal life, the forming and precipitating of clouds.

This infinite cyclicity appropriately dominates the plots and imagery of Shelley's "revolutionary" works: "If Winter comes, can Spring be far behind?" The anticipation of spring after winter, day after night, lends a great hopefulness to the frozen and benighted worlds of such poems as *Laon and Cythna, Prometheus Unbound,* "Ode to the West Wind," and *Hellas.* The alternative truth that night follows day, none the less powerful for its de-emphasis, receives some of its due in Demogorgon's valedictory acknowledgment that evil may regain its former ascendency:

> Gentleness, Virtue, Wisdom and Endurance,—
> These are the seals of that most firm assurance
>   Which bars the pit over Destructions's strength;
> And if, with infirm hand, Eternity,
> Mother of many acts and hours, should free
>   The serpent that would clasp her with his length—
> These are the spells by which to reassume
> An empire o'er the disentangled Doom.
>   [*PU* IV.562–69]

More strongly still, it comprises the dark countersong that so colors *Hellas,* the "dregs" of "the urn / Of bitter prophecy" (1098–99): granting that "The world's great age begins anew, / The golden years return" (1060–61), still the dawn of another Athens but foreshadows another sunset: hate and death, no less than Saturn and Love, will return.

Hellas ends, despairingly, with a lamentation over all cyclicity: "The world is weary of the past, / O might it die or rest at last!" (1100–01). The hope is ambivalent or even paradoxical, of course, for death itself makes part of a cycle with life; rest, with exertion.

Pursuing this paradox leads us quickly into the very weariness of which it speaks, the polytropic wearyingness that Schlegel found to be "the most fundamental irony of irony," the tiresomeness of the very *mise en abîme* from which the chorus longs to escape.[19] Considering it less self-indulgently, however, we might simply note that the world's cycle and mankind's do not coincide here. The cycles of human history constitute only a single day in the world's implicitly cyclical history. Their annihilation, then, would figuratively represent only an alternate pulse in that encompassing rhythm.[20] A potential *mise en abîme* can thus be terminated by the usurpation of another, by its absorption into some larger cycle.

Such a pattern of clashing and dying cyclical figures is in fact quite frequent in Shelley's poetry. Common as regress structures are, they often seem to be not infinite but finite. This seems particularly pronounced in that ultimately regressive and annihilative text, "The Triumph of Life," where the cycles of human life and death and time are absorbed into the apparently linear triumph of Life. Here the great crowd of Life's multitude give off shadowy phantasms that themselves "fling / Shadows of shadows . . . / Behind them" (487–89); but all this occurs in a realm that is already a figurative repetition and shadow, for it is a vision of the afterlife as a reenactment after death of life. Like Dante's *Commedia*, "The Triumph of Life" is anagogically about life after death even while being allegorically about life on earth.[21]

Triumphant Life's obliteration of life's cycles, variously signaled as the "light's severe excess" (424) which "obscured . . . The Sun as he the stars" (78–79) or as the "deep night" that "Caught them ere evening" (214–15; cf.289–92, 483–86), stands forth poignantly in Rousseau's account of his own victimization. As he drinks from the cup of nepenthe proffered by the beautiful "shape all light," the terrific vision of Life's triumph suddenly bursts upon him—

> "And the fair shape waned in the coming light
> As veil by veil the silent splendour drops
>   From Lucifer, amid the chrysolite
>
> "Of sunrise ere it strike the mountain tops—
>   And as the presence of that fairest planet
> Although unseen is felt by one who hopes

"That his day's path may end as he began it
In that star's smile, . . .

"So knew I in that light's severe excess
The presence of that shape which on the stream
    Moved, as I moved along the wilderness,

"More dimly than a day appearing dream,
    The ghost of a forgotten form of sleep,
A light from Heaven whose half extinguished beam

"Through the sick day in which we wake to weep
Glimmers, forever sought, forever lost.—
    So did that shape its obscure tenour keep
"Beside my path, as silent as a ghost. . . ."

                              [412–33]

Here Rousseau is likening the waned shape to Lucifer, the morning star, whose light is so pleasing and soothing—likening her, that is, to Venus, "The sphere whose light is melody to lovers" (479). Though the "shape all light" is extinguished by the greater light of Life's chariot just as is the morning star by the sun, Rousseau senses at first that her unseen presence continues beside him just as Lucifer remains invisibly present in the morning sky. And like "one who hopes / That his day's path may end as he began it / In that star's smile," Rousseau hopes that, once the extinguishing brightness of the chariot has passed, he will again be able to see the "shape all light," and draw comfort from her after the wearisome harshness of life. But—and this is the bitter irony of the passage—*no one* who begins his day in the light of that star's smile can ever so end it. When Venus is a morning star it is never—cannot be—an evening star also, but sets invisibly sometime during the afternoon. And though the shape may at first be moving invisibly down the stream beside Rousseau, it can hardly so accompany him when he follows Life's chariot up "The opposing steep of that mysterious dell" (470). His hope ultimately to regain his vision of her, then, is simply fond and delusive; having once faded away, she is now, as he secretly knows, "forever lost."

    If we now recall, however, that the poem represents Rousseau as here recounting his hopes, not in life, but in death, which symbolically reenacts and mirrors life, a still deeper import emerges. This new layer of meaning is perhaps best brought out by Shelley's 1821 translation of the pseudo-Platonic epigram that, in its Greek form, he had used as an epigraph for "Adonais":

> Thou wert the morning star among the living,
>   Ere thy fair light had fled;—
> Now, having died, thou art as Hesperus, giving
>   New splendour to the dead.

[SPW,p.720]

The Greek epigram addresses a youth named Aster, hence its play on the word "star." But more importantly, the epigram associates the world's passage from the light of Lucifer to that of Hesperus with the soul's passage from one realm to another, from life to death. Here again we find the suggestion that death is the image of life. Lucifer passes to Hesperus as does life to death; the change, for man as for Venus, is one not of essence but of phase. The path of a man's day, then, may indeed "end as he began it / In that star's smile"—but only if it ends in the mirror-land of death.[22] Thus Rousseau's hope for a twilight return to auroral bliss, a hope founded upon the analogy of morning and evening, is doomed by the overriding facts of a larger, diurnal cycle.

"All high poetry is infinite," Shelley writes in *A Defence of Poetry;*; "Veil after veil may be withdrawn, and the inmost naked beauty of the meaning never exposed." Like *The Cenci,* "The Triumph of Life" reminds us that what lies behind or beneath may be not beautiful but hideous: "Mask after mask fell from the countenance / And form of all" in Life's train (536–37), but these incessant sheddings of shadows and of "shadows of shadows" (527–28, 488) comprise a *shedding* of beauty:

> "From every form the beauty slowly waned,
>
> "From every firmest limb and fairest face
> The strength and freshness fell like dust, and left
> The action and the shape without the grace
>
> "Of life. . . ."

[519–23]

Much the same fate awaits the Morning Star "wan[ing] in the coming light" of day (412) or the "shape all light" waning in that of Life's

triumph: "veil by veil the silent splendour drops . . ." (413). This removal of veil after veil is a successive loss of splendour: the inmost
form is not a naked beauty, but an invisible abstraction from which
all beauty has been stripped away.

A related kind of regression into final obliteration appears in
"Adonais" when we try to pursue the fading trace of Keats's poetry or
Adonais's songs.

> [T]ill the Future dares
> Forget the Past, his fate and fame shall be
> An echo and a light unto eternity!
>
> [7–9]

So Shelley initially proclaims, though his elegy soon enough reminds
us that this assertion (which is, after all, hardly more than a tautology) holds little consolation (there are many immortals "whose
names on Earth are dark" [406]).[23] But what of Adonais's songs
themselves, now that "Death feeds on his mute voice" (27)? Momentarily, perhaps, they survive his death: these are the dreams and
thoughts "Who were his flocks, whom near the living stream / Of his
young spirit he fed, and whom he taught / The love which was its music" (75–77). Yet now that they are no longer communicable by him
"from kindling brain to brain," they "droop there, whence they
sprung" (78–79), and their mourning for him is simultaneously a
dying with him (73–117); in effect, his songs cannot now sing themselves.

Others, of course, can still sing Adonais's songs, and here Echo repeats them, "feed[ing] her grief with his remembered lay" (128), "Re-
kindl[ing] all the fading melodies" (16). But her sterile repetition of
Adonais's song serves chiefly to beguile Urania into a continued,
sleeping inattentiveness to his danger and fate. The echoed song becomes an inadvertent lullaby; only when the other listening "Echoes
whom their sister's song / Had held in holy silence" (195–96) can finally cry out—apparently the song is no longer there so to hold
them—does Urania wake. Formerly lulled by his song, she is now
awakened, it would seem, by the sound of his silence. And Adonais's
Echo, like his songs, does indeed seem to be fading away, as echoes
do. In her grief, she

> will no more reply to winds or fountains,
> Or amorous birds perched on the young green spray,

Or herdsman's horn, or bell at closing day;
Since she can mimic not his lips, more dear
Than those for whose disdain she pined away
Into a shadow of all sounds:—a drear
Murmur, between their songs, is all the woodmen hear.

[129–35]

Shelley's figure is very complex here. What is this "drear murmur"? In one sense, it is all that remains of the echo (and re-echoings) of Adonais's song, which has faded into an inarticulate, unintelligible near silence. In another sense, this murmur is what ought to have been the echo of the woodmen's songs, or at least comes when they would expect to hear that echo. Now that Echo is no longer responsive, however, what they hear are the blended, blurred, and to them unresponsive sounds of the natural world around them, the white noise of their phonic background. But this very background noise also drowns out whatever faint trace of Adonais's song might still be resounding in the world. This obscuration is all the more ironic in that the "drear murmur" comprises also the natural world's lamentations for Adonais—"Albion wails for thee" (151):

Afar the melancholy thunder moaned,
Pale Ocean in unquiet slumber lay,
And the wild winds flew round, sobbing in their dismay.

[124–26]

Shelley soon after this will cry, "Alas! that all we loved of him should be, / But for our grief, as if it had not been, / And grief itself be mortal!" (181–83). But grief, as appears on closer scrutiny, is mortal in more senses than one: not only does it die, it also kills. This is the same lesson that the ghost of Patroclos returns to teach the intensely but wrongly grieving Achilles: "You have forgotten me" (*Iliad* XXIII.69). What drowns out the fading but still repeated echo of Adonais's songs is the noise of the world's own grieving for its loss.[24]

Thus we encounter again here that clash of figures whereby one potentially infinite regress—this time, the continued echoing of Adonais's song—is overridden and obliterated by the interference of another—now, the continuum of nature's sounds. The implications for "Adonais" are darkly antagonistic to the poem's ostensible consolations. For if "there is heard / His voice in all [Nature's] music, from the moan / Of thunder, to the song of night's sweet bird" (370–72), there is nevertheless not heard his song or his words—indeed, Nature's music is precisely what has usurped Adonais's song, leaving him among what Earth calls in *Prometheus Unbound* "the *inarticulate* people of the dead" (I.183; my emphasis). The audible presence of Adonais's song, like the visible presence of the shape all light, is obscured and effectively annulled by an overriding, usurping intruder. Rousseau indeed describes this as the very essence of Life's triumph:

> "For deaf as is a sea which wrath makes hoary
>   The world can hear not the sweet notes that move
>   The sphere whose light is melody to lovers. . . ."
>
>   [477–79]

The world, like a sea stirred into whiteness by the wind, so deafens and ages itself with its own wrathful activity that it cannot hear the music of Venus's sphere, the cosmic song of love. As Jerome McGann notes of this passage, "Following upon his formulation of Dante's 'wonder'—that man must love to be saved—Rousseau's wonder affirms the inability of the world to love, hence to be saved.[25]

As these examples should already suffice to make clear, a cycle, seen in the full range of its oscillation, emphasizes the potential ambivalence (two-sidedness) and ambiguousness (having wandered about) of that which it figures: what suggests day can also suggest night; what life, death. This ambivalence, with its consequent potential for self-contradictoriness, is of course characteristic of all metaphor (and indeed all figuration), for the simple reason that, as Coleridge says, "No likeness goes on all fours." Always between an original and a trope there must, by definition, be a point of difference, so that, as Paul Weiss argues, any metaphor is implicitly akin to a counterfactual statement.[26] Nor can we simply dismiss any emphasis on this contrariness as transparent irony, as Coleridge does etymologically (following Quintilian) with Lucifer: "Old Scratch" is called Lucifer, i.e., Lightbearer, "*ut Lucus a non lucendo, vel ut Mons a non movendo* [as a grove is so called from not giving light, and a mountain from not moving], that is ironically & by contraries" (*CN* 3:4134).[27] The ambivalence is actually quite inescapable and fundamental, as Freud first notes is true of dreams themselves (*The Interpretation of Dreams*, *SE* 4:318) and then, following K.Abel, posits of language itself in "The Antithetical Sense of Primal Words": as he quotes Abel,

"The essential relativity of all knowledge, thought, or consciousness cannot but show itself in language. If everything that we can know is viewed as a transition from something else, every experience must have two sides; and either every name must have a double meaning, or else for every meaning there must be two names"(*SE* 11:159).[28] But this doubleness already implicit in figuration becomes especially obvious in a cyclical figure, whose very nature it is to pass back and forth between a condition and its opposite. Shelley's emphasis on such figures, then, constitutes a forceful acknowledgment of and even insistence on such ambivalence.

Where in all this ambivalence, though, does ultimate meaning lie; whence or whither does interpretation proceed? Since "Dreams feel themselves at liberty . . . to represent any element by its wishful contrary," Freud notes, "there is no way of deciding at first glance whether any element that admits of a contrary is present in the dream-thoughts as a positive or as a negative" (*SE* 4:318). Yet, with sustained study, Freud insists, dreams are indeed interpretable (though he will hedge importantly on this point, as when he speaks of the "navel" of a dream); and literary figurations, too, tradition tells us, are able to convey their meanings. In the present case of cyclical figuration, the preeminent way of settling on a meaning is the way of closure. "If Winter comes, can Spring be far behind?" While a cycle may continue forever, a figure cannot: a poet, then, must necessarily give a closing emphasis to some part of the cycle, though he may well weaken this emphasis by insisting upon its arbitrariness.[29] If the closure repeatedly and consistently privileges the same point of the cycle, however, the emphasis becomes very strong. So in Shelley's "The Serpent Is Shut Out from Paradise":

> Full half an hour, to-day, I tried my lot
>   With various flowers, and every one still said,
>   "She loves me, loves me not."
>
> [33–35]

As Freud notes, "this factor of involuntary repetition . . . surrounds with an uncanny atmosphere what would otherwise be innocent enough, and forces upon us the idea of something fateful and unescapable where otherwise we should have spoken of 'chance' only" (*SE* 17:237).

Shelley agrees of his petal picking, "there was truth in the sad oracle" (40). But is he not introducing yet another reversal here? For, more accurately, there is simply a sad oracle in the truth of the flowers' repeated assertion, in the uncanny sameness of their petals' parity. We might, too, want to call the conditions of Shelley's experiments into question. What flowers is he interrogating? A field of violets or anemones (five-petaled flowers), for example, would always give the answer, "She loves me," while a field of evening-primroses (four-petaled) would always say "She loves me not." Perhaps we should associate this Shelleyan persona with the narrator of Poe's "The Raven," who "experiences a phrenzied pleasure in so modeling his questions as to receive from the *expected* 'Nevermore' the most delicious because the most intolerable of sorrow" ("The Philosophy of Composition"). Such repetition may not, after all, be so "involuntary" as Freud's example assumes.

To summarize briefly: a metaphor is always ambivalent or ambiguous; and a cyclical metaphor, by making explicit the potential opposite extremes of the figure, serves to make particularly obvious this ambivalence. A repeatedly consistent closure of the cycle, however, serves to make particularly obvious the poet's choice of a pole of emphasis.

If, as Derrida argues, the metaphor par excellence is the sun, then the exemplary figure of insistently hopeful or faithful affirmation will be one of light usurping light, sun reemphasized by sun—Plato's sunlight stunning the eyes of the cave dweller heretofore accustomed only to firelight, Milton's "another morn / Ris'n on mid-noon" (*Paradise Lost* V.310–11), or Coleridge's "faith, which . . . must absolutely *put out* [a] mere poetic Analogon of faith, as the summer sun is said to extinguish our household fires, when it shines full upon them" (*BL* 2:134). Similarly, the exemplary figure of nihilism will be the contrary usurpation of darkness by darkness—"And for the morn of truth they feigned, deep night / Caught them ere evening" ("The Triumph of Life," 214–15);

> "as when there hovers
>
> A flock of vampire-bats before the glare
> Of the tropic sun, bringing ere evening
> Strange night upon some Indian isle. . . ."
> ["The Triumph of Life," 483–86]

Shelley's strategy of figuration seems thus to be one of emphasizing metaphor's "partial apprehension" (*DP*, p. 31): it apprehends but a part, and it evinces a willful partiality.

IV

Shelley's tropes of regressive eclipse thus reveal themselves as elaborate, pointedly insistent examples of stage managing or deck stacking: the poet chooses repeatedly to emphasize one pole of a figure's ambivalent potential, and so sets up and determines the dark conclusions to which his figures and his narrative tend. It can perhaps go without saying that Shelley's use of allusion in these works tends to much the same effect: to quote Satan, Francesca, and Lady Macbeth in support of one's putatively idealistic affirmations, as Shelley does in *A Defence of Poetry*, is, after all, to throw those affirmations terribly into doubt, however pious the quoted phrases themselves might in isolation seem to be. Still, we might well dwell for a moment on the nature of the trope of allusion itself, for its structure and character seem largely relevant to Shelley's, and perhaps poetry's, very enterprise.

What kind of a trope is a quotation or an allusion? (We may, I think, consider the two together; for while an allusion may change the tropings of its original, yet as a trope itself, it clearly includes exact quotation as a subset.) The question is notably absent from most taxonomies and theories of rhetoric.[30] Nonetheless, it is hugely important to the study of poetry, as Harold Bloom especially has recently emphasized.[31] A passage that quotes from or alludes to another text differs from the same passage when not regarded as a quotation or allusion precisely in that the former is recognized as having, and implying, an additional, particular voice and context. Once recognized, this voice and context inevitably reflect forward in some degree upon the passage newly evoking them; indeed, some such effect results even if the allusion is not recognized but merely suspected, or even if it is wrongly suspected. It is thus ultimately on this pair of contexts—of the earlier text no less than the present one—that we must found our interpretation.[32] Is the speech alluded to an angel's, or a devil's? (And if the latter, is this an instance of the devil's quoting scripture?) If a devil's, is it Job's, or Milton's, or Blake's, or Byron's? Is the present allusive speaker a desperado, an ironist, or a buffoon? Is the present work tragic or comic? The very structure and operation of this trope of allusion depend largely upon our (perhaps unconscious) responses to such questions as these.[33]

As both Bloom and John Hollander have indicated, allusion is a form of the trope traditionally called transumption or metalepsis, a vexed and complex trope which we may think of as a trope of a trope, often extravagant, with the intermediate stage or stages of the trope suppressed.[34] It bears a close and interesting relation, then, to metaphor—which, we remember, is itself a trope of a trope, a compounding of two synecdoches or cause-effect metonymies—and to pun.[35] In allusion, as in metaphor and pun, original meaning turns and turns again through its intermediate context—not without inevitable change.

Change is inevitable because, save perhaps in the extreme conditions posited by Borges in "Pierre Menard, Author of *Don Quixote,*" contexts themselves are always changing. As an ideal limit of unchanging meaning, though, we may take the example of analogy. Aristotle, as we have noted, considers analogy a species of metaphor (*Poetics* 1457b). Todorov, in his powerful integration, following Aristotle, of lexical and logical structures, curiously sets aside analogy from his analysis of the relation of tropes to propositions.[36] But analogy and metaphor would seem to bear, after all, a close and important relation to one another. Recall, for example, an observation by Coleridge that we have already had occasion to examine in chapter 1: "No one would say the lungs of a man were analogous to the lungs of a monkey, but any one might say that the gills of a fish and the spiracula of insects are analogous to lungs." What, let us ask, is unacceptable about Coleridge's first example? Clearly it is not false. It is simply trivial. Significantly, it is also a metaphor in the making— not a very interesting one, granted, but a metaphor nonetheless. A monkey is manageably a metaphor for a man (here, in that both are members of the class of lung-breathing animals) just as, traditionally, a lion is of a gallant soldier (both are members of the class of fierce and valiant creatures). All metaphors, accordingly, are collapsed analogies.[37] This is partly the point of Coleridge's witticism about "the inadequacy of every metaphor," that "no likeness goes on all fours" (*Logic,* p. 132; cf. p. 143).

I have said that we may take analogy as an ideal limit of unchanging meaning in allusion. Analogy asserts a changelessness not of things but of relations, ratios, and thus can accommodate changes—

"proportional" changes—in the things related. At this theoretical extreme of allusion, we might interpret an allusion as an assertion of parallel situations: for example, Keats, his poetic Muse, and the anonymous *Quarterly Review* reviewer of *Endymion* putatively relate to one another, mutatis mutandis (one of Coleridge's favorite phrases), just as do Adonis, Venus, and the boar. In practice, though, the parallels must sooner or later break down: *simile non est idem.* The eventually imperfect analogy lapses by virtue of its imperfection to the status of metaphor, with all the attendant ambivalence and ambiguity of that trope.

Nor, often, is there any certain end to the chain of an allusion. Transumption itself may be understood as a kind of chain. Quintilian's *cano-canto-dico* exemplifies this linkage in a semantic and punning mode, and Puttenham, in his *The Arte of English Poesie* (1596), provides a classic instance of a cause-effect metonymic chain in illustrating the trope:

> [A]s *Medea* cursing her first acquaintance with prince Jason, who had very unkindly forsaken her, said:
>
> Woe worth the mountaine that the maste bare
> Which was the first causer of all my care.
>
> Where she might as well have said, woe worth our first meeting, . . . and not so farre off as to curse the mountaine that bare the pinetree, that made the mast, that bare the sailes, that the ship sailed with, which caried her away. . . .[38]

Transumption, then, is itself a kind of regress structure. But when the transumption is an allusion, the regression is frequently no smooth catenary curve, but a wild zigzag and network of links. Here especially the catenarian Coleridge, with his privileging of scripture, differs from Shelley, who privileges no texts. Allusion, like regressive or cyclical metaphor, gives Shelley particular opportunity to emphasize the contrary, antithetical potential of his poetic arguments.

On the one hand, Shelley's readiness to allude ironically or perversely reveals how greatly an allusion's effect depends on its new context. This revelation is particularly forceful in the *Defence*, for example, when he quotes the damned Francesca in ostensible celebration of the poet's art or echoes Lady Macbeth's tauntings of her not yet sufficiently murderous husband to chide the inadequate spirit and commitment of contemporary poets; it impresses similarly in "Adonais" when he evokes Hell's reception of a vanquished tyrant

(Isaiah 14:9–10) to characterize the dead poets' welcome of Adonais (410).[39] On the other hand, though, Shelley's examples often remind us that allusions can be innately both ambivalent and regressive, even regardless of present context. Thus Rousseau's meeting with the "shape all light" in "The Triumph of Life" pointedly alludes to Dante's with Matilda in the Earthly Paradise of *Purgatorio* xxviii–xxix.[40] But Dante the poet, when he presents this "beautiful lady" who went "singing and culling flower from flower" (*"bella donna," cantando e scegliendo fior da fiore"* [*Purg.* xxviii.43, 41]), is already thus associating her with Leah, representative of the Active Life, of whom Dante the pilgrim had dreamed in the preceding canto, "a lady young and beautiful . . . gathering flowers and singing" (*"giovane e bella . . . / donna . . . / cogliendo fiori; e cantando"* [xxvii.97–99]). And when Dante the pilgrim perceives Matilda, he thinks, first, of Proserpine when she, another solitary flower-gatherer, was raped by Pluto; then, when he sees Matilda's eyes, of Venus when she was accidentally wounded by Cupid's arrow (the result was her passion for Adonis); and next, as he regrets being separated from her by the intervening river, of Leander's hatred of the Hellespont, which separated him from Hero. The classical, sexual, ultimately fatal allusions consistently counterpoint the biblical, spiritual one: Dante's text already contains the very ambivalence that Shelley's would later seem only to extrapolate from it. The presentation of Matilda, moreover, itself evokes an erotic, secular poem by Dante's friend Guido Cavalcanti "which celebrates the poet's erotic adventure with a shepherdess culminating with a joy that makes the poet believe that he has seen the very God of Love."[41] Shelley's antithetical use of the Matilda allusion, then, seems hardly more than a heightened sensitivity to some of its implications.

V

We are now ready to declare the argument of Shelley's rhetoric, and to discover, again, how mutually consistent are the plots of figures and the figures of plots. In its essence, the argument of Shelley's rhetoric is simply this—that to try to grasp or force meaning is to lose it and even to corrupt it. Meaning is that which cannot be grasped or forced. Inevitably, then, to attempt to regard one's—or any—metaphor as a truth is to be refuted, for the only ultimate truth is the principle of metaphoricity itself. All is, and is only, metaphor.

But this argument of Shelley's rhetoric is hardly distinguishable from the argument of his poetry itself—that to try to grasp or force *truth* (Bab-El) is to lose it (babble) and even to corrupt it (Babylon); that *truth* is that which cannot be grasped or forced. This is also Satan's experience, and Macbeth's, and indeed Captain Ahab's; it is the plot of Poe's "Ligeia" and Melville's *Pierre* and a hundred lesser works of dark Romanticism. Recurrently, insistently, Shelley's poetry comprises a dialectic of attempts to force and choices not to force a desired, "favorable" meaning. Jupiter, Rousseau, the poet and the narrator of "Alastor," and Urania are among those who try to force truth or meaning; it is Asia's strength that she does not, while Prometheus and Mahmud II learn not to.

Usually, in Shelley, the impossible attempt on truth assumes the form and plot of an attempt to possess a beautiful, ideal (or idealized) woman. As Pan sings,

> down the vales of Maenalus
> I pursued a maiden and clasped a reed.
> Gods and men, we are all deluded thus!—
> It breaks in our bosom and then we bleed. . . .
>   ["Song of Pan," 30–33]

Jupiter's perversely fulfilled rape of Thetis marks one extreme of this mis-taking; Rousseau's hesitant address, "between desire and shame / suspended" ("The Triumph of Life," 394–95), to the "shape all light" marks another. Other versions of the plot occur in Shelley's variations on the Actaeon myth—in "Adonais," of course, but also, surely, in his sonnet "Lift not the painted veil," which seems unmistakably allusive to Schiller's "The Veiled Image at Sais," about the fate of a youth who dares lift the veil hiding the statue of Isis at Sais.[42] If the maiden is ideal, she is unattainable: witness the poet's futile quest for his dream-maiden in "Alastor," or the implied poet's death (as the poem's "Advertisement" informs us) on the very eve of his elopement with Emily in "Epipsychidion." If she is attainable, on the other hand, she is no ideal: Pan's maiden becomes a reed (and the reed, figuratively, the shaft that pierces and breaks off in his heart), and Cenci's pure daughter feels herself (and so is) contaminated by his rape. And all these versions of plot have their analogues in rhetoric; every missing, mistaking, or corrupting of truth corresponds to an interpretative swerve of figurative meaning.

Shelley's most sustained confusion of the ideal with the attainable, the astonishing and embarrassing "Epipsychidion," eventually became for him a bitter object-lesson of the very argument he had wished in that poem to deny. "The 'Epipsychidion,'" he writes his friend John Gisborne in 1822, "I cannot look at; the person whom it celebrates was a cloud instead of a Juno; and poor Ixion starts from the centaur that was the offspring of his own embrace" (*SL* 2:434). His self-analysis here is both shrewd and devastating. As he soon elaborates, "the error, and I confess it is not easy for spirits cased in flesh and blood to avoid it, consists in seeking in a mortal image the likeness of what is perhaps eternal." In idealizing Emilia (Teresa) Viviani, he had posited, impossibly, an attainable, immanent perfection. But again, as necessarily always, the mortal's attempt to grasp the transcendent is baffled.[43] Emilia is no divinity, however ideal she appears to be (so Ixion, striving to win Juno, deludedly seizes a phantom double of her which Jupiter had shaped from a cloud); and by identifying himself with Ixion, Shelley belatedly drops the moralistic pretenses of the poem (and of his own position: Shelley had earlier avowed to Claire Claremont of his interest in and attachment to Emilia, "There is no reason that you should fear any mixture of that which you call *love*" [*SL* 2:256]) and figures himself as a selfish rapist, and the poem born of this deluded union as (what Jupiter calls his own frightful child in *Prometheus Unbound*) a "detested prodigy" (III.i.61). "Epipsychidion" as centaur—that is, as monster, an arbitrary yoking of disparate elements: Shelley's figure hereby further suggests that the poem is inferior in that despite its pretenses to imagination and transcendental aspiration it is, in Coleridge's sense, merely fanciful, "a counterfeit product of the mechanical understanding" (*SM*, p. 30).[44] The allusion becomes, then, something of a figure for the fate of figuration itself.

VI

Rhetorical suicide is a dead end. Rhetoric, like that arch-rhetorician Cleopatra, is never more vital than when it bids to die. The suicidal close of "Adonais" makes this no less clear than does *Antony and Cleopatra*: "that su*staining* Love" (481; and cf.378) evokes, paradoxically, Life's very "staining" of it (463); "The fire for which all thirst" (485)—a thirst that "the eclipsing Curse / Of birth can quench not" (480–81)—plays grimly, not for the first or the last time in Shelley's writings, upon the English idioms whereby water quenches both thirst and fire, so that to quench the thirst is self-defeatingly to put out the fire.[45] And to be "extinguished"—a fate

Shelley almost always associates with fire[46]—is, its etymology reminds us, to be deeply "tinged" (the word is a cognate of "stain"—which itself, however, etymologically connotes a *losing* of color). It is as if one has not died, but been dyed—with, doubtless, the colors of rhetoric.[47] "Adonais" endlessly calls into question its own rhetoric, and simply will not allow its own questions ("What Adonais is, why fear we to become?" [459]; "Why linger, why turn back, why shrink, my Heart?" [469]) to be merely rhetorical.

Not when suicide is espoused, then—and this is an espousal: "No more let Life Divide what Death can join together" (477) almost grotesquely parodies the familiar phrase of the marriage ceremony—but when it, too, is questioned, might we expect to find the more honest testing of the end of rhetoric. Shelley's preeminent essay in such a testing is *The Cenci*. Like its companion play, *Prometheus Unbound*, this work explores the limits of expression, approaches the verge of the ineffable, the "imageless." But now, Shelley insists, his subject is no "dream[] of what ought to be, or may be," but "a sad reality"—"that which has been" (*SPP*, p. 237); and in reality, the ineffable proves to be all too truly the unspeakable.

The question of suicide repeatedly surfaces in *The Cenci,* and always in a context that makes clear the question's association with rhetoric. The first hint of it comes from Count Cenci himself, in the first vague intimation of his plan for Beatrice:

> Aye, we must all grow old—
> And but that there remains a deed to act
> Whose horror might make sharp an appetite
> Duller than mine—I'd do,—I know not what.
>   [I.i.99–l02]

To Giacomo, who perhaps raises the question only rhetorically, suicide is not something unspoken but instead a response to a silence. Hearing from Orsino that Beatrice's petition for help has been rejected—"returned unanswered" (II.ii.62)—by the Pope, he concludes,

> My friend, that palace-walking devil Gold
> Has whispered silence to his Holiness:
> And we are left, as scorpions ringed with fire,
> What should we do but strike ourselves to death?
>   [II.ii.68–71]

This "whispered silence," however, is not merely an advised response, but the original message, which Orsino in fact has not delivered at all. Beatrice herself, after her father's assault upon her, is held back from suicide by a word: "Self-murder . . . no, that might be no escape, / For [God's] decree yawns like a Hell between / Our will and it" (III.i.132–34); as she elaborates just after to Orsino,

> I thought to die; but a religious awe
> Restrains me, and the dread lest death itself
> Might be no refuge from the consciousness
> Of what is yet unexpiated.
>   [III.i.148–51]

But she is baffled in another direction by the lack of a word to be her weapon and instrument:

> If I could find a word that might make known
> The crime of my destroyer; and that done
> My tongue should like a knife tear out the secret
> Which cankers my heart's core; aye, lay all bare. . . .
>   [III.i.154–57]

What she contemplates here is a self-murdering to dissect; for the peculiarly Cencian trick of "self-anatomy" (II.ii.10) is figuratively just such a surgical dissection (just so Orsino earlier speaks of Beatrice's "anatomiz[ing] me nerve by nerve / And lay[ing] me bare" [I.ii.85–86]). The one actual suicide of the play, Marzio's self-suffocation in defiance of the papal court of inquisition, constitutes an absolute refusal to speak: having reversed his earlier, torture-wrung confession of Beatrice's complicity to proclaim with "my last breath" that "She is most innocent!" (V.ii.165), he end-punctuates this revised, exclamatory testimony with his unexclaiming death. As the torturer who had hoped to force a further confession from him reports,

>   As soon as we
> Had bound him on the wheel, he smiled on us,
> As one who baffles a deep adversary;
> And holding his breath, died.[48]
>   [V.ii.180–83]

Suicide in *The Cenci* is bound up with the issues of speech and silence, we see, even as words (and, Marzio demonstrates, silences) are implicated as deadly weapons. Giacomo, threatening Orsino, blusters, "Coward and slave! But, no, defend thyself; [*Drawing.*]/Let the sword speak what the indignant tongue/Disdains to brand thee with" (V.i.54–56). Orsino can easily turn aside such thrusts; not the speaking sword, but the "tongue . . . like a knife" of which Beatrice has already spoken is, he knows, the severer threat in this world— especially, perhaps (and Beatrice learns this, too), if the weapon is one's own. As he prepares to flee in disguise from the ruins of his plot, he wonders,

> Have I not the power to fly
> My own reproaches? Shall I be the slave
> Of . . . what? A word? which those of this false world
> Employ against each other, not themselves;
> As men wear daggers not for self-offence.
>
> [V.i.97–101]

He has reason to doubt. For weapons in this world are typically two-edged (cf. IV.iv.115, V.ii.97), and blade-tongues not only speak messages but declare, sometimes to betray, their speakers. When Beatrice, chiding the recalcitrant murderers, snatches a dagger from one and proclaims, "Hadst thou a tongue to say, / 'She murdered her own father,' I must do it!" (IV.iii.31–32), she is addressing the weapon as much as the man.[49]

Blades speak; words wound. But what of those wounds for which there are no words? This is the ultimate trial of argument and rhetoric in *The Cenci*.

Michael Worton, rightly emphasizing the play's "linguistic preoccupation," has noted that "there are two kinds of silence in *The Cenci*—the silence of repression and the silence of inadequacy."[50] It remains to observe that *The Cenci* clothes and "impersonates" each of these silences in a single word. The word of repressed thought is "parricide"; the unutterable word of imageless thought is—and let the brackets indicate that the word is not in the text—"[incest]."

Though Giacomo once ambivalently alludes to parricide as among "such phantasies / As the tongue dares not fashion into words, / Which have no words, their horror makes them dim / To the mind's eye" (II.ii.84–87), he soon effectively retracts the latter claim. The thought may be terrifying and shameful, but it has a word. Nor is Giacomo, nor even Beatrice, the first to say it: it enters the play with Count Cenci himself (II.i.132), and ultimately, by report, is on the tongue even of the Pope (V.iv.20). "Parricide"—word and thought—is like a murderer (II.ii.96), like fear (III.i.341), like a monster (V.i.23): it is foul, but it is there. The Judge's reaction to Marzio's admission of the parricide characterizes the word perfectly: "This sounds as bad as truth" (V.ii.19).

"[Incest]," in pointed contrast, is defined by the conventions of *The Cenci* to be both unutterable and unimaginable: it simply "[can] not be told, not thought" (V.ii.141).[51] Stunned and traumatized by the rape, Beatrice discovers that there is no word for her plight, for she "can feign no image in my mind / Of that which has transformed me": "there are deeds / Which have no form, sufferings which have no tongue," wrongs which are therefore innately "expressionless" (III.i.108–09, 141–42, 214). Where "parricide" is figuratively unnatural, monstrous, "[incest]" is figuratively supernatural, so that Beatrice's "thought / Is like a ghost shrouded and folded up / In its own formless horror" (III.i.109–11).

To these conventions of thought and language in *The Cenci*, however, as to those of morality and action in the world it presents, we must add one more: Count Cenci, he whom words cannot wound, is not bound by these conventions. Cenci alone can think the unimaginable. As he first plans to confront Beatrice with his intent for her, he is wary of eavesdroppers:

> I think they cannot hear me at that door;
> What if they should? And yet I need not speak
> Though the heart triumphs with itself in words.
> O, thou most silent air, that shalt not hear
> What now I think!
>
> [I.i.137–41]

These, clearly, are not unformed thoughts, merely unspoken ones: "such mischief as I now conceive," "my purpose," "the act I think" (II.i.125, 193, 188), is to him simply what "parricide" is to Giacomo, daunting but imaginable. If he finds [incest] difficult to say, so that he first broaches it to Beatrice in "inarticulate words" (II.i.112), yet he does know the word and can communicate it to her. "What did your father do or say to you?" Lucretia asks her after that interview; and Beatrice can only answer, "It was one word, Mother, one little word; / One look, one smile" (II.i.59, 63–64). Her immediately subsequent raving in this scene pointedly anticipates her words and behavior after the rape itself (one "act" later), even as her imaginational parallels her physical violation.

Count Cenci impersonates a dark variation of Shelley's usual plot: he grasps and forces with the *intent* that the true and beautiful, the "light of life" (Bernardo's phrase for Beatrice [V.iv.134] is also Prometheus's for Asia [*PU* III.iii.6]), shall be made false and corrupt. Her "atonement" is similarly an attempt to grasp and force a meaning for his forcing of her. In resisting him, she becomes like him. As many critics have noted, her relation to her father is a sustained repetition of the bound Prometheus's to Jupiter: her very resistance to his tyranny adopts and perpetuates the hatred that empowers it.[52] But the interrelation of the two plays is of course no simple reflexiveness. In *Prometheus Unbound,* the repressed word divinely corresponding to *The Cenci*'s infernal "parricide" is the secret of Jupiter's vulnerability, which Prometheus will not "Cloathe in words" (*PU* I.375).[53] The unimaginable word or language corresponding to "[incest]" is beyond Prometheus's or Asia's ken; "the deep truth is imageless" (II.iv.116), as Demogorgon declares, and only the "tremendous Gloom" (I.207) of shapeless Demogorgon can convey it. But it is the final convention of *The Cenci* that Count Cenci *can* speak the unspeakable word. He is thereby, and thus far, defined as supernatural within the world of the drama. Not only does he play Jupiter to Beatrice's bound Prometheus, he also in this respect plays Demogorgon to her Jupiter. Demogorgon and his deep truth, "[incest]" and its meaning—each is that which grasps and forces, but cannot be grasped.

We have already seen that allusions and regresses or cycles signal the attractions of entropic corruption in Shelley; and in *The Cenci* their pull is terribly strong. Here Shelley's allusions are so numerous, various, and complex as to approach the condition of pastiche: fragments and echoes of *Paradise Lost,* the Bible, the *Aeneid,* Shelley's own writings (especially *Prometheus Unbound*), Byron, Godwin, Webster, and, above all, a number of Shakespeare's major tragedies, crowd bewilderingly through the text.[54] Beatrice is allusively linked to Desdemona, but also to Lady Macbeth, and yet again to Hamlet; Cenci speaks like Macbeth, but also like Lear; if she is Thetis to his Jupiter, she is also Sin (incestuously impregnated with incestuously inclined Death) to his Satan (cf. IV.i.145–57), but also Satan to his Jehovah. Similarly, the cyclical metaphors and regresses of Shelley's customary imagery here accelerate into the dizzying spin of a vortex: "I / Slide giddily as the world reels" (III.i.11–12) captures succinctly the moral and imaginative vertigo of the play.

In this vertigo, however, the play's rhetorical and argumentative disparities begin to sort out and coalesce. We are on the brink of an abyss, or in the depths of a cave, or both. A correlative of this figurative locus is the Cenci Palace itself, "a vast and gloomy pile of feudal architecture," with one particularly striking gate "formed of immense stones and leading through a passage, dark and lofty and opening into gloomy subterranean chambers" (*SPP*, p. 242); another is the precipitous chasm in the Apennines—"a gulph," a "dread abyss" (III.i.250, 254)—where the conspirators first intend to kill Cenci. Figuratively, this brink is the limit of what we know, "the giddy verge / Of life and death" (V.ii.115–16; cf.V.iv.100–01). Again, it is possibly the lip of Hell, of that "gulph / Of Hell" that Beatrice sees yawning between herself and her father (IV.i.98–99); so the passage from Calderon on which Shelley explicitly models his description of the Apennine chasm describes the mouth of Hell.[55] But most importantly, this dark and deep place is what Orsino calls "the inmost cave of our own mind" (II.ii.89), and Shelley, "the most dark and secret caverns of the human heart" (*SPP*, p. 239).

The exploration of this "inner cave of thought" (*SP*, p. 199) is the ultimate objective of *The Cenci*. "The highest moral purpose aimed at in the highest species of the drama, is the teaching the human heart, through its sympathies and antipathies, the knowledge of itself . . ." (*SPP*, p. 240); or, as he says in making the same point in his "Treatise on Morals," "[The] deepest abyss of this vast and multitudinous cavern, it is necessary that we should visit" (*SP*, p. 192). But this visiting is none other than that "self-anatomy," figuratively suicidal, which proves so dangerous in *The Cenci* (and is implicitly so, perhaps, to Shelley himself, "a strict anatomist of his own [heart]" [*SL* 2:324]). And Shelley warns, in phrases freshly borrowed from *The Cenci*, that this necessary visit can be to no positive effect: "How vain it is to think that words can penetrate the mystery of our being!" "We are on that verge where words abandon us, and what wonder if we grow dizzy to look down the dark abyss of how little we know" (*SP*, pp. 172, 174).[56]

To totter on this brink of self-knowledge, however, is to experience not merely vertigo, but fear. The "gloomy passion for penetrating the impenetrable mysteries of our being," as Shelley says in his

Preface to *The Cenci,* "terrifies its possessor at the darkness of the abyss to the brink of which it has conducted him" (*SPP,* p. 240). Whence this fear? In this sublime *topos,* as Burke recognizes, it has two sources: not only the terrible and seemingly infinite precipice, but also the obscuring darkness, wherein "it is impossible to know in what degree of safety we stand" (*Enquiry,* p. 143).

> [N]ight increases our terror more perhaps than any thing else; it is our nature, that, when we do not know what may happen to us, to fear the worst that can happen us. . . .

And again,

> To make any thing very terrible, obscurity seems in general to be necessary. . . . Every one will be sensible of this, who considers how greatly night adds to our dread, in all cases of danger, and how much the notions of ghosts and goblins, of which none can form clear ideas, affect minds, which give credit to the popular tales concerning such sorts of beings. (*Enquiry,* pp. 83, 58–59)

But just such a ghost, we remember, lurks in the abyssal cave of Beatrice's mind, "whose thought / Is like a ghost shrouded and folded up / In its own formless horror." Perhaps, Shelley suggests, it lurks in those "dark and secret caverns" of *every* human heart. As he writes in his "Treatise on Morals,"

> [T]hought can with difficulty visit the intricate and winding chambers which it inhabits. It is like a river whose rapid and perpetual stream flows outwards—like one in dread who speeds through the recesses of some haunted pile and dares not look behind. The caverns of the mind are obscure and shadowy; or pervaded with a lustre, beautifully bright indeed, but shining not beyond their portals. (*SP,* p. 186)

The mind, it seems, is horribly haunted; thought is in *dread* of its secret springs. This is what rhetoric no less than argument teaches in *The Cenci.*

This ghastly haunting lurks everywhere in Shelley's Preface to *The Cenci* as well, even—especially—in its finest and most moral affirmations. Consider:

> Undoubtedly, no person can be truly dishonoured by the act of another; and the fit return to make to the most enormous injuries is kindness and forbearance, and a resolution to convert the injurer from his

dark passions by peace and love. Revenge, retaliation, atonement, are
pernicious mistakes. If Beatrice had thought in this manner she would
have been wiser and better. . . . (*SPP*, p. 240)

We well know what Count Cenci's ultimate "dark passions" were.
But what, then, of this phrase's subsequent evocation in that
"gloomy passion"—significantly, "a gloomy passion for
penetrating"—of which Shelley soon after speaks? The play itself
makes the implications of the Preface unmistakable, in that very
scene and passage immediately following Beatrice's rape wherein she
also speaks of her thought as "like a ghost shrouded and folded up /
In its own formless horror." "Oh, my lost child," Lucretia exclaims,
"Hide not in proud *impenetrable* grief / Thy sufferings from my
fear"; and Beatrice replies,

> I hide them not.
> . . . .
>   Of all words,
> That minister to mortal *intercourse,*
> Which wouldst thou hear? For there is none to tell
> My misery: if another ever knew
> Aught like to it, she *died* as I will *die,*
> And left it, as I must, without a name.
>   [III.i.104–16; my emphasis]

There is no avoiding such cumulative suggestiveness. The "gloomy
passion" of metaphysical speculation that so drives Shelley is figuratively incestuous; and the words that minister to such intercourse
are mortal indeed, not merely human but deadly.

And what, finally, of Beatrice's one supposedly valid alternative,
that "fit return" she is unwilling or unable to make? "Revenge, retaliation, atonement," the "pernicious mistakes" that all in *The Cenci*
adopt, sort together oddly—the first two relate to a sense of being
wronged; the last, to one of being wrong—but at least proceed from
a common assumption that one can indeed, notwithstanding Shelley's prefatorial denial, be dishonored by the act of another—that
the world's slow stain is indeed contagious ("Adonais," 356), that the
"disguise" of impersonation "Stain[s] that within" which wears it
("The Triumph of Life," 204–05).[57] Yet Beatrice herself consistently
speaks of her revenge and retaliation on her father as an atonement
and expiation, whether his or hers: as she says in proposing her fa-

ther's murder, "I have endured a wrong, / Which, though it be expressionless, is such / As asks atonement" (III.i.213–15; cf. III.i.151, IV.iv.91). Clearly such language evinces her own casuistry. Yet Shelley knew Coleridge's *Statesman's Manual*,[58] and would have read his meditative etymology there:

> Am I *at one* with God, and is my will concentric with that holy power, which is at once the constitutive will and the supreme reason of the universe?—If not, must I not be mad if I do not seek, and miserable if I do not discover and embrace, the means of *at-one-ment*? (*SM*, p. 55)

The misery and madness of an unholy at-one-ment, a hellishly incestuous embrace, is precisely the violation Beatrice has endured. To seek "atonement," as she does, is, horribly, thus to repeat the crime.

But has she, really, that better alternative of which Shelley speaks? "Kindness and forbearance": such are, after all, Beatrice's valedictions to Bernardo as she departs to her death:

> And though
> Ill tongues shall wound me, and our common name
> Be as a mark stamped on thine innocent brow
> For men to point at as they pass, do thou
> Forbear, and never think a thought unkind
> Of those, who perhaps love thee in their graves.
>
> [V.iv.149–54]

But the formless horror haunts even these bright passages. We may recall the first dark words we hear Hamlet mutter, when Claudius hails him as "my cousin Hamlet and my son": "A little more than kin, and less than kind." Unkind and unforbearing though he be, Count Cenci *is* Beatrice's kind and forbear: the very phrasing of Shelley's moral prescription reeks of the corruptive ghost within. Our dark passion for a beautiful meaning will corrupt both it and us: when forced, rhetoric cannot forbear retaliating upon us with this unkind atonement.

Romantic Argument, Freud's Metapsychology, and The Deconstructionist Debate

I

After so long an examination of how Coleridge's and Shelley's rhetorics differ, it is time to insist on how much they have in common, and on how distinctively Romantic is their common ground.

Whatever their ostensible quarrels with each other, Coleridge's and Shelley's rhetorics prove to be structurally indistinguishable. Beneath the celebrations of symbol, the privilegings of cause-effect metonymy, the various tricks of metalepsis, both rhetorics are ultimately metaphorical. What distinguishes them is not structure but attitude—whether we call it style or psychology: in multiple senses of the phrase, they mean to serve very different ends. I have found it convenient—and illuminating—to identify these ends, life and death, with the two basic instincts that Freud names Eros and the death instinct, and the pathways to these ends with Freud's two principles of mental functioning, the reality principle and the pleasure principle. These namings are clarifying conveniences: I do not offer them as Freudian interpretations, but as instruments for interpretation—of Freud himself no less than of his Romantic predecessors. In so doing I have implicitly supported, and drawn support from, those contemporary critics who find the structures of psyches and texts to be analogous.[1]

We have seen the rhetorical and argumentative implications of these two pathways, the tensions of these two principles, in the divergent writings of Coleridge and Shelley. I would like briefly now to explore their workings in Freud's own project.

II

The divergence between Coleridge's and Shelley's rhetorics, to repeat, is a tension between two antagonistic attitudes toward the text. Neither man's rhetoric, neither's argument, is what it apparently claims to be. Both men's texts can of course be deconstructed; but where Coleridge himself continually resists such a course, Shelley continually invites and impels it. Thus while Coleridge's argument is continually undercutting itself (Bab-El into babble), Shelley's is continually inverting itself (Bab-El into Babylon).

This divergence, in the language of Freud's metapsychology, marks the distinction between the reality principle and the pleasure principle. In the language of criticism, and in the tradition of Plato and Sidney, it marks the distinction between philosophy and literature.

This latter, critical phrasing of the distinction also appears frequently in Freud. In discussing "secondary revision" in *The Interpretation of Dreams,* for example, he notes,

> The thing that distinguishes and at the same time reveals this part of the dream-work is its *purpose.* This function behaves in the manner which the poet maliciously ascribes to philosophers: it fills up the gaps in the dream-structure with shreds and patches. As a result of its efforts, the dream loses its appearance of absurdity and disconnectedness and approximates to the model of an intelligible experience. (*SE* 5:490; cf. *SE* 22:160–61)

This function, moreover, seems identifiable with "the activity of our waking thought" (*SE* 5:499; cp. 5:489): there seems in fact to be no difference between "secondary revision" and the "secondary process," the reality principle. As Freud elaborates,

> Our waking (preconscious) thinking behaves towards any perceptual material with which it meets in just the same way in which [secondary revision] behaves towards the content of dreams. It is the nature of our waking thought to establish order in material of that kind, to set up relations in it and to make it conform to our expectations of an intelligible whole. In fact, we go too far in that direction. An adept in sleight of hand can trick us by relying upon this intellectual habit of ours. In our efforts at making an intelligible pattern of the sense-impressions that are offered to us, we often fall into the strangest errors or even falsify the truth about the material before us. (*SE* 5:499)

So it is that, confronted by a "tricky" or enigmatic text—a scurrilous jest, for example, disguised as a Latin inscription—the "philosopher" will become the butt of the joke:

For this purpose the letters contained in the words are torn out of their combination into syllables and arranged in a new order. Here and there a genuine Latin word appears; at other points we seem to see abbreviations of Latin words before us; and at still other points in the inscription we may allow ourselves to be deceived into overlooking the senselessness of isolated letters by parts of the inscription seeming to be defaced or showing lacunae. If we are to avoid being taken in by the joke, we must disregard everything that makes it seem like an inscription, look firmly at the letters, pay no attention to their ostensible arrangement, and so combine them into words belonging to our own mother tongue. (*SE* 5:501)

As Samuel Weber notes, "Such a process of reading presupposes that the readiness to play with language is strong enough to check the desire to recognize the familiar (the pseudo-Latin of the 'inscription'), and thus to accede directly to meaning."[2] The difference between philosophy and literature, in this sense, would be that of unwillingness or willingness to play with the text—in other words, to be *allusive* (from *ad* + *ludere*). Freud's characterization of the philosopher also recalls a passage from Nietzsche we considered in chapter 2: "the so-called instinct of causality is nothing more than the *fear of the unfamiliar,* and the attempt at finding something in it which is already *known.*—It is not a search for causes, but for the familiar."

How does Freud write and read texts? How willing is he to play with them, how anxious is he to recognize the familiar in them? The answer is by no means straightforward. On the one hand, adamantly insistent as he is on the scientific status of psychoanalysis, he emphatically identifies his position with the reality principle: his purpose is thus "to transform *metaphysics* into *metapsychology*" (*SE* 6:259), and to oppose to the pleasurable illusions of religion, philosophy, and art the scientist's recognition and acceptance of the real world (*SE* 22:158–75). On the other hand, as an interpreter of dreams, of word-slips, of symptoms, Freud has to be willing and able to enter into the play of the text. The interpreter must reverse the distortions of the dream, but he may also participate in them.[3] Hence Freud's curious admission when he offers as an everyday example—the only available example, he says—of such psychical distortion precisely the power-relationship from which we have derived our own metapsychological schema, the interaction of an individual with a more powerful other:

In such a case the [less powerful] person will distort his psychical acts or, as we might put it, will dissimulate. The politeness which I practice every day is to a large extent dissimulation of this kind; and when I interpret my dreams for my readers I am obliged to adopt similar distortions. (*The Interpretation of Dreams, SE* 4:142)

A similar admission occurs in *Beyond the Pleasure Principle* when Freud explains the "bewildering and obscure" character of his speculations on the life and death instincts as "merely due to our being obliged to operate with the scientific terms, that is to say with the figurative language, peculiar to psychology. . . . We could not otherwise describe the processes in question at all, and indeed we could not have become aware of them" (*SE* 18:60).

We may note, too, the curious shifting of philosophy in Freud's pairings. In contrast to science, it belongs to the pleasure principle; then again, partly scientific itself, it is a blend of realism and illusion (*SE* 22:160–61); but on another level, it is identifiable with his own scientific project. "When I was young," he wrote Fliess in 1896 (he had then already worked out his theory of *The Interpretation of Dreams*), "the only thing I longed for was philosophical knowledge, and now that I am going over from medicine to psychology, I am in the process of attaining it."[4]

But that Freud aspires to truth, or admits to figuration, still tells us little of his rhetorical attitude. We need to know more of the relative strengths of these competing impulses in his work. I would like now first to reconsider his willingness or unwillingness to play with the text in an essay we have already considered, "The 'Uncanny,' " and then to track his argument and its rhetoric through a crucial passage in "Analysis Terminable and Interminable"—something of a "nodal point" (*SE* 4:283), in the phrase of *The Interpretation of Dreams*—where many of the issues we have been considering converge.

III

"The 'Uncanny' " itself necessarily seems uncanny in a certain sense, insofar as it brings to light what the subject, "the uncanny," conceals; indeed, Freud himself notes along the way, "I should not be surprised to hear that psycho-analysis, which is concerned with laying bare these hidden forces, has itself become uncanny to many people for that very reason" (*SE* 17:243). Pursuing this line of thought, Freud would soon come to see clearly, as perhaps he did not in 1919, the relativity of uncanniness (to inferior canniness), its status as a relationship of power. This is especially apparent in *Group Psychology and the Analysis of the Ego* (1921), where he speaks of the uncanniness of the hypnotist and the primal father or group leader (and, by parallel, the psychoanalyst), attributing it to their supposed dangerous power over the subject (*SE* 18:125–27 and n). At this one point of "The 'Uncanny,'" however, Freud's mastery of his subject (if not of his audience) fails; the relativity of the uncanny is not brought to light, but remains hidden.[5]

What hides this hiding from the reader is Freud's rhetoric; and his paragraph on the evil eye, where we explored this obscuration in chapter 2, is by no means its only or even its primary covert. Ultimately that which is repressed but recurs in this essay is Freud's very notion of the uncanny, borrowed from Schelling's surprising but finally satisfying definition, which Freud quotes or cites no fewer than four times: "something which ought to have remained hidden but has come to light" (*SE* 17:241; cf. 224, 225, 226). Schelling's recurrence in this essay on recurrence is in itself perhaps only mildly interesting; but when we note additionally that Schelling's definition is actually an allusion and that Freud represses or suppresses this fact, its relevance to the uncanny becomes strikingly prominent.

The allusion, moreover, is transcendental. "For there is nothing covered, that shall not be revealed; neither hid, that shall not be known." This saying of Jesus, itself allusive to a prior, Old Testament text (Job says of God, "The thing that is hid bringeth he forth to light" [Job 28:11]), recurs several times in the Synoptic Gospels, always in the immediate context of illumination that Schelling—and Job—stress: "Therefore whatsoever ye have spoken in darkness shall be heard in the light." Its contexts and applications are various. Once it is a warning about the Pharisees' hypocrisy (Luke 12:2–3, the version I have just quoted); once, an exhortation to his disciples to preach openly, despite persecution, what Jesus has privately taught them (Matthew 10:26–27); twice, elaborating upon the homely truth that "No man, when he hath lighted a candle, covereth it with a vessel, or putteth it under a bed; but setteth it on a candlestick," it is a reference to and promise of the coming of the kingdom and of judgment (Luke 8:16–17; cf. Mark 4:21–22). The Jobean and Gospel proverb, then, is consistently relevant to Freud's concerns—and indeed, to his own ambitions. Yet consistently he fails to confront this source of Schelling's allusive definition, which thus remains uncannily beyond his interpretation, secretly rebuking dissimulation and insinuating transcendental promise in the very presence of the text that would claim to be abjuring all dissimulation and refuting such promise.

Helene Cixous has suggested that Freud's essay is "less a discourse than a strange theoretical novel," a "search whose movement constitutes the labyrinth which instigates it";[6] and we see here a central way in which this is surely true. Insofar as Freud refuses to play with Schelling's biblical allusion, he is treating Schelling and the uncanny philosophically; he seeks to master the problem of the uncanny, but by virtue of his very rigor fails to perceive the uncanniness of his own text. But perhaps he does, after all, recognize the allusion. Then, we can only conclude, he is deliberately, rather than inadvertently, shaping his essay to be uncanny; he is assuming the role not of philosopher but of poet, and he is playing with his text and with us.

IV

My text from the striking late essay "Analysis Terminable and Interminable" (1937), one of Freud's very last works, is from the penultimate section. Freud's concern at this point of the essay is with the innate *relativity* of psychoanalysis: for not only the analysand, after all, but also the analyst, has a psyche. It is important, then, that the analyst be a specially and particularly talented person, not merely a mentally normal and correct one (*SE* 23:248): "in addition," Freud says,

> he must possess some kind of superiority, so that in certain analytic situations he can act as a model for his patient and in others as a teacher. And finally we must not forget that the analytic relationship is based on a love of truth—that is, on a recognition of reality—and that it precludes any kind of sham or deceit. (*SE* 23:248)

So speaks Freud in his most scientific vein. "But where and how is the poor wretch to acquire the ideal qualifications which he will need in his profession? The answer is, in an analysis of himself, with which his preparation for his future activity begins." And this initial submission to analysis is in fact the *rite de passage* of psychoanalysis, the test that determines if a candidate will be admitted into training for the profession. "It has accomplished its purpose," Freud continues,

if it gives the learner a firm conviction of the existence of the unconscious, if it enables him, when repressed material emerges, to perceive
in himself things which would otherwise be incredible to him, and if it
shows him a first sample of the technique which has proved to be the
only effective one in analytic work.

Ideally, the neophyte analyst, thus stimulated, will continue sponta-
neously and interminably to remodel his own ego in the light of his
new awareness. More than almost any other man, then, the psychoanalyst knows firsthand the *relativity* of the uncanny and the canny.
Lured by the prospect of being uncanny to others, the candidate
analyst—the "cannydate," perhaps we should call him—must first
submit to the uncanniness of his teacher.

There is no need to dwell on the important contradiction already
built into Freud's prescriptions here—that the analyst is a lover of
truth, a recognizer of reality, free from all sham or deceit, but that
nevertheless no nonbelievers need apply, or at least none will be accepted. I have likened it to a rite of passage advisedly; for clearly this
pass/fail oral examination, in which the submissive candidate either
does or does not attain a firm conviction, either does or does not
learn to acknowledge the otherwise incredible, has more in common
with religious initiation than with scientific apprenticeship. Rather
than pursue such implications now, however, I would like to follow
Freud's argument a bit farther.

This stimulus to spontaneous self-remodelling "does in fact happen," Freud notes, "and in so far as it happens it makes the analysed
subject qualified to be an analyst himself." And then Freud continues
in a remarkable paragraph: "Unfortunately something else happens
as well. In trying to describe this, one can only rely on impressions.
Hostility on the one side and partisanship on the other create an atmosphere which is not favourable to objective investigation."—Let
me interrupt here to interject editorially, Not favorable, then, to scientific investigation. Freud is speaking, of course, of a highly politi-
cized situation, with the opponents and partisans of psychoanalysis
arrayed against each other. But consider: is not this equally the situation of the Freudian psyche itself? "Thanatos on the one side and
Eros on the other create an atmosphere which is not favorable to objective investigation." More succinctly still, "The psyche—as Freud
has imagined it—does not admit of objective investigation."

"It seems," Freud continues,

that a number of analysts learn to make use of defensive mechanisms
which allow them to divert the implications and demands of analysis
from themselves (probably by directing them on to other people), so
that they themselves remain as they are and are able to withdraw from
the critical and corrective influence of analysis. Such an event may justify the words of the writer who warns us that when a man is endowed
with power it is hard for him not to misuse it. (*SE* 23:249)

What are we to make of these powerfully defensive analysts who so
trouble Freud; are they endangered, or are they instead dangerous?
Their defenses against the demands of a more powerful other, their
insistent maintenance of self ("they themselves remain as they
are")—these, after all, are self-expressions that our Freudian model
teaches us to read as demonstrating an allegiance to the reality principle. And can this be what Freud suggests it is, a misuse of power?
Evidently not; for by Freud's own estimate, such an analyst *does* direct these demands of analysis on to other people, presumably his patients. Rather than a misuse of power, this seems to be a refusal to
submit to the power he wields.

Freud's next trope is even more strikingly dangerous to his argument:

> Sometimes, when we try to understand this, we are driven into draw-
> ing a disagreeable analogy with the effect of X-rays on people who
> handle them without taking special precautions. It would not be sur-
> prising if the effect of a constant preoccupation with all the repressed
> material which struggles for freedom in the human mind were to stir
> up in the analyst as well all the instinctual demands which he is other-
> wise able to keep under suppression. These, too, are "dangers of
> analysis," though they threaten, not the passive but the active partner
> in the analytic situation; and we ought not to neglect to meet them.
> There can be no doubt how this is to be done. Every analyst should pe-
> riodically . . . submit himself to analysis once more, without feeling
> ashamed of taking this step. (*SE* 23:249)

Freud implicitly likens the analyst's troubled patients to dangerously
radioactive packages of id capable of harming anyone who handles
them carelessly. But what does Freud's prescription have to do with
providing immunity to such a threat? The analogy resists his interpretation, and demands to be reread. In context, Freud's analogy actually insists on our reading the X-rays—a power that the doctor

therapeutically wields, a power that reveals what was always there but had otherwise remained hidden—as a trope for psychoanalysis itself. But insofar as the supposedly self-endangering behavior of these incautious X-ray manipulators comprises a greater skill in *defense* against psychoanalysis's penetration (they *divert* it, they withdraw from its *influence,* they *remain as they are*)—insofar as it seems, that is, actually a particular *cautiousness*—Freud's foreboding analogy turns against itself and darkly bespeaks the ultimate perverseness and predisposition of psychoanalysis's secret agenda. A disagreeable analogy, indeed: Freud might well find it so, for it most certainly does disagree with him.

We might ask, too, by which drive (*Trieb,* instinct) Freud is "*driven*" into drawing this analogy. *Is* he "try[ing] to understand," putting forth one of those "efforts at making an intelligible pattern" that leave the philosopher so liable to error? Or does Freud take a subversive pleasure in his playful sabotaging of his argument?

Like Coleridge, Freud seems to preach and practice an interminable adherence to the reality principle, a compulsive repetition of sane defense: There are dangers of analysis, and we ought not to neglect to meet them. But like Shelley, Freud also silently acknowledges the higher, rather than lower, calling of the wish to *submit* to a greater power, and insinuates the dark possibility that his truths are fictions, and his fictions deadly. He thrives and struggles, he lives and dies, in the curious space between psychoanalyzing and psychoanalysis. Like Coleridge, I will suggest finally, as a would-be transcendental philosopher Freud is instead actually one of our great critics; like Shelley, as a would-be interpreter he is actually instead important as a major poet.

V

The Romantic, chiastic tension between Coleridgean and Shelleyan rhetorics, between "philosophical" (reality-principle) and "literary" (pleasure-principle) attitudes toward the text, thus informs Freud's argument as well. But surely it informs all texts. Jerome Christensen, approaching Coleridge from quite a different direction, writes finely that "the chiasmus is the blessed machine of Coleridge's language";[7] I would universalize this to argue that we may sense it in all language. What varies is the overtness of the tension, and the interpreter's awareness of it. That awareness is today again acute. The tension between philosophy and literature builds at the very center of the deconstructionist debate.

The terms of this current debate are, from the perspective of this book's argument, too familiar to need much rehearsing here. When Derrida speaks of the "two interpretations of interpretation," one which "dreams of deciphering a truth or an origin which escapes play and the order of the sign," the other which "is no longer turned toward the origin, affirms play, and tries to pass beyond man and humanism,"[8] we recognize the irreconcilable alternatives of rhetoric that we have traced respectively from Coleridge and Shelley, even as Derrida has respectively from Rousseau and Nietzsche. When Culler, considering Derrida's attention to philosophy as a literary genre, concludes, "To read a text as philosophy is to ignore some of its aspects in favor of particular sorts of argument; to read it as literature is to remain attentive even to its apparently trivial features,"[9] we again recognize the very style and substance of Freud's comments (to which Culler is surely alluding) on dream interpretation as analogous to the grasping of a pseudo-Latin jest. In de Man's analysis of "the problem of the relationship between literature and philosophy" to the end that "Rhetoric is a *text* in that it allows for two incompatible, mutually self-destructive points of view," an "aporia between performative and constative language," and in Miller's argument that "metaphysics, the obvious or univocal meaning," and nihilism, its deconstructive enemy, are bound up reciprocally with each other, the same rhetorical insights we have been deriving from Coleridge and Shelley recur and recur.[10]

If every text, as I have been arguing, contains this tension between contesting attitudes, still most texts—how else have we been led for so long to categorize specific works as "philosophical" or "literary"?—seem to privilege one side or the other. Such, I particularly realize, will seem to be the case with the present text.

Hillis Miller has shrewdly noted that "If nihilism is the parasitical stranger within the house of metaphysics, 'nihilism,' as the name for the devaluation or reduction to nothingness of all values, is not the name nihilism has 'in itself.' It is the name given to it by metaphysics. . . ."[11] A similar truth obtains in the Freudian terminology I have utilized in this study. The borrowed vocabulary of my entire chiastic schema expresses the viewpoint of "philosophy," which sees "literature" as adhering ultimately to a death (that is, a death-to-philosophy) drive. From the point of view of "literature," of course, matters bear quite a different construction, and now "philosophy" denotes that which adheres to a death (that is, a death-to-literature) drive: in Harold Bloom's gnomic formulation, "Eros or libido *is* figurative meaning: the death-drive *is* literal meaning."[12] Philosophy regards literature as errant, extravagant, "parlous"; literature regards philosophy as rigorous; both ways—each seen from the other's perspective—lies death.[13]

But then again, the consequence of these antithetical claims is also that both ways—each seen from its own perspective—lies life. And now there looms a question we have not previously asked, and this shall be our final one: what is the life toward which literature strives? I shall take my clue or cue here whence Freud took his when he first assumed the separateness and distinctness of the sexual and the self-preservative instincts.[14] Certain pleasures—in biology, sexual pleasures—serve the preservation, not of the individual, but of the species. Sexuality, as Freud notes,

> is the single function of a living organism which extends beyond the individual and is concerned with his relation to the species. It is an unmistakable fact that it does not always, like the individual organism's other functions, bring it advantages, but, in return for an unusually high degree of pleasure, brings dangers which threaten the individual's life and often enough destroy it. (*Introductory Lectures on Psycho-Analysis*, SE 16:413)

While Freud, in his vexed efforts to reconcile the various elements and terms of his shifting theories, tries to retain both instincts, of self-preservation and of the preservation of the species, within the field of Eros (*SE* 23:148), it is very clear that in so doing he is again blurring instincts with principles; as Laplanche and Pontalis insist, "In fact the self-preservative functions ought instead to be assigned to the side of the reality principle from the start, and the sexual instincts to the side of the pleasure principle."[15] And as with biology, so, it would seem, with texts: the poet, in his unrealistic pursuit of textual pleasure, of the "wild West Wind," may endanger or harm or destroy himself, but his pursuit serves the ulterior purposes of the preservation of the species—of poetry itself. It contributes to, and sustains, "that great poem, which all poets, like co-operating thoughts of one great mind, have built up since the beginning of the world"; and it is thus and only thus that the poet himself is "washed in the blood of the mediator and the redeemer, Time" (*DP*, pp. 51, 76).

It remains now only to remember that, since literature and philosophy are not separable texts but inextricably entangled attitudes within a text, to preserve the life of one is to preserve that of the other. So the Arab-Quixote of Wordsworth's dream in Book 5 of *The Prelude* goes to save shell and stone together; and it is but a dream to think that we might ever separate them.

VI

Let us finally sketch again the outlines of the interpretative position to which our study of Romantic transcendental rhetoric and argument has brought us. "Philosophy" and "literature" name, not different kinds of texts, but different attitudes toward a text. When the text has transcendental aspirations or implications, the difference between philosophy and literature is a difference in psychological allegiances (to the reality principle or to the pleasure principle) in the face of this greater other. A transcendental text inevitably is metaphorical, and so indeterminate: "philosophy" means to ignore this uncertainty; "literature" means to acknowledge it. The text, then, is something of an Oedipus—(rhetorically) redundant;[16] (philosophically) guiltless but (literarily) polluted. Driven by univocal interpretation of ambivalent oracle to attempt to impose a favorable meaning on itself, it discovers the impossibility of such singlemindedness; alternatively resigning itself to the play of deeper, controlling forces, it finds however that it cannot, after all, withdraw from the world of reality, the necessity of interpreting and of being interpreted.

Notes

Preface

1. Tzvetan Todorov, "On Linguistic Symbolism," trans. Richard Klein, *New Literary History*, 6 (1974–75): 121–22, 129. Cf. Paolo Valesio, *Novantiqua: Rhetorics as a Contemporary Theory* (Bloomington: Indiana University Press, 1980), p. 187.

2. *Atheneum* fragment 116; *Friedrich Schlegel's Lucinde and the Fragments*, trans. Peter Firchow (Minneapolis: University of Minnesota Press, 1971), p. 175.

3. See Tzvetan Todorov, *Theories of the Symbol*, trans. Catherine Porter (Ithaca: Cornell University Press, 1982), pp. 34, 129–46.

4. A.W. Schlegel, *A Course of Lectures on Dramatic Art and Literature*, trans. John Black (London: Bohn, 1846), p. 340.

5. Certainly metonymy of clothing is very highly motivated indeed: clothing does suggest much of the form of its wearer, just as a guitar case suggests much of the form of the guitar, a glove much of the shape of the hand. But the guitar may instead rest in a suitcase, the hand in a mitten or a muff; or the guitar case may contain the gangster's machine gun. However greatly motivated, Shelley's vesture-metonymies are not determined.

6. The divergence is primal: the Latin *arguere* can mean variously "to make clear, prove, assert, accuse, or blame," as it shades gradually from logic to persuasion. While *arguere* itself typically crowds toward the logical end of this spectrum, moreover, its frequentative form, *argutare,* whence the English "argue" derives, means "to prattle, prate" (cf. the obsolete "argutation" [cavilling, cavil, quibble] and the colloquial "argufy"): the frequent, repeated argument loses its aura of referential, logical purity and stands increasingly revealed in its suasive, conative character.

7. Biedermann 1601; quoted by Bruno Snell, *The Discovery of the Mind: The Greek Origins of European Thought,* trans. T. G. Rosenmeyer (1953; repr. New York: Harper, 1960), p. 31.

8. J. Laplanche and J.-B. Pontalis, *The Language of Psycho-Analysis,* trans. Donald Nicholson-Smith (New York: Norton, 1973), p. 249.

Chapter 1

1. See Rene Wellek, *A History of Modern Criticism: 1750–1950* (New Haven: Yale University Press, 1955–), 1:211; 2:42, 76; Patricia A. Ward,

"Coleridge's Critical Theory of the Symbol," *Texas Studies in Literature and Language*, 8 (1966): 15–25; Kathleen Wheeler, *Sources, Processes, and Methods in Coleridge's Biographia Literaria* (Cambridge: Cambridge University Press, 1980), pp. 67, 75–76.

2. For some important exceptions calling into question Coleridge's discrimination of fancy from imagination and allegory from symbol, see Paul de Man, "The Rhetoric of Temporality" (1969), now republished in his *Blindness and Insight: Essays in the Rhetoric of Contemporary Criticism*, 2nd ed., rev. (Minneapolis: University of Minnesota Press, 1983), pp. 187–228, esp. 191–98; John Gatta, Jr., "Coleridge and Allegory," *Modern Language Quarterly*, 38 (1977): 62–77; Jerome C. Christensen, "The Symbol's Errant Allegory: Coleridge and His Critics," *ELH*, 45 (1978): 640–59; Frances Ferguson, "Coleridge on Language and Delusion," *Genre*, 11 (1978): 191–207; and Steven Knapp, *Personification and the Sublime: Milton to Coleridge* (Cambridge: Harvard University Press, 1985), pp. 10–50. More generally, see Christensen, *Coleridge's Blessed Machine of Language* (Ithaca: Cornell University Press, 1981).

3. Ralph Waldo Emerson, "Art," *Essays: First Series, The Complete Works of Ralph Waldo Emerson*, 12 vols. (Boston: Houghton Mifflin, 1903), 2:355.

4. Charles Lamb, "Christ's Hospital Five and Thirty Years Ago," *The Works of Charles and Mary Lamb*, ed. E. V. Lucas, 5 vols. (New York: G. P. Putnam's Sons, 1903), 2:24–25.

5. On *symbolon* and its implications, see James A. Coulter, *The Literary Microcosm: Theories of Interpretation of the Later Neoplatonists* (Leiden: E. J. Brill, 1976), pp. 43–51, 60–72, and Marc Shell, *The Economy of Literature* (Baltimore: Johns Hopkins University Press, 1978), pp. 33–36.

6. Coulter, p. 61.

7. Coulter, p. 60. For a sense of Proclus's usage as it enters the English tradition in Coleridge's time, see the first section of Proclus, "An Apology for the Fables of Homer," trans. Thomas Taylor (1804), in *Thomas Taylor the Platonist: Selected Writings,* ed. Kathleen Raine and George Mills Harper (Princeton: Princeton University Press, 1969), pp. 450–61.

8. *SM,* p. 70; cf. *The Philosophical Lectures of Samuel Taylor Coleridge,* ed. Kathleen Coburn (New York: Philosophical Library, 1949), p. 367.

9. Coulter does argue interestingly, however, that Proclus in some respects "anticipated the important distinction between allegory and symbol, whose formulation is customarily assigned by historians of literary theory to critics of the late eighteenth and early nineteenth century" (p. 45); and Wellek notes that A. W. Schlegel's idea of poetry's "symbolic relationship to

the whole universe . . . has its ultimate roots in neo-Platonism" (2:42; cf. 1:232, 2:75). Wellek's comment on Coleridge's notion of "Idea" seems equally applicable to his idea of "symbol": "It is true, of course, that some of these ideas have their ultimate source in antiquity and can be found occasionally in the English neo-Platonists. Coleridge was acquainted with Plato, Plotinus, Cudworth, Henry More, and others, but still he draws on the Germans, for only they use the same dialectical method as he, the same epistemology and the same critical vocabulary" (*A History of Modern Criticism* 2:156–57).

10. Coleridge, *Lectures 1795: On Politics and Religion,* ed. Lewis Patton and Peter Mann (Princeton: Princeton University Press, 1971), p. 158. Cf. the clearly Platonic or Neoplatonic characterization in "The Destiny of Nations" (1796) of all natural phenomena as "Symbolical, one mighty alphabet / For infant minds" (lines 19–20).

Coleridge already knew Proclus (who was particularly responsible for the Neoplatonic emphasis on *symbolon*) in the 1790s; see Thomas McFarland, *Coleridge and the Pantheist Tradition* (Oxford: Oxford University Press, 1969), pp. 356–57.

11. *LL* 1:325. Coleridge repeats a version of the assertion in his *Lay Sermon:* "Religion is the Poetry and Philosophy of all mankind" (in *Lay Sermons,* ed. R. J. White [Princeton: Princeton University Press, 1972], p. 197).

12. *TT,* 3/31/1832. Cf. Coleridge's marginalium criticizing interpreters of the Book of Revelation for "their utter want of . . . all Eye Taste and Tact for Poetry generally . . . Hence, they forget . . . that the Apocalypse is a POEM, and a Poem composed by a Hebrew Poet, after the peculiar type of Hebrew Poetry" (Cited in Coleridge, *On the Constitution of the Church and State,* ed. John Colmer [Princeton: Princeton University Press, 1976], p. 140n).

13. The word *tautegorical,* formed as a counterpart to *allegorical,* is Coleridge's coinage, and means "expressing the *same* subject but with a *difference*" (*AR,* p. 199/197).

14. The absolute comprehensiveness of this hierarchy, implicit in the present passage, becomes quite explicit in Coleridge's exactly contemporary *Theory of Life;* see Coleridge, *Miscellanies, Aesthetic and Literary,* ed. T. Ashe (London: Bell, 1885), pp. 384–385, 409–424.

15. The inconsistent figurativeness of Coleridge's mention of "translucence" here is noted by de Man, "The Rhetoric of Temporality," pp. 191–93. Coleridge himself is elsewhere sensitive to just this inconsistency: "It would be easy to explain a thought from the image on the retina, and that from the geometry of light, if this very light did not present the very same difficulty" (*BL* 1:137).

Coleridge's use of *translucence* in this *Statesman's Manual* passage has confused some commentators who have taken the word, in accordance with modern usage, to refer to a medium through which light imperfectly passes. Coleridge's actual meaning is "shining through," referring not to the medium but to the light passing through it. An instance from the *Table Talk* confirms this unambiguously: "As to what Captain Hall says about the English loyalty to the person of the King—I can only say, I feel none of it. I respect the man while, and only while, the king is translucent in him: I reverence the glass case for the Saint's sake within; except for that, it is to me mere glazier's work—putty, and glass, and wood" (8/20/1830). See also "The Destiny of Nations," draft I (1796), line 19 (*CPW* 1:522); "On Poesy and Art," in *Biographia Literaria*, ed. J. Shawcross (Oxford: Oxford University Press, 1907), 2:263; *AR*, p. 391/393; "The Two Founts," line 27 (*CPW*, 1:455). The *OED* cites Coleridge as the first to use "translucence," but cites no instance earlier than the 1827 "Two Founts" occurrence.

16. In line with his notion of the universal hierarchy Coleridge imposes a qualification on these latter tropes: a lower form or species may symbolize only a higher in the same kind (*AR*, p. 254n/253n). No member of a species may symbolize a lower in the same kind, and only the lowest form may symbolize the entire genus. These restrictions derive straightforwardly from Coleridge's unempirically hierarchical, chain-of-being notion "that the Definition of a Genus or Class is an *adequate* definition only of the lowest *species* of that Genus: for each higher species is distinguished from the lower by some additional character, while the General Definition includes only the characters common to *all* the Species. Consequently it *describes* the lowest only" (*AR*, p. 238/236). See also *Friend* 1:467n.

17. Coleridge, *Confessions of an Inquiring Spirit,* ed. H. StJ. Hart (1956; Stanford: Stanford University Press, 1957), p. 42.

18. See Jacques Derrida's meditation upon the sun as the paradigmatic and ultimate metaphor, the metaphor of metaphor, in "White Mythology: Metaphor in the Text of Philosophy," trans. F. C. T. Moore, *New Literary History*, 6 (1974–75), 5–74, esp. 18, 46–60, 68–71. Cf. J. Hillis Miller, "A 'Buchstabliches' Reading of *The Elective Affinities,*" *Glyph*, 6 (1979): 16. See also Jerome C. Christensen, "The Symbol's Errant Allegory," who argues that "in Coleridge the undeniable and pervasive wish for a metaphysical continuity that is involved in his promotion of the symbol is typically breached by a discourse that divulges the obdurate discontinuities of signification. Coleridge's metaphysical symbolism is transgressed by a discursive allegory" (p. 644).

For a view the converse of Christensen's and mine, see Leslie Brisman,

"Coleridge and the Supernatural," *Studies in Romanticism* 21, (1982): 123–59, which avowedly "treat[s] Coleridge the poet [but apparently Coleridge the critic and theologian also] as though he were always of the 'symbolist' party without knowing it" (p. 129n).

19. Another notably allegorical rejection of allegorizing occurs in an 1805 notebook entry: "The understanding of Metaphor for Reality (Loaves and Fishes = Apostles, Fisherman, Christ's Doctrine/&c&c) one of the Fountains of the many-headed River of Credulity which overflowing covers the world with miscreations & reptile monsters, & then gives its huge supply thro' its many mouths into the Sea of Blood" (*CN* 2:2711; cf. 2:2724). As Brisman notes, "Perhaps the most striking thing about this passage is that in saying *no* to the allegorical mode Coleridge releases a surprising rush of allegorical imagery, as though he momentarily turned the spigot to demonstrate the work that the valve of literalism must do" ("Coleridge and the Supernatural," p. 135).

20. Coleridge anticipates his new thinking on metaphor here possibly as early as 1807–12, in reading and reacting to Johann Friedrich Jacobi's antagonistic edition of Bahrdt's *Glaubens-Bekanntniss:* "a Metaphor does not express the Thing: (for how then is it a Metaphor[?)] but the *effect* of the Thing. When I call the Sonun the Lam[p] of Heav[en] I mea[n] that [the] effec[t] on us is th[e] same as tha[t] of a Lamp[,] not t[hat] the Su[n] is itse[lf] a Lam[p]" (*Marginalia* 1:200; as the brackets suggest, the page has been cropped). As Whalley notes, Coleridge "evidently consulted [this note] when he was writing *AR*" (1:197).

21. If, as Coleridge sometimes suggests, the effects in question are similar but not identical, this figural combination becomes even more complex: it will now also contain in its middle a metaphoric figuration of one effect by the other.

22. They are arbitrary—illogical or alogical—because they are formed from two conversely related synecdoches and thus involve the sophism of transition into a new kind. On metaphor as a combination of synecdoches see Jacques Dubois et al., *A General Rhetoric,* trans. Paul B. Burrell and Edgar M. Slotkin (Baltimore: Johns Hopkins University Press, 1981), especially pp. 106–10, and the brief summary by Jonathan Culler, *Structuralist Poetics* (Ithaca: Cornell University Press, 1975), pp. 180–81; also Umberto Eco, "Metaphor, Dictionary, Encyclopedia," *New Literary History,* 15 (1984): 255–63. For Coleridge on the sophism involved, see *SM,* p. 99 and n; *AR,* pp. 215/213, 311/314; *Logic,* p. 90. I shall discuss the logical status of determined metaphor in the next chapter.

23. While most of the marginalia in this volume date from 1831–32, else-

where on this same page (the first of the text proper) Coleridge records the date "1816"; and one later note to this same, first sermon seems to anticipate a not-yet-written *Theory of Life*, and thus almost certainly also dates from 1816 (*Marginalia* 2:268).

24. Notebook 29, f. 59; quoted in J. Robert Barth, *The Symbolic Imagination: Coleridge and the Romantic Tradition* (Princeton: Princeton University Press, 1977), p. 5n. For the date of the entry (c. September 1821), see *Marginalia* 1:345n.

25. "On the Prometheus of Aeschylus," in *The Complete Works of Samuel Taylor Coleridge*, ed. W. G. T. Shedd, 7 vols. (New York: Harper, 1884), 4:351, 361.

26. See the *Critique of Pure Reason*, B299–315; *Prolegomena to Any Future Metaphysics*, secs. 30, 34.

27. *Literary Remains*, in *The Complete Works of Samuel Taylor Coleridge*, ed. Shedd, 5:402; see also *CL* 2:1193; *SM*, p. 67; *Friend* 1:515.

28. *Theory of Life*, in *Miscellanies, Aesthetic and Literary*, p. 404; see also *CN* 1:2319.

29. Cf., conversely, the suggestion of analogy sometimes present in Coleridge's description of determined metaphor—for example, his characterization of the Redemption's effects as "the same for the Sinner *relatively to* God and his own Soul, as the satisfaction of a debt for a Debtor *relatively to* his Creditor" (*AR*, p. 327/329; my emphasis).

30. Immanuel Kant, *Critique of Judgment*, trans. J. H. Bernard (New York: Macmillan, 1951), p. 315 (footnote to section 90). See also Kant's brief discussions of analogy in section 59 of this same *Critique* (pp. 197–200) and in section 58 of the *Prolegomena to Any Future Metaphysics*.

31. While the recognition that analogy is a (perhaps especially elegant) form of metaphor goes back at least to Aristotle (*Poetics*, 1457b6–33; *Rhetoric*, III.10–11, 1411a1–1411b20) and thoroughly informs the entire Neoplatonic tradition, Coleridge's pointed privilegings of determined metaphor and particularly of analogy may well owe something also to a source he did not often mine, St. Thomas Aquinas. In the *Summa Contra Gentiles* I, xxviii-xxxiv, St. Thomas argues that the perfections found in other things can be attributed to God "only according to likeness and metaphor," and specifically "in the same way as effects are found in their equivocal causes," "since we cannot know Him naturally except by arriving at Him from His effects"; that this predication is yet not equivocal, because we can and do "come to a knowledge of God from other things," from effect to cause; that, finally, such knowledge is possible because this predication of God is not merely metaphorical, but analogical (*On the*

Truth of the Catholic Faith: Summa Contra Gentiles Book I: God, trans. Anton C. Pegis [Garden City, New York: Doubleday, 1955], pp. 135–48). Another version of Aquinas's argument appears in his *Summa Theologica;* see especially I. xiii.5.

32. Coleridge recurs to this example in his *Logic,* p. 117, where he acknowledges Mendelssohn as his source, and in an appendix to *On the Constitution of the Church and State,* pp. 178–79. He seems also to have had it in mind as a figure for his planned *magnum opus:* see *CL* 5:239.

Chapter 2

1. Hume advances the argument especially in *An Inquiry Concerning Human Understanding* (1748), sections 6 and 7, and *Treatise of Human Nature* (1739–40), Part III, sections 14 and 15. The observation quickly became a skeptical commonplace; compare William Drummond, *Academical Questions* (London: Bulmer, 1805), p. 157.

2. Friedrich Nietzsche, *The Will to Power,* trans. Anthony M. Ludovici, III.1.h.551, in *The Complete Works of Friedrich Nietzsche,* ed. Oscar Levy (New York: Gordon Press, 1974), 15:56–57, 58.

3. Jonathan Culler, *The Pursuit of Signs: Semiotics, Literature, Deconstruction* (Ithaca: Cornell University Press, 1981), p. 183.

4. To his rule that "Reason cannot exist without Understanding" Coleridge does elsewhere offer a single, fictitious exception, Don Quixote, who personifies "the reason and the moral sense divested of the judgment and the understanding" (*LL* 2:162; cf. *Omniana,* p. 183). Again, the suggestion that at least some dreams evince reason without understanding is implicit in Coleridge's musings that "Nightmair is . . . a state not of Sleep, but of Stupor of the outward organs of Sense . . . while the volitions of *Reason* . . . are awake, tho' disturbed" (*CN* 3:4046) and that certain vision-like dreams tap not the sensations and memory but an inner sense, a spiritual "divining power in the human mind" (*SM,* pp. 80–83).

5. Thomas Carlyle, *The Life of John Sterling,* in *Works,* ed. H. D. Traill, 30 vols. (London: Chapman and Hall, 1898–1901), 11:57.

6. "On the Prometheus of Aeschylus," in *The Complete Works of Samuel Taylor Coleridge,* ed. Shedd, 4:359.

7. Kant, *Critique of Judgment,* pp. 99–104 , esp. pp. 100, 103. The quotation on Burke is from p. 119.

8. As Frances Ferguson notes more generally, "the problem that haunts Burke's *Enquiry* is the possibility that repeated exposure to the sublime may annihilate it altogether"; "The sublime . . . dwindles as soon as familiarity converts the necessary distance of danger and death into an absolute banish-

ment of those dreads" ("The Sublime of Edmund Burke, or the Bathos of Experience," *Glyph*, 8 [1981]: 70, 71).

9. Thomas Weiskel, *The Romantic Sublime: Studies in the Structure and Psychology of Transcendence* (Baltimore: Johns Hopkins University Press, 1976), pp. 93–106; the quotation is from p. 94.

10. Edgar Allan Poe, "The Purloined Letter," in *The Collected Works of Edgar Allan Poe*, ed. Thomas Ollive Mabbott (Cambridge: Harvard University Press, 1969–), 3:984–85.

Despite the schoolboy's first example, his strategy would meet its match in a truly arrant simpleton. As Senator Snort quite validly advises a colleague in Wagner's syndicated "Grin and Bear It" cartoon of 9 December 1985, "Always keep your opponent guessing. . . . If you don't know what you're doing, neither can he."

11. These assumptions are more generally those of the eighteenth-century moral philosophers, for whom "sympathy" was a fundamental moral (and, increasingly, aesthetic) virtue; so Erasmus Darwin, for example, notes that if we assume "the attitude that any passion naturally occasions, we soon in some degree acquire that passion" ("Of Instinct," *Zoonomia* [1794–96], 146–47; cited by Walter Jackson Bate, *From Classic to Romantic: Premises of Taste in Eighteenth Century England* [1946; New York: Harper and Row, 1961], p. 139).

It is worth noting that recent psychological research tends to confirm Campanella's supposed insightfulness: his rhetorical strategy may be none the less effective for all its deductive illogic. Apparently human facial expressions can indeed produce corresponding emotions as well as express them. See Paul Ekman et al. in *Science* (9/16/1983), and a report on Ekman's work in the *Chronicle of Higher Education* (6/5/1985), p. 30.

12. For further discussion of Freud's obscurantism in "The 'Uncanny,'" see below, Afterword, section III.

13. Burke analyzes a similar confusion and reversal in his account of "the new monied interest" of France, "long looked on with rather an evil eye by the people" (for "They saw it connected with their distresses, and aggravating them," as if it in fact were an evil eye to them) and "no less envied by the old landed interests": the monied interest in turn resents its felt inferiority to the latter and manages to redirect against them the popular envy originally directed at its own "obnoxious wealth" (*RRF*, pp. 125–29).

14. Barbara Johnson, *The Critical Difference* (Baltimore: Johns Hopkins University Press, 1980), p. 118, anticipates me in this point, taking a hint from Lacan.

15. Yet notwithstanding his absolute rejection of this absurdity, Coleridge's own philosophical system is founded upon just such an infinite regress. As Grosvenor Powell has pointed out, "Coleridge cannot resolve the conception of self-consciousness as an absolute ground. . . . In fact, Coleridge was unable to define self-consciousness since he was unwilling to accept a definition which acknowledged the regress . . . present in his use of the notion" ("Coleridge's 'Imagination' and the Infinite Regress of Consciousness," *ELH*, 39 [1972]: 275–76).

16. The allegorist to whom Coleridge here alludes is Coleridge himself. The allegory is his "Allegoric Vision," and the irrational insistence that "infinite blindness supplied the want of sight" is the credo of the Janus-headed priest of Superstition/Atheism therein. See *Lay Sermons*, pp. 131–37; *CPW* 2:1091–96. Coleridge rejects the imputation that he himself is "The Blind offering to lead the Blind" at the beginning of *The Friend* (1:10).

17. So he speculates in his *Logic*: "The mind is distinguished from other things as a subject that is its own object, an eye, as it were, that is its own mirror, beholding and self-beheld" (p. 76).

18. Contrast Friedrich Schlegel's celebration of such endless mirroring as the very apotheosis of Romantic poetry: "it can . . . hover at the midpoint between the portrayed and the portrayer, . . . on the wings of poetic reflection, and can raise that reflection again and again to a higher power, can multiply it in an endless succession of mirrors" (Athenemum Fragment 116; *Friedrich Schlegel's Lucinde and the Fragments*, p. 175). But Schlegel, too, when he comes to acknowledge "the irony of irony" in his essay "On Incomprehensibility," finds in this endless repetitiveness, as de Man argues, no "higher power" after all, but only the multiplication of the void (cf. de Man, "The Rhetoric of Temporality,"pp. 221–22).

19. Cf. the moral of "The Fable of the Madning Rain"—"It is in vain to be sane in a world of madmen"—and Coleridge's response (*Friend* 1:9–10).

20. Cf. Frances Ferguson, "Coleridge on Language and Delusion," *Genre*, 11 (1978): 193–95.

21. See *BL* 1:272–86 *passim;* cf. *Marginalia* 2:291 ("The Christian Preacher should abjure every argument, that is not a link in the chain of which Christ is the Staple and Staple Ring"), 2:466.

22. I discuss some rhetorical implications of allusiveness in chapter 4, section IV.

23. Coleridge frequently, as here, offers this knot in the line as a figure alternative to that of the staple at the end of the chain; but cutting the knot thus subversively looses the chain. Thus the dissolving rock of ice that fails to sup-

port the staple of Spinoza's chain corresponds to Pantheism's "cutting the
Knot, which it cannot untwist" (*Friend* 1:522n). Cf. *CL* 4:864, *Marginalia*
1:557, 2:628.

Chapter 3

1. *The Complete Works of Percy Bysshe Shelley,* ed. Roger Ingpen and
Walter E. Peck, The Julian Edition, 10 vols. (New York: Scribner's, and London: Ernest Benn Limited, 1926–30), 7:336. This manuscript note is also directly relevant to the *Defence of Poetry,* for the passage to which it is ap-
pended is that which Shelley later adapted as the concluding paragraph of
the *Defence.*

2. *DP,* pp. 56, 73; "Preface" to *The Cenci,* in *SPP,* p. 241. Compare Shelley's assertion to Hunt that "the Imagination . . . is the master of them both
[the passions and the understanding], their God, and the Spirit by which they
live and are" (*SL* 2:152).

3. Cf. Earl R. Wasserman, *Shelley: A Critical Reading* (Baltimore: Johns
Hopkins University Press, 1971), pp. 208–9.

4. Cf. Paul H. Fry, *The Poet's Calling in the English Ode* (New Haven:
Yale University Press, 1980), p. 207. It is noteworthy that Coleridge, in contrast, follows Bacon in asserting that the understanding is such a distorting
mirror (*Friend,* 1:491; *Logic,* pp. 39–40).

5. Shelley's most explicit statements of his skepticism appear in his "Essay
on Life," "Essay on a Future State," and note 2 to *Hellas.* Our present critical
sensitivity to Shelley's skepticism derives especially from C. E. Pulos, *The
Deep Truth* (Lincoln: University of Nebraska Press, 1954). An awareness of
Shelley's skepticism informs, though does not dominate, such diverse studies
as Wasserman, *Shelley*; James Rieger, *The Mutiny Within* (New York:
George Braziller, 1967); and Judith Chernaik, *The Lyrics of Shelley* (Cleve-
land: The Press of Case Western Reserve University, 1972). More recently,
such an awareness is central to Lloyd Abbey, *Destroyer and Preserver: Shel-
ley's Poetic Skepticism* (Lincoln: University of Nebraska Press, 1979); Jean
Hall, *The Transforming Image: A Study of Shelley's Major Poetry* (Urbana:
University of Illinois Press, 1980); Tilottama Rajan, *Dark Interpreter: The
Discourse of Romanticism* (Ithaca: Cornell University Press, 1980); and
Richard Cronin, *Shelley's Poetic Thoughts* (New York: St. Martin's Press,
1981).

6. Some of the subversive implications of Shelley's shift here to *we* from
Milton's *ye* are explored by Margaret W. Ferguson, *Trials of Desire: Renaissance Defenses of Poetry* (New Haven: Yale University Press, 1983), pp.
176–78. Others, I will suggest in passing, lurk in Shelley's play on *stoop*—a

condescending to those on a lower level (*stupid* ones—the words are cognate), but also a hawk's or falcon's (a *soaring* bird's) stunning, *stupefying* plunge onto its prey.

Responding to an antagonistic critic, Shelley identified himself with Satan via this same quotation in a letter dating from this same period: "But I feel in respect to the writer in question, that 'I am there sitting where he durst not soar—'" (*SL* 2:251).

7. On Macbeth's "humankindness," see Ruth Nevo, *Tragic Form in Shakespeare* (Princeton: Princeton University Press, 1972), pp. 221–27.

8. Cf. Paul H. Fry's conclusion, "there is an intellectual honesty peculiar to Shelley that makes one feel that the defeat of metaphor by metaphor in his poems amounts to a confession, an unhappy confession that is impossible to ignore in the 'Ode to the West Wind,' and that constantly subverts his attraction to the ode and to the celebratory manner" (*The Poet's Calling in the English Ode*, pp. 193–94).

9. Richard Cronin makes a similar but narrower point about the relation of "Adonais" to "Lycidas" in the elegiac tradition: "*Adonais* works with *Lycidas* rather than against it. And yet this statement, though true, is somewhat paradoxical. To be in harmony with Milton is to be in harmony with a predecessor quite as fierce as Shelley in his relations with received literary tradition" (*Shelley's Poetic Thoughts*, p. 201).

10. Pulos, *The Deep Truth*, pp. 106–7; cf. Cronin, *Shelley's Poetic Thoughts*, pp. 199–200.

11. William Drummond, *Academical Questions*, p. 192. On Drummond's influence on Shelley, see Pulos, *The Deep Truth*, chapter 3.

12. On Shelley's suicidal impulses and insinuations see especially Rieger, *The Mutiny Within*, pp. 229–35, and Richard Holmes, *Shelley: The Pursuit* (New York: Dutton, 1975), pp. 70, 627, 725–29.

13. Weiskel, *The Romantic Sublime*, also investigates the connections between Burke and Freud, though his emphasis falls on Freud's psychoanalytic psychology, not on the metapsychology; see pp. 83–104, esp. pp. 92–96.

14. As Laplanche and Pontalis observe, "the intrasubjective field [of Freud's 'second topography' of id, ego, and superego] tends to be conceived of after the fashion of intersubjective relations, and the systems are pictured as relatively autonomous persons-within-the-person" (*The Language of Psycho-Analysis*, p. 452). Cp. Freud's assertion in *The Psychopathology of Everyday Life* that much of mythology and religion "*is nothing but psychology projected into the external world*" (Freud's emphasis; *SE* 6:258).

Burke's matrix not only anticipates Freud but also suggestively foreshadows Lacan's interpretation of Freud, especially Lacan's attention to "the unconscious [as] the discourse of the other." Cf. Jacques Lacan, *Speech and Language in Psychoanalysis*, trans., with notes and commentary, Anthony Wilden (Baltimore: Johns Hopkins University Press, 1968), pp. 27, 106–8 n. 49, 263–69.

15. Jacques Derrida, "Coming into One's Own," trans. James Hulbert, in *Psychoanalysis and the Question of the Text*, ed. Geoffrey H. Hartman (Baltimore: Johns Hopkins University Press, 1978), p. 138.

16. See Laplanche and Pontalis, *The Language of Psycho-Analysis*, pp. 51–52, 242; and cf. pp. 272–73.

17. Despite Freud's occasional practice, we cannot properly speak of the Nirvana *principle;* it is not a principle, but a state or condition. Nirvana is to be identified neither with the pleasure principle nor with the death instinct, but, schematically speaking, with their intersection.

18. For a quite differently grounded but ultimately compatible analysis of Freud's theory of the drives, see Jean Laplanche, *Life and Death in Psychoanalysis*, trans. Jeffrey Mehlman (Baltimore: Johns Hopkins University Press, 1976), pp. 103–24. I refer especially to pp. 122–24, where Laplanche analyzes "the genealogy of the final instinctual dualism" of Eros and the death drive as "tak[ing] the form of a strange chiasmus" (p. 124). While there are important differences between Laplanche's scheme and my own (most notably, his is diachronic while mine is synchronic), in many respects each schema seems convertible into the other.

19. Cp. Freud's ambivalent analysis of that other example of the uncanny, the evil eye: that which he originally takes as an expression of aggressive envy actually seems to signal a *defensiveness* against such envy. See above, chapter 2, section IV.

20. Hence, for example, those dreams during traumatic neuroses, "dreams which, with a view to the psychical binding of traumatic impression, obey the compulsion to repeat" (*SE* 18:33). By "binding," Freud here means what I have termed *bounding* (above, section VII).

21. Freud can be seen working toward this position in the early *Psychotherapy of Hysteria* (1895): "A picture which refuses to disappear is one which still calls for consideration, a thought which cannot be dismissed is one that needs to be pursued further. Moreover, a recollection never returns a second time once it has been dealt with; an image that has been 'talked away' is not seen again" (*SE* 2:296).

22. Jacques Lacan, "The Agency of the Letter in the Unconscious," in *Ecrits: A Selection*, trans. Alan Sheridan (New York: Norton, 1977), pp. 166, 175.

23. Carlyle, *The Life of John Sterling*, in *Works* 11:55–56.

24. I note that Harold Bloom in his "Introduction" to Samuel Taylor Coleridge, *Selected Poetry*, ed. Bloom (New York: New American Library, 1972), p. 27, asks, "What is the total situation of the Ancient Mariner but a repetition-compulsion, which his poet breaks for himself only by the writing of the poem and then only momentarily?" Elsewhere, though, Bloom follows Freud's initial impulses in associating repetition-compulsion with the death drive (Bloom, *Agon: Towards a Theory of Revisionism* [New York: Oxford University Press, 1982], pp. 97, 136, 138), while I am instead arguing that it serves the *life* instinct.

Chapter 4

1. Harold Bloom, *A Map of Misreading* (New York: Oxford University Press, 1975), p. 91. Cf. similar comments in his *Agon*, pp. 124, 139.

2. Roland Barthes, *Writing Degree Zero*, trans. Annette Lavers and Colin Smith (London: Cape, 1967), p. 74.

3. Tzvetan Todorov, *Introduction to Poetics*, trans. Richard Howard (Minneapolis: University of Minnesota Press, 1981), p. 22. Cf. J. Hillis Miller, "The Critic as Host," in Harold Bloom et al., *Deconstruction and Criticism* (New York: Seabury, 1979), p. 223. More generally, see Paul Ricoeur, *The Rule of Metaphor*, trans. Robert Czerny (Toronto: University of Toronto Press, 1977), pp. 138ff.

4. Chernaik, *The Lyrics of Shelley*, p. 41. Cf. Harold Bloom, *Shelley's Mythmaking* (1959; repr. Ithaca, N.Y.: Cornell University Press, 1969), p. 23.

5. The most forceful exponent of this "One Mind" reading is Earl R. Wasserman, whose interpretation of "Mont Blanc" in *The Subtler Language* (1959) recurs in his *Shelley: A Critical Reading*, pp. 221–38. Harold Bloom advances a similar "universal mind" reading of the poem in *Shelley's Mythmaking* and again in *The Visionary Company: A Reading of English Romantic Poetry* (Garden City, N.Y.: Doubleday, 1961), p. 309. Wasserman and Bloom are anticipated in this aspect of their explications by C. D. Locock in his edition, *The Poems of Percy Bysshe Shelley* (London: Methuen, 1911), 2:489–90.

6. Hence Wasserman: "Since each human mind is also one of the 'things' of the universe, it too pours its tributary stream into the universal river of the One Mind . . ." (*Shelley*, p. 223). And similarly Bloom: "The ravine masks and metaphorically represents universal mind; the Arve river, the 'everlasting Universe of things,' and the 'feeble brook,' the human mind . . ." (*The Visionary Company*, p. 309).

7. As Paul H. Fry notes, Shelley "takes it for granted almost from the be-

ginning that 'things' are *mental*. . . . He will often write 'things' when he
means 'thoughts' (in the opening sentences of the *Defence* there are two
manuscript changes from 'things' to 'thoughts'), but that is simply because
the nominalist habit of expression is difficult to get over and too handy to do
without" (*The Reach of Criticism: Method and Perception in Literary Theory* [New Haven: Yale University Press, 1983], p. 132).

8. More subtly, this same distinction also informs the poem that is something of a companion piece to "Mont Blanc," the "Hymn to Intellectual
Beauty." Shelley there addresses Intellectual Beauty as "Thou—that to human thought art nourishment, / Like darkness to a dying flame!" (44–45). It
is nourishing only in that, as does darkness a burning candle, it reveals that
there *is* such a flame of thought—a flame that would be effectively obscured
by the vastly greater light of common day, just as in "Mont Blanc" the internal contribution of "human thought" is nearly obscured by the vastly greater
flow of external impressions.

9. David Hume, *An Inquiry Concerning Human Understanding,* ed.
Charles W. Hendel (Indianapolis: Bobbs-Merrill, 1955), p. 28.

10. David Hume, *An Enquiry Concerning the Principles of Morals;*
quoted by M. H. Abrams, *The Mirror and the Lamp* (New York: Norton,
1958), p. 64.

11. I follow the text of "Mont Blanc" established by Chernaik, *The Lyrics
of Shelley,* in understanding a comma at the end of line 45.

12. Though several critics have pointed to the myth of the cave in Plato's
Republic as a source of Shelley's cave of the witch Poesy, I suggest that we
should trace it back there mediately through Bacon. I have in mind particularly Shelley's observation in his "Essay on Christianity" that "Every human mind has what Lord Bacon calls its *idola specus,* peculiar images which
reside in the inner cave of thought. These constitute the essential and distinctive character of every human being" (*SP,* p. 199). Bacon uses the phrase in
the course of an explicit reference to Plato's cave; see *De augmentis scien-
tiarum* V. iv.

13. Jacques Derrida, "Coming into One's Own," in Hartman, *Psycho-
analysis and the Question of the Text,* p. 120.

14. The Arve/rave/aver anagram is strongly implicit in Shelley's transition
from section I to section II, with its striking phonetic links: "ever / . . . vast
river / Over . . . rocks . . . bursts and raves. / . . . Ravine of Arve" (9–12).
William Keach notes the Arve/rave link in *Shelley's Style* (London: Methuen,
1984), p. 197. I am grateful to Nelson Hilton for his suggestion about the relation of "river" to "riving." In French, alternatively (and Chamounix is a

French-speaking area), *river* means just the opposite—"to attach" or "to rivet" (the latter is a cognate).

15. On the "vale"/"veil" homophone, cf. Keach, *Shelley's Style*, pp. 198–99.

The underlying pun on "bound" in "Mont Blanc" 90–91 is enriched by the deeper allusive presence of a prior context and pun, Satan's entrance into Eden in *Paradise Lost:* disdaining to enter by the gate, he "At one slight bound high overleap'd all bound" (IV.181).

16. Shelley's scriptural allusion here seems all the more certain in that he repeats it in similar terms four years later in the verse "Letter to Maria Gisborne." He is speaking of Spanish, "The language of a land which now is free," which "winged with thoughts of truth and majesty / Flits round the tyrant's sceptre like a cloud, / And bursts the peopled prisons—cries aloud, / 'My name is Legion!'" (176–80).

17. Wasserman, *Shelley*, p. 235n; Chernaik, *The Lyrics of Shelley*, p. 59 n.10.

18. But Leslie Brisman, who further relates "Mont Blanc" allusively to numerous biblical, prophetic voices, seems to have noted and appreciated the allusion to John the Baptist; see his *Romantic Origins* (Ithaca: Cornell University Press, 1978), pp. 382–83.

19. Friedrich Schlegel, "On Incomprehensibility," in *Friedrich Schlegel: Lucinde and the Fragments*, p. 267.

"Polytropic wearyingness" I borrow from Odysseus—*Odysseus polytropos*, "Odysseus of many turns" (*Odyssey* X.330), as one of his characteristic epithets proclaims him—whose many turnings bespeak both resourcefulness and long-suffering.

20. Cf. the encompassing cycle of the Platonic year; the notions of pre-Adamite races and prehuman worlds introduced by Byron in *Cain;* the pulsatingly expanding and contracting universe of Poe's *Eureka.*

21. For a fuller discussion, see John A. Hodgson, "The World's Mysterious Doom: Shelley's 'The Triumph of Life,'" *ELH*, 42 (1975): 595–622, esp. pp. 601, 603–4.

22. Cf. Vergil, *Georgics* I.242–51; Wordsworth, *The Excursion* IV.699–717.

23. As Cronin notes of a similar crux in stanza V, "The confusing metaphors distract the attention from a question that the stanza begs: how can one rely on mortal fame as a compensation for one's sufferings when the world has forgotten some suns, and yet retains the memory of some tapers?" (*Shelley's Poetic Thoughts*, pp. 180–81).

24. Cf. the poet of "Alastor," who "shall live alone / In the frail *pauses*" of the narrator's song (705–6; my emphasis). With this "But for our grief," cf. "Mont Blanc," 79 ("But for such faith . . ."): Shelley's "but" here in "Adonais" 182, I would suggest, repeats the syntactic ambiguity of that earlier passage.

25. Jerome McGann, "The Secrets of an Elder Day: Shelley after *Hellas*," *Keats-Shelley Journal*, 15 (1966): 38–39. See also Hodgson, "The World's Mysterious Doom: Shelley's 'The Triumph of Life,' " 596–97.

26. Paul Weiss, *Nine Basic Arts* (Carbondale, Ill., 1961), pp. 164–66; cited in Douglas Berggren, "The Use and Abuse of Metaphor, I," *Review of Metaphysics*, 16 (1962–63): 240.

27. Cf.*The Watchman*, ed. Lewis Patton (Princeton: Princeton University Press, 1970), p. 318; *Inquiring Spirit*, ed. Kathleen Coburn (London: Routledge and Kegan Paul, 1951), p. 153.

28. Coleridge himself also notes the contrariness of dreams: "The *Praegustatores* among the luxurious Romans soon lost their Taste; and the verdicts of an old Praegustator were sure to mislead, unless when, like Dreams, they were interpreted into contraries" (*CL* 2:317).

29. So Cronin notes that the question closing "Ode to the West Wind" "bravely attempts to be rhetorical, but in it affirmation coincides with wistfulness. The certainty that the seasonal cycle will continue its round . . . is not matched by a similar certainty of the imminence of the apocalyptic spring that Shelley prophesies. . . . Ode to the West Wind is, in a sense other than Shelley intended, a 'congregated might', a grand *peut-être*" (*Shelley's Poetic Thoughts*, p. 242).

30. For two important exceptions, see V. Voloshinov [probably a pseudonym for Mikhail Bakhtin], *Marxism and the Philosophy of Language*, trans. L. Matejka and I. R. Titunik (New York: Seminar Press, 1973), pp. 109–59, on quotation, and Ziva Ben-Porot, "The Poetics of Literary Allusion," *PTL*, 1 (1976): 105–28. Barbara Johnson, *The Critical Difference*, p. 111, touches on the question interestingly at the beginning of her consideration of Derrida reading Lacan reading Poe's "The Purloined Letter." For Romantic poetry particularly, James K. Chandler, "Romantic Allusiveness," *Critical Inquiry*, 8 (1981–82): 461–87, argues cogently that Romantic allusiveness is not fundamentally different from Augustan or any other kind, but that "the threshold [of recognizability] is lower for most Romantic poetry; that is, the echo admits of a greater degree of muffling" (485).

31. Harold Bloom, *The Breaking of the Vessels* (Chicago: University of Chicago Press, 1982), p. 13; *A Map of Misreading*, pp. 102, 126.

32. As Ben-Porot observes, "In a literary allusion . . . the . . . sign points

towards another text . . . in which the symbol constituting the sign may acquire different denotation(s). These . . . are independent of, and may even be incompatible with, the reconstructed world of the alluding text" ("The Poetics of Literary Allusion," 108). But this independence, of course, is not mutual; and any important incompatibility with the referent will necessarily introduce a significant strain (potentially analogous to the anxious tension of the sublime itself) into the dependent, alluding text.

33. For a sustained sensitivity to the significance, and the subversive potential, of allusive context, see Robert F. Gleckner, *Blake's Prelude: Poetical Sketches* (Baltimore: Johns Hopkins University Press, 1982), pp. 10–12, 90, and especially *Blake and Spenser* (Baltimore: Johns Hopkins University Press, 1985), pp. 1–3, 173, 194. Blake's "significant allusions," Gleckner demonstrates at length, "[draw] with them into his context an appropriate borrowed context, one that more often than not inverts, subverts, or otherwise comments upon the significance or direction of the Blakean context into which it has been inserted"; Blake's "manipulations of contextualized allusions . . . provide various angles of perception by which to construe his own poetry as well as to probe its 'greater truth' " (*Blake and Spenser*, pp. 2, 173).

34. John Hollander, *The Figure of Echo: A Mode of Allusion in Milton and After* (Berkeley: University of California Press, 1981), pp. 133–49, provides an extended discussion.

35. That puns are close cousins of transumptions is already implicit in Quintilian's "commonest example" of transumption: "*cano* is a synonym for *canto* and *canto* for *dico*, therefore *cano* is a synonym for *dico*, the intermediate step being provided by *canto*" (*Institutio oratoria*, trans. H. E. Butler, Loeb Classical Library [London: Heinemann, 1921], VIII. vi.38); see further Hollander, *The Figure of Echo*, pp. 135, 142–43. As my attention to Shelley's puns and verbal ambivalences in "Mont Blanc" and elsewhere implies, I regard the pun as a significant crossing of argument and rhetoric. Clearly it seemed so to Coleridge, whose interest in puns was both deep and sustained. For an analysis of Coleridge's concerns with puns suggesting how for him the pun succinctly relates rhetoric to argument, wit to allegory or symbol, see John A. Hodgson, "Coleridge, Puns, and 'Donne's First Poem': The Limbo of Rhetoric and the Conceptions of Wit," *John Donne Journal*, 4 (1985): 181–200.

36. Todorov, "On Linguistic Symbolism," 111–34, esp. 118–29; represented in part and with significant revisions in Todorov, *Symbolism and Interpretation*, trans. Catherine Porter (Ithaca: Cornell University Press, 1982), pp. 72–76. Although Todorov pointedly refrains from making the suggestion, there would seem to be a strong connection between analogy and

his last category of propositional symbolism, "the evocation of a general proposition by another" ("On Linguistic Symbolism," p. 124), which he further associates with the propositional relations of "implication" and "allusion" ("On Linguistic Symbolism," pp. 124–25; *Symbolism and Interpretation,* p. 75). In this context it is also worth noting that while Todorov associates this category and these relations with the trope of metonymy, they are instead clearly, according to the analysis of Dubois *et al.* (which Todorov claims to be adapting), related to "referential metaphor" (*A General Rhetoric,* pp. 109–10).

37. Cf. Eco, "Metaphor, Dictionary, Encyclopedia," 258–59.

38. Quoted by Hollander, *The Figure of Echo,* pp. 135, 142. Samuel Clemens offers a classic American alternative to Puttenham's paradigm: "A body might stump his toe, and take pison, and fall down the well, and break his neck, and bust his brains out, and somebody come along and ask what killed him, and some numskull up and say, 'Why, he stumped his *toe*'" (*Adventures of Huckleberry Finn,* ch.28).

39. William Michael Rossetti, ed., *Adonais* (1891; rev. ed. London: Oxford University Press, 1903), p. 142, notes this last allusion.

40. A. C. Bradley, "Notes on Shelley's 'Triumph of Life,'" *Modern Language Review,* 9 (1914): 442–43; Bloom, *Shelley's Mythmaking,* pp. 254–55, 270–71.

41. Giuseppe Mazzotta, *Dante, Poet of the Desert: History and Allegory in the Divine Comedy* (Princeton: Princeton University Press, 1979), p. 115.

42. Coleridge in his *Philosophical Lectures,* p. 91, refers to "the whole world as a kind of language—as the painted veil of Isis," which further confirms the likely occasion for Shelley's sonnet.

43. For an analysis of "Epipsychidion" as "a proleptic hope which is forbidden by the words which express it," see J. Hillis Miller, "The Critic as Host," pp. 236–47 (the quotation is from p. 241).

44. Tetens had already analyzed Pegasus, a similarly compound creature, to just such an effect: see James Engell, *The Creative Imagination: Enlightenment to Romanticism* (Cambridge: Harvard University Press, 1981), p. 120. For a similar elaboration by Coleridge, see *LL* 2:147.

45. The metaphysical *double entendre* on "quench" appears as early as "Alastor," the Preface to which suggests that the more influences of the Power one imbues, the sooner one's life will be extinguished: in quenching one's spiritual thirsts with the Power's influences (flowings-in), one quenches one's flame of life as well. At the end of Shelley's career, the "quench" pun riots through "The Triumph of Life," where Rousseau, in quenching his thirst for knowledge—"Shew whence I came, and where I am, and why," he

asks the "shape all light" (398), to which she replies by inviting him to "quench thy thirst" (400) with her cup of nepenthe—is also quenching "the spark with which Heaven lit my spirit" (201). Already her fountain-treading feet had seemed to trample the embers of his thoughts into dust (382–88); now, when he drinks, "my brain became as sand" (405) on a wave-washed beach.

46. A few memorable examples: "[T]hat Power which strikes the luminaries of the world with darkness and extinction . . ." ("Alastor," Preface); "Scatter, as from an unextinguished hearth / Ashes and sparks, my words among mankind!" ("Ode to the West Wind," 66–67); "The soul of man, like unextinguished fire, / Yet burns towards Heaven with fierce reproach and doubt" (*PU* III. i.5–6); "[Dante's] very words are instinct with spirit; each is as a spark, a burning atom of inextinguishable thought" (*DP*, p. 63); "The splendours of the firmament of time / May be eclipsed, but are extinguished not; / Like stars to their appointed height they climb . . ." ("Adonais," 388–90); "If I have been extinguished, yet there rise / A thousand beacons from the spark I bore" ("The Triumph of Life," 206–07); "A light from Heaven whose half extinguished beam / Through the sick day in which we wake to weep / Glimmers, forever sought, forever lost" ("The Triumph of Life," 429–31).

47. In his Advertisement to "Epipsychidion" Shelley quotes Dante on the "*colore rettorico*" (*SPP*, p. 373). Elizabeth Sewall, *The Orphic Voice: Poetry and Natural History* (New Haven: Yale University Press, 1960), p. 31, and Paul H. Fry, *The Poet's Calling in the English Ode*, pp. 192, 313 n.25, both associate the "colouring" Shelley speaks of in the *Defence* with rhetoric.

48. Marzio's suicide shows Shelley departing pointedly from his source, which says simply that Marzio "obstinately died under his torments" (Shelley, *Works*, ed. Ingpen and Peck, 2:162). Something of Shelley's purpose in making the change appears in his blackly comic contemporary "Essay on the Devil and Devils": "[The Devil] is forever tortured with compassion and affection for those whom he betrays and ruins; he is racked by a vain abhorrence for the desolation of which he is the instrument; he is like a man compelled by a tyrant . . . to appear as the witness against and the accuser of his dearest friends and most intimate connections. . . . As a man, were he deprived of all other refuge, he might hold his breath and die—but God is represented as omnipotent and the Devil as eternal" (*SP*, p. 270).

49. Beatrice is also anticipating her career. Though Count Cenci is finally strangled rather than stabbed (and here again Shelley departs from his source, according to which the murderers "with a hammer drove a nail into his head, . . . and another they drove into his neck" [Shelley, *Works*, 2:160]),

yet one of these men does become what Beatrice calls "this two edged instrument / Of my misdeed; this man, this bloody knife / With my own name engraven on the heft . . ." (V. ii. 97–99).

As with Marzio's death, so with Count Cenci's, Shelley departs from his source to insist on a *stifling,* a stopping of breath and so of speech.

50. Michael Worton, "Speech and Silence in *The Cenci,*" in *Essays on Shelley,* ed. Miriam Allott (Totowa, N.J.: Barnes and Noble, 1982), pp. 106, 114.

51. Shelley does use the word "incest" in his letters, and even his Preface to the play speaks of Cenci's "incestuous passion." Interestingly, though, Mary Shelley pointedly and explicitly refuses to write or even paraphrase the word in her translated "Relation of the Death of the Family of Cenci," excising this part of the story with the plea that "the details here are horrible, and unfit for publication" (Shelley, *Works* 2:160).

52. On the interrelation of *Prometheus Unbound* and *The Cenci,* see especially James Rieger, *The Mutiny Within,* pp. 105, 125–28; Stuart Curran, *Shelley's Annus Mirabilis: The Maturing of an Epic Vision* (San Marino, Calif.: Huntington Library Press, 1975), pp. 121–30; Earl Wasserman, *Shelley,* pp. 95–101, 128.

53. On another level, this repressed word is also the curse that Prometheus had once pronounced on Jupiter.

54. It is George Steiner, in *The Death of Tragedy* (New York: Hill and Wang, 1961), pp. 147–48, who has claimed that in *The Cenci* "pastiche is carried to the level of art" (cited by Paul A. Cantor, "'A distorting Mirror': Shelley's *The Cenci* and Shakespearean Tragedy," in *Shakespeare: Aspects of Influence,* ed. G.B. Evans, Harvard English Studies, 7 [Cambridge: Harvard University Press, 1976], p. 92n). For listings of Shelley's borrowings and allusions, see Ernest Sutherland Bates, *A Study of Shelley's Drama "The Cenci"* (New York: Columbia University Press, 1908), pp. 54–55; David Lee Clark, "Shelley and Shakespeare," *PMLA,* 54 (1939): 278–86; Stuart Curran, *Shelley's Cenci: Scorpions Ringed with Fire* (Princeton: Princeton University Press, 1970), p. 38n. Critics particularly sensitive to the confusion and potential or actual contradictoriness of Shelley's allusions include Carlos Baker, *Shelley's Major Poetry: The Fabric of a Vision* (Princeton: Princeton University Press, 1948), p. 150; Milton Wilson, *Shelley's Later Poetry: A Study of His Prophetic Imagination* (New York: Columbia University Press, 1959), pp. 86–88; and Cantor, pp. 94–108.

55. For a discussion of the reverberations of this passage in *The Cenci,* see Curran, *Shelley's Cenci,* pp. 120–27.

56. Wilson notes that Shelley's work "shows clearly how well he knew

the thinness of the line that separates "the dark idolatry of self" from self-knowledge. . . . [I]t is self-knowledge that Shelley invokes as the end for which *The Cenci* is designed. . . . But a paradox or two lie hidden in this statement if we read it in the light of the play. For Cenci analyzed his own and other minds, and through his knowledge did not become just, tolerant, or kind, but 'fell into the pit'; and Orsino, fearful of what he sees within, exits crying, 'Where shall I / Find the disguise to hide me from myself . . . ?' Beatrice seems to have found her disguise and stands trial, fiercely proclaiming her innocence, but Shelley, however he may admire her, does not find her innocent" (*Shelley's Later Poetry*, p. 92). Though Wasserman has tried to save Shelley from this paradox by discriminating between "pernicious casuistry" (associated with self-anatomy) and "sublime casuistry" ("the artistic management of casuistry" to "promote . . . self-knowledge") (*Shelley*, pp. 115–26, esp. 117–20; the quotations are from p. 119, 118), not even this plea can resist Rieger's conclusion that Shelley here claims to have "created a work of art to which the only valid responses are, paradoxically, illegitimate" (*The Mutiny Within*, p. 126).

57. So Shelley again, as Wasserman notes (pp. 94–95n), groups these terms to similar effect in his "Essay on the Punishment of Death": "revenge, retaliation, atonement, expiation . . . are the chief sources of a prodigious class of miseries in the domestic circles of society" (*SP*, p. 155). Leslie Brisman's observation on the grouping is precisely to the point: "Shelley's most radical insight about traditional Christianity is that the theology of atonement is based on revenge and retaliation: man's disobedience struck God as a slap in the face, and rather than turn the other cheek, God himself exacted retribution in approving of the Son's suffering for mankind" ("Mysterious Tongue: Shelley and the Language of Christianity," *Texas Studies in Literature and Language*, 23 [1981]: 395).

58. Mary Shelley records the book in her list of Shelley's reading for 1816 (*Mary Shelley's Journal*, ed. Frederick L. Jones [Norman: University of Oklahoma Press, 1947], p. 74).

Afterword

1. See Jacques Derrida, "Freud and the Scene of Writing," *Writing and Difference*, trans. Alan Bass (Chicago: University of Chicago Press, 1978), p. 199, and Harold Bloom, *Poetry and Repression*, p. 1; and cf. Bloom, *The Breaking of the Vessels*, pp. 63–64.

2. Samuel Weber, *The Legend of Freud* (Minneapolis: University of Minnesota Press, 1982), pp. 11–12. I am indebted to Weber's entire discussion of secondary revision on pp. 10–12.

3. Weber, *The Legend of Freud,* is especially attentive to this coloring of Freud's interpretations by the very texts and psychic rhetorics on which they operate. "[T]o what extent is the theory of Entstellung [distortion, dislocation] itself an Entstellung?" (p. 85). "What if the analysis of the dream as Entstellung points to the fact that the interpretation of meaning . . . is itself only part and parcel of a larger process, one of *verstellenden Entstellung (dissimulating dislocation)?*"(p. 68). See also Margaret W. Ferguson, *Trials of Desire,* pp. 164–84.

4. Freud, *The Origins of Psychoanalysis: Letters to William Fleiss, Drafts and Notes: 1887–1902,* ed. Marie Bonaparte, Anna Freud, and Ernst Kris (New York: Basic Books, 1954), p. 162; quoted by Stan Draenos, *Freud's Odyssey: Psychoanalysis and the End of Metaphysics* (New Haven: Yale University Press, 1982), p. 77. Draenos offers a powerful analysis of "the odyssey of Freud's thought" as a "striving to return, via the circuitous route of natural science, to his spiritual place of origin—philosophy" (p. 2).

5. Interestingly, at just this point—both this kind of putative uncanniness in another and also this very period of Freud's life (early 1919)—Freud's own claimed invulnerability to the emotion or the experience of the uncanny also breaks down. Though he insists in the essay, "It is long since [the writer] has experienced or heard of anything which has given him an uncanny impression" (*SE* 17:220; see also 248 and n., but cf. 237), there is independent testimony that at just this time Freud spoke of the "uncanny" impression that Victor Tausk, an ephebe but also an intelligent and ambitious potential rival, made upon him. See Paul Roazen, *Brother Animal: The Story of Freud and Tausk* (New York: Knopf, 1969), p. 77; cf. pp. 171, 182. See also Neil Hertz, "Freud and the Sandman," in *Textual Strategies,* ed. Josue Harari (Ithaca: Cornell University Press, 1979), pp. 296–321, and especially pp. 314–317, on Freud and Tausk.

6. Helene Cixous, "Fiction and Its Phantoms: A Reading of Freud's *Das Unheimliche* (The 'uncanny')," trans. Robert Dennome, *New Literary History,* 7 (1976): 525.

7. Jerome Christensen, *Coleridge's Blessed Machine of Language,* p. 27; on the chiasmus as the motivating figure of Coleridge's rhetoric, see esp. pp. 260–67. "The blessed machine of language" is Coleridge's phrase; see *Friend* 1:108.

8. Jacques Derrida, "Structure, Sign, and Play in the Discourse of the Human Sciences," *Writing and Difference,* p. 292.

9. Jonathan Culler, *On Deconstruction: Theory and Criticism after Structuralism* (Ithaca: Cornell University Press, 1982), p. 182.

10. Paul de Man, *Allegories of Reading: Figural Language in Rousseau,*

Nietzsche, Rilke, and Proust (New Haven: Yale University Press, 1979), esp. pp. 103–131 (the quotations are from p. 131); J. Hillis Miller, "The Critic as Host," pp. 222–32 (the quotation is from p. 222).

11. Miller, "The Critic as Host," p. 228.

12. Bloom, *Agon,* p. 139; cf. pp. 107, 136; *A Map of Misreading,* p. 91; *Poetry and Repression,* p. 10. That Bloom criticizes and interprets from the point of view of literature is, I think, the essential characteristic of what he calls his "antithetical criticism."

13. For some thoughts on the deathly implications of philosophical "rigor," see Jonathan Arac, "To Regress from the Rigor of Shelley: Figures of History in American Deconstructive Criticism," *Boundary* 2, 8 (1980): 249, 251–53.

14. Draenos, *Freud's Odyssey,* pp. 57–62, offers an important analysis of Freud's "utilization of the biological hypothesis."

15. Laplanche and Pontalis, *The Language of Psycho-Analysis,* p. 221.

16. Cf. Geoffrey Hartman, "The Voice of the Shuttle: Language from the Point of View of Literature," *Beyond Formalism: Literary Essays 1958–1970 (New Haven: Yale University Press, 1970), p. 348.*

Index

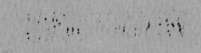